PIECES OF THE PUZZLE

Volume 1 – Psychic Phenomena

Trinda Latherow

~UCWS~
The Universal Center for
World Spirituality, LLC
www.UCWS.org

~Becky,
In God we Trust,
Trinda

D0968081

PIECES OF THE PUZZLE
Volume 1-Psychic Phenomena

An exploration into the unseen world around us.

Trinda Latherow

Author's Note:

Portions of transcribed conversations and interviews for this book have been edited for space and clarity.

Published and distributed in the United States by:
The Universal Center for World Spirituality, LLC.
www.UCWS.org

Editor: Sid Versaci, Izora, Inc.   Cover Design: Trinda Latherow
                                          Cover Graphics: J. Ryan Sanders

Library of Congress Control Number: 2006907002

Latherow, Trinda
    Pieces of the Puzzle, Volume 1 – Psychic Phenomena / Trinda Latherow.

ISBN 13: 978-0-9787898-1-7
ISBN 10: 0-9787898-1-4

1st Printing, September 2006

Printed in the United States of America

In Loving Memory of Gloria
Beloved Mother and
Kindred Soul Forever

Gloria, 1960

Contents

Forewords

"Everybody is intuitive to one extent or the other."
- - James Van Praagh, Survival Evidence Medium, Speaker, Author and
      Producer

*"I believe that people that are old, old energies that have lived before who come back
into life, seem to be blessed with some psychic ability."*
- - Allene Cunningham, America's No. 1 Radio Psychic-Counselor

*"The difference between a psychic and a lay person is not getting the information to
begin with; it is the fact that they recognize it."*
- - Sandy Anastasi, Psychic-Channel, Astrologist, Author, Owner and
      Operator of Starchild New Age Books & Gifts

*"If you're a sentient being, you're psychic. I think that everybody has a good degree of it
naturally."*
- - Lauren Thibodeau, Ph.D., Speaker, Author, Business Intuitive,
      Psychic-Medium and Intuition Development Mentor

Acknowledgements

Guided by God, my first and foremost acknowledgement and deepest appreciation must be to God and all those in divine spirit, especially *The Team*, who has helped to bring about this first volume of *Pieces of the Puzzle*. I am humbled to have been their tool for this communication.

They have also led me to a number of insightful, earthly guides as well. In particular, one of the noblest souls I have been blessed to know and love, my husband Richard. He continues to teach, help, and inspire others, leading by example. Another blessing in this life is my much, loved daughter and friend, Tamisan, a dreamer in her own right, named from a fictitious character by author, Andre' Norton (1912-2005).

My sincerest thanks to (in no particular order):

Sandy Anastasi: I am forever grateful for the initial shot of confidence, which led to my beginning this work. You are one of the brightest stars in an infinite sky of light and love.

Allene Cunningham: May God bless you, Allene, for giving so much of yourself for the betterment of others, and my sincerest thanks to Pat for his trust.

James Van Praagh: Thank you for your generous gift of support. May *you* be forever surrounded by unconditional love as a blessing and valuable *piece of the puzzle*.

Reverend Janet M. Reynolds and Blue Feather for their benevolent contributions.

Reverend Phyllis Dee Harrison for reminding me that perseverance can bring meaningful rewards.

To the kindest of Cassadaga, and all the lovely ladies of Lily Dale, my prayers for continued blessings, particularly Lauren Thibodeau for your initial assistance.

In addition, my appreciation goes out to all the others who have participated, including family and friends who have given their support and prayers, but especially to Theresa, and all the girls at the hospital, for their interest early on. Prayers of healing go out to all those you and your co-workers help to care for.

To all those who have been an aid in helping to bring about the mechanics of this book, especially Gill at TwinTrak and everyone at A&A Printing, I give my sincerest gratitude. My thanks go out once again to Ryan, Celeste, and Laura for their efforts as well.

Last, but not least, my heartfelt thanks go out to *you*, for joining us on this journey. I know that by your reading this book, you have already found that within, which truly knows we are so much more, that we *never* walk alone, and that we are all, like *pieces of a puzzle*, connected to one another in a bigger and brighter picture that is our existence.

Introduction – The Unseen World

Orchestrated by spirit, *Pieces of the Puzzle, Volume 1 - Psychic Phenomena* affirms the unseen world to those living in this world. While I never sought to discover the paranormal while living a normal life, it has happened nonetheless. In the still of the night, I heard noises not attributable to my husband or the dogs. I felt a presence, as if someone had touched my shoulder. The tiniest of hairs on my arms stood up with unexplainable chills. I knew the phone would ring, or if someone had important news. After decades of these types of experiences, I began to suspect spirit had made repeated attempts to communicate with me. Those mystifying moments in my life led me to begin an exploration of the unseen world around us, including psychic phenomena, our sixth sense, and spirit communication.

In the search for answers to some of life's greatest mysteries, I sought after the most intriguing and insightful souls in both the body and spirit who may hold valuable, *pieces of the puzzle* to our existence, particularly, who we are and why we are here. Joining me in the beginning of my journey are famous and notable psychic-mediums, authors, celebrities, and gifted laypeople throughout the U.S. Together in candid conversations and enlightening interviews, they share their psychic experiences, thoughts and beliefs of the unseen world and all that it entails for the betterment of others. From these experiences, we may find ourselves one step closer to the realization that the paranormal is normal and that there is a great deal more to both our surroundings and us.

Thankfully, with their guidance, we will not only learn of spirit messages and develop a keen awareness of an unseen world, but also discover much about ourselves in the process. For all those who may have ever asked, "Am I all that I am?" I invite you to join me now in search for answers. My only request is that you keep an open mind along the way.

Preface – My Mystical Memoirs

I knew of God's love early in my life, but it was not until I experienced personal tragedy, and yes, psychic phenomena, that I found my spirituality and faith. It caused me to ask those age-old questions: who are we, and why are we here? Determined to find the answers, I started out on the quest of a lifetime.

The first of many discoveries are in this book—true stories of the supernatural and miraculous, which may bring us all a little more hope, faith and love. More of a personal journal that enlightens than a story, this book is a collection of real-life experiences and answers to some of the most familiar and haunting age-old questions. They are the mystical memoirs of one soul's search for answers to some of life's greatest mysteries, including our purpose in life, and the seemingly supernatural aspects to it.

Hello, my name is Trinda, and I am neither a psychic nor a scientist. Nor do I have a doctorate. However, I do not believe you have to have a title behind your name to have a better understanding of this life, or the next. Those with and without higher degrees have explored the most complex theories of man's existence. Countless of individuals with varying backgrounds have taken a similar journey toward *personal enlightenment*, and found the answers they were seeking. In addition to psychics and scientists, they have been priests and rabbis, authors and philosophers, and yes, even laypeople whose higher self has found that which brings them peace and purpose. More times than not, it is a purpose greater than they are. While many are still discovering the endless possibilities to our being, some certainties are clearly identifiable. Like *pieces of the puzzle* to our existence, their answers may lead us all to a bigger picture, a greater awareness of this life, our reality, the afterlife, and a better understanding of ourselves—who we are and why we are here. Through their concepts of life and amazing experiences, others may gain greater insight into their own beliefs. While some of their interpretations may be familiar to you, others may indeed challenge your whole perception of the seen and unseen world around you.

My own personal journey began twenty-four years ago with both the birth of my daughter and the death of my mother. Until then, my world was well grounded; I knew who I was and what I wanted out of life, or least I thought I did. Afterward, the normal reactions occurred at first—grief, confusion and anger at the loss of my mother. Then the questions poured out, why her, why now, why God, why? Then slowly, little by little, the answers came, one piece of the puzzle at a time, until an astonishing picture began to form. The answers came from the most unusual and surprising sources. I met people I never thought I would ever meet, or had needed to meet. Yet, I did find them. They are an eclectic group of spirit and earthly guides and teachers. They were there for me, and now, they are here for you, too. They share their beliefs, experiences, and comments candidly and willingly—all for the betterment of others.

Even though my quest does not end with this first book, I did find many wondrous answers. Those answers have given me both a new look at life and inner peace. Until recently, I never really knew of this peace. Some think of it as being born-again while others have described it as an inspired awakening. All I know is that the journey has changed my life, thankfully for the better.

Now, after all the years of psychic phenomena and supernatural experiences, as well as countless hours of interviews, research, and study, I am able to share my findings with you. I invite you to join me in the quest of a lifetime, a spiritual quest toward personal enlightenment, purpose, inner peace, and true unconditional love. I only hope that it may help you in your own journey. Many blessings to you and those you meet along the way.

Chapter 1 – Psychics

"They want you to write. Are you aware of that?" Her words struck me somewhere around the fifth charka. The fifth or throat chakra rules the faculty of speech, being part way between the tongue and heart. It is also associated with clairaudience (hearing spirit words and sounds).

Without hesitation, my mouth moved and I heard myself answering, "Yes, yes." It was all I could do to not come out of my chair and hug this woman. Finally, someone I did not know was saying that which I only suspected. Even though we had never met before, I did know her. She was not only the owner and operator of this quaint, mystic bookstore, but also the well-known psychic and once teacher to John Edward, himself a famous psychic-medium. He speaks highly of Sandy in his book, *After Life: Answers from the Other Side* (Princess Books, 2003). My impression of her did not differ much; she was indeed "very good" and our meeting was one that has since helped shape my own life's work.

This is what good psychics do: they give confirmation to voice and truths of your inner self. They also give you those all-important validations that deceased loved ones are still with us. I was hanging onto her every word. If her tape recorder had not been on, I would have been hard-pressed to recall my shorthand. I continued to listen as if my life depended on it, and in some ways, it actually did. She was expressing my innermost thoughts and desires. I kept thinking; how *does* she do that? She spoke of my good—and not so good—personality traits, some of which I will blame on my previous lives, of course. "Past life drags," I believe were her exact words. She explained a few of my life issues, some astrologically influenced as well. Whew, for a minute there, I thought I was completely responsible. At least my joy guide says it is never my fault. Then in a flash, Sandy viewed my early childhood and my future. She recalled the past and foretold the future, all in little over an hour. It was all so overwhelming. However, she was the first psychic to talk of my writing. Perhaps it just had not been time to hear it until then, but I was grateful to her. I was at that juncture in my life when I knew something needed to change. Trust me, you will usually know when someone tells you a truth or not. It is like telling a young person that they will just know it when the right person comes along. It is an intuitive thing and we all have it (and not just women either). Interestingly enough, my soul knew what I was ready for before I did. Someone else was just expressing the voice from within. Now that she spoke of the writing, I could consciously grab hold of it as well. I felt more than ready to be busy with the next phase of my life, and began writing.

When I look back over all the years of psychic counseling and readings, I realize that most were simply validations. I never received more than a little bit of personal history, some of the present and perhaps a few possible paths for the future. When I was a young mother, a number of wonderful psychic-mediums talked of my family, home, and of those things that mattered most in my life. A few years later, others noted changing events, career and personal interests. They were all good experiences, never a bad moment. Sure, some psychic-mediums were somewhat off with a name or date now and again, but surprisingly most were very accurate. Nearly all of them had amazing intuitive capabilities. Even though I did have a few notable psychics like Sandy Anastasi and John Edward present some of the most incredible psychic readings of my life to me, many other psychics were equally amazing. Those not-so-famous psychic-mediums were also truly gifted, particularly, a sweet, older woman, whom I shall call Hazel. She gave my very first psychic reading in 1983, but more on Hazel a little later on.

As far as intent goes, I have heard of more concerns over celebrity evangelists than I ever have of psychic-mediums. Obviously, not all psychics are saints; they are human too, but I do believe that many of them are indeed the real deal and most have sincerely good intentions. However, I use the word *psychic* as a general term when in fact, some may be a channel, medium, or gifted intuitive counselor. To varying degrees, everyone possesses psychic or intuitive abilities, which are sometimes referred to as our sixth sense. Therefore, while a medium must be psychic, not all psychics would be mediums. I understand that a medium is one who can somehow alter their energy waves in order to receive communication from spirit. The information is to be from God, a God source, or a Divine Intelligence, given through spirit, like spirit guides, teachers, and even our deceased loved ones who may stay with us for emotional support until we ourselves cross over.

A spiritualist medium is one who believes in God, commonly understood to be an Infinite Intelligence, an infinite creative force that governs all things by *natural laws*, basically, *love* through *compassion, faith,* and *unity,* among others. They believe Jesus to be one of the greatest teachers and leader that the world has ever known. They also maintain that the Bible contains God's word given to humankind. Some also include other great works such as the Torah, Koran and Bhagavad-Gita. Incarnation is a divided belief among spiritualists as well. However, a spiritualist does not believe in a devil or a place such as hell, only that a state of consciousness can be hell. Hell can be our experiences here on earth, but a more in depth understanding of the hereafter and spirituality are in later volumes.

While mediums may be at different skill levels, some have honed their psychic abilities to be honestly deserving of professional titles such as clairvoyant, psychic-medium, psychic-channel and so forth. A clairvoyant is someone who possesses the ability to perceive beyond our normal senses, including visions and mental pictures, as well as foresee possible future paths. A clairsentient *feels* as if through great empathy. A clairaudient generally hears sounds, voices or words. It may even come in as creative thought through writing. Many authors, songwriters, and poets are usually somewhat clairvoyant, if not clairaudient as well.

Yet, no matter what type of psychic or psychic-medium I met, I often felt a true genuineness. Nearly all my personal psychic readings were well-intentioned messages from caring individuals (the majority being women). The feeling was as if the messages were from a kind and loving source. Afterward, the experience always seems to take me to a place of great peace and comfort. I think it is because after so many years of readings, I finally came to recognize an underlying theme in all the messages, quite simply, love.

Now, after more than two decades of personal experience with psychic phenomena, including spirit messages, I am no longer the virgin sitter. (Psychic phenomena being supernatural events and spirit messages, the communication from our deceased loved ones, divine entities, guides and teachers in the world of spirit. The psychic is the reader and the person read is the sitter.) As I began to reflect upon all of the messages, I recognized similar themes, all having to do with great love through spiritual guidance.

Surprisingly, professional psychic-mediums number many more than one would think. If you were to search the World Wide Web for professional psychics, you would find over 75,000 hits on any given day in just one Internet search engine alone. There are a number of those not listed, perhaps even those with greater abilities who shy away from fame or who are somewhat hesitant to use their abilities. While there are a number of well-known mediums overseas, I have kept this collection of conversations, interviews, and psychic readings to those located throughout the U.S.

Nearly all the psychic-mediums that I have personally spoken with seemed to be genuinely gifted and some with specialized skills. However, most mediums do not consider their psychic ability a gift, but rather an extension of themselves and their natural-born sixth sense. In addition, those mediums I met throughout my research not only cared about the sitter's well-being, but the betterment of others. They see a bigger picture and those interviewed included their hopes that their work would help the masses, thus using their mystical powers for good and not evil.

Psychic-mediums around the nation have told me everyone wants them to prove themselves and that of the unseen world, as well as reassurances that our deceased loves are still with us. Mediums are continually demonstrating spirit messages, proving to us that their ability is not magic or trickery, yet there is still doubt, or perhaps fear. It is that very fear of the unknown and the unseen that limits us to a better understanding of our existence. Mediums continue to travel the globe in outreach efforts to demonstrate their abilities. Yet, after they prove it, what will happen? Will we be ready for a leap of faith in an unseen world? What will it take to prepare us for such a realization that there is more to life than what is perceived through the five senses? Can we look to God and perhaps modern day prophets, as well as psychic-mediums? More like spiritual leaders than fortunetellers, dedicated mediums focus their energy on healings of the mind, body, and soul, with the knowledge that life is not only continual, but also a blessing. Perhaps they are simply, just intuitive souls with a straightforward message of divine love. Are we *all* a part of God, a divine love? Do we all not have this natural intuitiveness within us? Is there really an unseen world?

I promise to explore those possibilities and questions with you in this volume. Perhaps our earthly guides, from psychic to priest, and all those in between, can help us along the way to finally, recognize, that which was previously unseen. Religious leaders might say God is always with us, as are our guardian angels. However, there may be those among us here who can also help. In truth, we are all here to help one another. Through the experiences and intuitiveness of various insightful souls, living here and *out there*, we can begin to discover some of the greatest truths of life. Yet, who are these guides and where do we find them?

Finding them is easy; you know them already. They are the individual spirits in and out of flesh, our brothers and sisters in life that show us unconditional love, forgiveness, and kindness in numerous ways. They give us guidance without judgment. They are everywhere. I know how hard it is to see them in times of stress, fatigue, and fear. However, believe me; they are among us. Whenever we can open our eyes and hearts completely, we will also notice those spiritual guides who are always with us. Like Jesus' footsteps in the sand, when you thought you were alone, it was then that you were carried.

I hope to help introduce you to those in spirit who are with you through my own experiences. Trust me when I say there are those in both spirit and flesh that can and do walk with us every day of our lives. We are never alone, nor should we ever feel as if we are. If not with family or friends here, know that those in spirit are always with you. The loved ones that you think have left you can be closer than you ever imagined. They are with you in good times and in bad and are there to lean on should you need them. Much of what I have witnessed proves that they are always with us. It has brought me much comfort and I hope it will for you, too. However, nothing is truer than the saying of moderation in all things, especially in leaning too heavily on spirit guides or psychic-mediums as you walk through this life. After all, it is still your life. No one else can live your life or experience your life's lessons other than you. You must take that responsibility on yourself. I learned that myself the year my mother passed from a brain aneurism at the young age of forty-seven years old.

I grieved greatly after my mothers passing, but I did get through it. During my time of healing, I also leaned on the shoulders of others, mostly my husband, family, and a few close friends. Sadly, however, I questioned God instead of listening for divine explanations. Then I unexpectedly met Hazel. Hazel was the first psychic to reunite me with my mother and with my first spiritual messages from the other side. I had never been to a psychic-medium before, and frankly, I never had the desire to meet one. Up until then, I thought I had it all. I was a young, happily married woman and new mother. However, like the car on a roller coaster ride, my life turned upside down when my mother unexpectedly passed away. The emotional upheaval that followed her passing was long and fearful. There I was with a newborn baby and Ma was gone. I needed her help and guidance and I thought I was alone. It was the lowest part of my life, and I never saw it coming. However, as you know, life does go on. Somehow, I went back to work and rejoined the living; at least I was going through the motions anyway. Not long after, subtle events began to happen that would lead me on a path like nothing ever imagined. Within the year of her passing, I made contact with the spirit world and experienced the first of many psychic phenomena. It was the beginning of an unbelievable adventure, which would unfold over the next two decades. Little did I know then that spirit would lead me on the journey of a lifetime. It would be one filled with validations and remarkable reunions—with not only my mother and other deceased loved ones—but with spirit guides, angels, saints, and yes, even Jesus and the Blessed Mother.

Chapter 2 - The Virgin Sitter

Psychic Reading, March 6, 1983

It was not quite a year after Ma's death when I overheard coworkers talking around the water cooler about a woman who could communicate with the dead. I heard she could even foretell the future, and see the past. The woman was a psychic-medium. One conversation lead to another and before I knew it, I was writing her name down. Soon I would be standing at her door, looking for answers to the first of many questions. It was then that I began my own personal journey.

After some hesitation, I found myself knocking on the door to a modest little ranch home downtown. It was in the part of town where I was not at all surprised to find iron bars on the doors and windows. I understood that this psychic, whom I shall call Hazel, perhaps in her seventies, lived alone. A coworker whom I hardly knew had referred Hazel to me, and now, after arriving at her house, I was beginning to feel a little unsure about being there. I rarely ventured off on my own, especially far from home. I would not have ever thought to go downtown, never mind to see a complete stranger and a psychic at that. Yet, there I was.

I had envisioned all sorts of things on my drive to see Hazel that morning. Not only had I never been to a psychic-medium before, but also I was not clear on what services they actually preformed. Did they read minds or see ghosts or what? Was it wrong for me to visit with this woman? Questions of my sanity came to mind. This was quite an adventurous undertaking on my part, and even though I was a little hesitant about going to her, curiosity got me to her front door.

I remember knocking and hearing a little voice telling me to wait a minute. No one went to Hazel without being personally referred to her, and no one entered her home without that referral's name. Finally, the door behind the barred-locked screen door opened a crack and a petite woman appeared. After I told her my first name and who had referred me, she unlocked the doors and escorted me into her parlor. She asked if

I would wait a moment or two. She was just finishing up with another client. As I sat on the plastic covered sofa and looked around, it reminded me of a television sitcom where the décor was definitely early 1960s and under the influence of an elderly woman. It was neat and tidy with everything covered in plastic or lace.

It was not long before she was showing her previous client to the door and after their good-byes that Hazel promptly locked both doors again. It was my turn next, but I was not sure if I was ready. She asked me to follow her into her office, the second bedroom of her home, and to have a seat. There were two large, white leather recliners, a small table with a basket of money in it, and a lamp. Behind one of the recliners hung a life-size painting of Jesus showing his out stretched arms. I assumed that recliner was for Hazel. She escorted me into the room and said that I could leave my contribution in the basket. I asked her how much she charged and she simply said, "Whatever you can afford will be all right." I put a ten-dollar bill in the basket, hoped it was enough, and sat down nervously in the recliner.

As we sat, Hazel leaned toward me, gently held my arms with her thin, frail hands and said, "I would like to start off with a little prayer first, if you don't mind." She asked for the Lord's blessing and prayed that her words would be from God. She hoped that they be of help, comfort, and not in any way harmful to me. After a soft Amen, she began immediately in her first describing my husband. She talked of his physical appearance, his health; that he currently had a foot problem. I said she was correct as he was recuperating from a foot injury at the time. She said that he wanted a truck, a used one, and that it would be okay, and to go ahead and get it. Amazingly, my husband was indeed thinking of purchasing an old Willies pickup truck at the time to help clear a future home-site. He actually ended up buying that old, floorless truck. He used it for more than hauling tree stumps, and it ended up being a great buy for the work we got out of it. Hazel revealed that she saw us trying to sell our own home. She went on to tell me that we would be successful by June of that year. She saw the small for sale by owner sign out front, and commented that we wanted a little too much for the house, to lower the asking price by a few thousand dollars and it would sell quickly. We had bought a few acres in the next county in the hopes of building a new home, and did indeed have our house for sale at the time. She questioned my wanting land as much as a nice house. She saw it as a mobile home, a very nice mobile home, but a mobile home nonetheless. Well, she was partially right anyway. The house we built was a very nice, masonry home surrounded by mobile homes in the community. I always felt like it did not belong in that neighborhood. She also recommended that we buy quickly as she believed the economy would go soft after the next election.

Hazel next commented on our current home, and the fact that we had family living next door. Correct again, we were living next door to my in-laws. She told me what my faith was (meaning religion, which actually changed with marriage) and a few more minor facts that were all true. I questioned Hazel about traveling to see a friend in Australia, but she said that due to both the economy and my own personal finances at the time that I would not be going in the near future. In fact, it was another eight years before I was actually able to travel there.

She then told me that if I were to have another child, it would be a son and delivered by cesarean, but that I really did not want any more children. She mentioned I had only the one child, a daughter who was a blonde, with blue eyes like myself, and that that she had a temper like her mother and father, only more so. Here again, Hazel was correct on all counts. She also warned me that my daughter currently had a foot problem, and to watch her for a fall. She saw that one foot was turned in somewhat, but that she would out grow it. It was a great gift to hear of Hazel's warning. I had never noticed the problem with my daughter's foot before. When I arrived home, I purposefully stood in the front entry and watched her walk toward me. Sure enough, one foot turned slightly inward, amazing, I thought. It was something I had just never noticed before, but on a psychic's advice, we took care of her foot until she finally outgrew the problem.

Hazel did not end there. She went on to give me names of people that I knew now and would know later. As clearly as the rest, she gave me the name of a very close friend, the middle name of nearly all the women in our family, a few others close to me, and one other I have not yet met. However, four out of five is a high percentage, so I would say she was very accurate. She did the same thing with names of states, declaring that she saw two in particular, New York and Pennsylvania. Indeed, we had very close family in both those states and nowhere else at that time. Interestingly enough, when I asked about my sister-in-law, she saw the state of Texas, and yes, her husband and his family were from the state of Texas.

Before we ended our time together, she also asked if I played an instrument, as she saw music all around me. At the time, I was attempting to learn the flute; unfortunately, I never kept it up. I wondered about her remarks though. Did she see images of notes and sheet music or what exactly? I am sorry I never asked her how she saw the indication of music around me. Truthfully, bewildered by all her comments, I barely spoke, sitting there dazed throughout most of her reading.

After all the details about my family and myself (more than I have given you here due to length), I sat quietly during her final words to me. Our time together had ended, and while I wanted to know more, I just thanked her and stood up. As we left the bedroom, my eyes glanced up again at the image of Jesus, and I asked of her interest in psychic counseling. She told me that her own sister begged her not to do readings out of fear for her personal safety, especially living alone. However, Hazel felt it necessary to give, in her words, God's messages to those who needed to hear them. I later found out that she once told a woman of a fatal illness, only to help her to best prepare for the end of her life. Hazel told another of an unexpected pregnancy, only to best prepare for the coming birth. She told me of these things only to best prepare me for the rest of my life. These messages and more are for all of us, only to best prepare us. I thanked her again and left to make my drive home. It was a few minutes into my drive before the scope of what actually happened hit me. This sweet elderly woman, whom I had never met before, had just told me things that no one else but immediate family could know, all within just minutes of our meeting. Gratefully, my first encounter with a psychic-medium and the spirit world was with Hazel, truly one of God's messengers. My thanks go out once again to Hazel, who herself has long since gone home, but who will never be forgotten.

That first experience with a psychic-medium led me to dozens more throughout the next two decades. Even though it was not at all what one would expect, no rituals, no candles and no crystal balls, it was still, truly amazing and will be forever memorable. It was my first impression of what a psychic-medium did and only an inkling of the unseen world around us.

Chapter 3 – A Mother's Touch

The Burglary, December 1991

It was during the holiday season of 1991, and I had not finished wrapping gifts or decorating the house for Christmas. This year's gifts would be a little different. I had taken a trip to Australia earlier that summer and brought back many Aussie trinkets for family and friends. Most of them were various souvenirs, including some costume jewelry and small gold pins shaped of koalas and kangaroos. Nothing was too costly, but they were something different that year for family and friends. I thought everyone would enjoy getting them as gifts. I had wrapped them up in small boxes with holiday paper, and placed them in the corner of our bedroom floor until we trimmed the tree. I had begun wrapping a few other small incidentals when I ran out of wrapping paper. I needed to get more paper, and thought I would run down to the local store to pick some up. The store was only about five minutes from the house; I knew it would not take me long to run the errand. I left a few unwrapped gifts on the bed and headed out. I locked up the house and closed the shades in the dining room before leaving. The back wall to the dining room had sliding glass doors to the small patio and a backyard that led to an open field and adjoining road. The single bedroom window was tall, but narrow and faced the backyard. New to the neighborhood, we were renting until we became familiar with the area. The house was nice enough, but on a very busy and winding road. It was next to a small trailer park, yacht club, and an assisted living facility.

I believe my whole trip to the store took less than a half hour. When I parked in the driveway, I grabbed my package and went up to the double, front doors. They were double doors with privacy stained glass panels. As I put the key into the door lock, I felt someone tap me on the shoulder. I turned around quickly. I had not thought anyone followed me up to the door from the driveway. No one was there and it made me a little uneasy. My hand was still on the key in the lock. As I turned the key, I slowly pushed the door in. Peering cautiously into the house, I first looked left toward the master bedroom. The room was a wreck, and I knew it was a robbery. I quickly closed the door, slipped the key out and ran to the next-door neighbor to call for the police. This all took place in but only a few brief moments, as if I trained specifically for just an occurrence. It was as if I knew what happened before it happened. For being so scared, I was impressed with my own quick reactions. The local police must have been close by because they were there in only three or four minutes. After they entered to secure the house, I was allowed in. The robbers had come in through the back sliding doors, and left the same way. The sliding door was partially open and the blinds were still clanging together from their abrupt exit. The police detective said that my return must have startled them. They apparently ran out the back after hearing me insert the key in the door lock.

The robbers searched for gold, and for the most part stole only jewelry. They ripped open all the small Christmas boxes, dumped both jewelry boxes on the bed taking only gold and diamonds. They even took our daughter's jewelry, some of which was only gold tone. In addition to the real and sentimental items, they even took a recent wedding favor, almonds wrapped with two gold colored plastic rings as its ornamentation. The officers said that they were probably looking for anything gold to pawn for drug money. How sad it was that they felt they had to take the contents of a little girl's jewelry box.

Our bedroom was a mess; things were everywhere, drawers pulled out and the closet ran-sacked. Then I noticed the bed's headboard drawers were open, and the worst of all, empty. They had taken a gun. My husband had just returned late the night before from a hunting trip. He was so tired that night that he placed his cash in his sock drawer, rifles in the closet attic, and the handgun in the bed's headboard drawer. He planned to clean and empty the handgun the next day. Had he not taken the time to put the rifles up in the attic, they would have found those too. However, knowing the robbers had a loaded 9mm gun made me physically sick. Even though the police thought they would simply pawn the gun, the fact that it was loaded still upset me. Everyone should adhere to gun safety measures at all times, no excuses, please! I could have been shot with my husband's own gun had I entered the house while the robbers were inside.

Thankfully, I paid attention to that intuitive feeling and paused long enough for those critical few seconds, which meant the difference between leaving this earth then or later. I knew the tap on the shoulder had been spirit's effort at saving my life. It was an example of *clairsentience*, which is clear sensing or feeling. Spirit's touch had let me to know someone was there. However, who was that someone in spirit that saved my life? While I had always felt as if my mother had been there that afternoon, I never really knew for sure until many years later.

More than another decade had passed when I would ask the question of spirit, "Who warned me of the burglary"? Since that day, I have grown to know and believe that I have many in spirit who watch over and guide me in this life, including an angel and an Indian protector. Perhaps it was one of them. I felt I would never really know for sure until a church service nearly fifteen years later. I thought of asking the question of a psychic-medium giving messages at a local spiritualist church service. I rarely attend, but found myself in the first pew one Sunday in March of 2006. It was that time of the service when a medium would give messages from spirit through questions. The Reverend selected my question on a folded slip of paper (a billet) from a basket of many others, paused for a moment, and simply said, "Your mother." I was so surprised, as I thought it might have been my protection guide. However, I was delighted to know it was my mother then, nearly ten years after her passing. I sat quiet, reflecting on the moment. However, the Reverend had not finished her message. She continued with, "She asks that you light a candle for her." Yes, it is the eve of her birthday, absolutely, I will tomorrow. "She's happy you remembered and I see lots of cake." I thought not, as my husband and I rarely have a whole cake in the house, it is just too tempting to indulge in.

On the way home, I wondered about the message and was happy once again to hear from my mother. I did not know how to thank her for a mother's touch that day long ago. While we lost much that afternoon, especially my mother's wedding band, I did not loose my life over stolen jewelry. I was so thankful to the Reverend for her message that I called her on my cell phone on the ride home from church. How can I ever thank you? She would not accept an offering, and more impressive yet, she invited me to her home the next day for another complementary reading with a few other close friends. I was delighted and offered yet another donation only to her quick, no thank you. It was her pleasure to give back to others whenever she could. I accepted her invitation and then thought to offer the evening's refreshments, and of course, cake came to mind. I would bring cake and a candle for my mother's birthday. She cheerfully accepted with the cake as my donation to the gathering.

After I hung up, I realized I would be having cake for my mother's birthday after all, and even better, on her birth date. My wish had come true even before blowing out the candle.

Chapter 4 – Clairvoyant Cases

Clair, is French meaning clear, and voyant is to see, or as psychic-mediums simply describe as clear seeing. Clairvoyant was not part of my normal vocabulary much before the writing of this book. It is not commonly used, if you have never heard of someone with clairvoyant abilities or experienced such things for yourself. However, after now having recognized those things beyond our normal range of senses, I can identify with the definition of clairvoyant and similar terminology. Yet, to better explain such instances of clairvoyance to others, I have included some of those real-life clairvoyant cases, which might be considered as clairknowing (clear knowing), clairsentience (clear sensing), clairfactory (clear smell), clairaudient (clear hearing) and clairvoyance (clear seeing).

Clairknowing – Clear Knowing
Tin Can, June 19, 2003

My career as a risk management professional often took me to a number of locations across the U.S., especially throughout Florida. This particular week, my schedule called for me to travel throughout central Florida. There were branch offices in over one hundred locations and two of them were on my list to see that day in Sanford and Leesburg. That Thursday, I was supposed to visit the Sanford branch when a few last-minute changes caused some rescheduling. I decided I would visit the Leesburg branch instead as it was not as far to travel to. There was a heavy rainstorm that morning, and I really did not want to drive too far from home. It was also the day after my father's funeral. Even though working was healthy for me, I wanted to be sure I was home early that evening.

The rain eventually let up as I entered the next county and the sun began to peek through the clouds. It was going to be a nice day after all. The country back roads, lined with huge oaks and dangling moss, were soothing scenery and made for a pleasant drive. My thoughts drifted in and out of recalling the prior day's services. The Air Force representatives presented an impressive service, even if it did rain the whole day. I hoped that Dad was finally at peace after his long battle with cancer. I started to get a little teary eyed and thought I should concentrate more on my driving and plans for the next couple of days. I had much work ahead of me, but also had a number of social events planned.

One evening I went to see a famous psychic-medium in town. I knew there would be hundreds in attendance. However, like everyone else, I was hopeful of a personal reading. With Dad just gone, I was anxious to hear that he was well on the other side. Perhaps he would even come through and give me some sort of validation that would prove the continuance of life after death. I wondered if it did happen, what validation could I hear that would allow me know for sure that it was indeed Dad. In that instant I imagined that the psychic would say that I have a father figure coming through while looking my way and saying *Tin Can*. It was my father's nickname for me, and no, it does not have anything to do with my backside. I cannot believe I am telling the world that silly nickname, but I did promise to give you the truth. I remember visualizing the appearance of a tin can on the ground and the words *Tin Can*, as if I could make it so. Again, the teary eyes came with the reality of the moment. I told myself to quit daydreaming and concentrate on the day ahead of me.

I went on to the Leesburg office for a full day of auditing and training. Afterward, I took the same roads out of town that I had taken before. Even though it was getting late, the weather was nice and the roads were dry. I headed for I-75 south, the quickest way home. Once on the highway, I thought I could pick up speed and be home at a reasonable hour. I had traveled that same route several times before, but not for some time. The highway exit was only a few lights away when I completely changed direction.

For some unknown reason, I took a wrong turn. I saw the exit ahead of me and yet, I took the next right turn before it onto a highway heading west. Why would I do such a thing? It was almost ten minutes and several miles down the road before it dawned on me that I actually headed in the wrong direction. As if waking from a dream state, I realized my error and decided to quickly turn around and head back. I took the next available wide shoulder space on the road, and made a u-turn. As I turned the car around and looked ahead, there was a sign as big as a billboard. In large bold print, it read TIN CAN (café). I nearly drove off the road in shock. I could not believe my eyes. Somehow, I kept driving until I finally got on the correct highway toward home.

What was that all about? Was it just a *coincidence* or something more? All I know is that I had hoped to receive a validation from Dad, specifically with my unusual nickname, Tin Can, and actually did. It was such a shocking and emotional moment, even more so than his funeral services the day before. The funeral was real—that I could deal with—but this was something else. At any other time, I would have just called it coincidence and a billboard, but at that moment in time, it was obviously a sign of another type.

Trucking for Jesus, June 23, 2003

It was suppose to be just another road trip, but it turned out to be one that would give "Trucking for Jesus" a completely new meaning. The week after my father's funeral services was an emotional one to say the least. I thought nothing could top seeing the sign with my nickname on it.

Never the less, I saw hundreds of miles before me in the coming weeks, and my next stop was Orlando, Florida. On Monday, I headed toward Tampa and Interstate 4 to Orlando. The roads were busy, but the weather was clear and sunny.

Once again, thoughts of Dad raced through my mind; it had only been a week since his services. Thinking of all the moments over the past few months of his illness, I was surprisingly at peace with his passing. With his long years of illnesses and several near-death moments, we had many opportunities to say all the things we could while he was alive. We had said our good-byes, given our hugs, and had several talks. We were at peace with our time together. Since Dad was retired military, he had often told us he was ready to join God's army. He knew his time was drawing near, and we told him he could go home when he wanted to. It all went as well as one could imagine a passing could go. Yet, here I was weeks later still grieving my father's death. Thankfully, there was work, and lots of traveling.

I was well on my way that morning, driving in the far left lane of I-4 when I felt the wind from large semis passing me. Just as I firmed my grip on the wheel, I knew the next one coming up was bigger than the other trucks. The wind pushed against my car even more and I braced to keep my wheels straight. As the truck approached closer, I tapped my brakes to slow down just a little. Speed is not always your friend at times like this. Just as I was slowing, the semi began to pass by. I glanced over toward it. Behind the cab was a huge trailer with only two words on its side panel, "Gilbert Express." No logo, no other markings, just Gilbert Express, and yes, you have guessed correctly, Gilbert was my father's name. I do not know how many times you have seen the name Gilbert for a trucking company, but this was a first for me. I did not even know one existed by that name. Admittedly, with my attention taken away from the road, I saw his name on the side of the truck. That was an impressive validation if ever I saw one. Yet, there was another truck behind it.

I heard the wheels, felt the wind of the next truck behind it, and this time, tried to control both my emotions and my car. This one was going to be even bigger. The wind was stronger and the roar of the engine even louder than the last. The cab moved up to pace me for a while and then as he slowly moved ahead, I saw the trailer behind it. In large letters again, read, "Jesus is the way." I nearly swerved off the road at that point. There were no other markings on the trailer, no placards, no writing, nothing other than those big black letters so clearly written for me to notice.

One after the other, the trucks read Gilbert Express…Jesus is the way. How wonderful a validation it was I thought, or was it simply a coincidence? I guess it depends on whether or not you believe in coincidences. Either way, that just about did it for me that day. Both came together on the highway just as I was thinking of Dad. With my eyes filled with tears, both messages seemingly meant to tell me that he had most assuredly found his way home and with Jesus. Some say we planned the coincidences in our life before reincarnating to give us validations. I am not sure if that is true or not, but this day would once again give me cause to ponder that very thought.

The Gazebo Promise, July 2003

Daily drives on the highways of Florida were becoming a routine this particular summer. It was audit time for all our branch offices, so the boss told us to hit the roads. I had a newer car, so the vehicle was not a concern. Actually, the driving was nice if the weather held out. This particular morning was unusual for Florida in July, clear sky and open road. I had left early to head north toward Ocala. This was going to be a long day, as I usually preferred not to stay over night if I could make it home the same day.

As I leaned back and headed up the highway, my thoughts returned to the incidents of earlier weeks. With Dad's passing came several validations of life-after-death, or so I wished them to be. Had I made more what they really were? Validations or not, I continually wanted proof. Other than Dad materializing before my eyes, I relentlessly prayed for proof of his existence after death. I wanted more, another sign that Dad and the rest were indeed still alive. Should I have dared to ask for more? Could I receive yet another validation? When grief is still in its early stages, you constantly want more. Validations of life-after-death are impressive enough whether one is grieving or not. However, when you are grieving, there never seems to be enough to completely comfort you. Psychics warn us of this dependency and suggest you might give both adequate time to grieving and perhaps seek grief counseling before looking to them for such comfort. It had been more than a year after my mother's passing before I spoke to a psychic. Yet, with both of my parents gone now, I wanted further proof.

Still, when you contemplate such things as life and death, you tend to look for miracles and heavenly answers when there may be none visible to you. You may even make deals with God as if He was a Vegas gambler. Lord, if you do that for me, just this once, I will do this for you. I know you have thought about it at some time or another. It is natural to want control over those periods of fear or sadness in your life. Dad had only been gone a short while and I wanted to make those types of deals with God as well.

I prayed that if I were indeed seeing signs and messages from spirit, loved ones or my father, that I would have yet one more sign to confirm it. If I were not making it all up in my mind or simply seeing those things as mere coincidences without purpose, I would need yet one more validation. Of course, the deal would not be worth anything if it did not have a value of some sort connected to it. I promised that if I were to see another sign, I would write another check to my favorite charity. I really do not believe one would receive signs with promises of payment, but I made it nonetheless. It was a weak moment and I look back at it as being somewhat sad and silly to put it kindly. However wrong it was at the time, I made the deal anyway.

I needed a sign of some sort to barter with, but wondered what it could be? I had just finished playing a CD that gave me the idea. Part one on the CD was a collection of readings by a famous psychic and part two was a meditation exercise, which led you to a gazebo in a peaceful field. It was there that you would meet your spirit guides or loved ones in the meditation. I had just listened to part one and was pulling out the CD before the meditation section came on. Meditation while driving is obviously not a good combination. Then it came to me, I would ask to see a gazebo. Not just one gazebo, mind you, or even two, but I wanted three, and only three, during my traveling that day. There it was; the deal was made, three gazebos for the price of a charity check. I just know psychics and psychiatrists alike are shaking their heads about that logic. However, it was just a thought; what harm could come from a simple thought or silly, inconsequential wish?

However, it was not an hour after my wish when I saw my first gazebo. It was not really a surprise either. I almost expected it, actually. The first gazebo was a large white wooden structure out in the middle of a grassy field off the highway. I spoke aloud, "Okay, that's one." The miles added on and the likelihood of seeing two was beginning to seem slim. I was nearing my destination and still no other gazebos. Yet, just minutes before I got to the branch office in Ocala, I spotted another. I dropped my head and said, "Whew, okay, that's two." I finally arrived at the office and began my audit. Surprisingly, my work went quickly and I was able to leave earlier than I thought. Since it was still rather early in the afternoon, I thought I would try to squeeze in just one more office visit before heading home. The schedule change would only put me a few hours late and I could avoid duplicating the same long drive the following day. With the change, however, came an alternate route, and one that I had not consciously planned. The second audit took a little longer than I hoped, but finally, I was on the road again and headed home. This time the route took me south on another highway. It was close to dark then and to stay alert, I put in a CD. I was listening to tunes for quite a while, and had actually forgotten about the third gazebo, until suddenly, there it was. The third gazebo was off the right side of the road, along with a few sheds and swings for sale. That one gazebo made three for the day. I could hardly believe it. Wow, that was three.

Well, at this point, I began laughing and thanking God and my spirit guides for leading me to see the three gazebos. I was feeling lucky when I realized I still had a number of miles ahead of me. What if I saw more gazebos, I only needed three to confirm the validation. I think I was nervous for the next hundred miles after that. I know this all sounds so foolish to you, and I thought that as well, believe me. I tried to tell myself to forget it and just listen to music the rest of the way back. Yet, after hours on the road, I finally arrived home and settled in for the night. As I laid my head on the pillow, it dawned on me; I had actually only seen three, and only three, gazebos all day. I could not have been happier until I remembered my promise. Now I needed to write my charity check. Spiritually driven or not— I would like to think some greater influence, some previous plan perhaps—was at work that day. Either way, the charity got a little extra help, and I got a little extra motivation to keep praying.

Rune Stones, January 15, 2005

I never really had a strong desire to have past-life regression counseling. I always thought, what is done, is done. However, many have found it extremely helpful to understand their current life's habits and views by knowing those influences of the past. I am sure a psychologist would find this story even more interesting than most. However, I share it with you to show you how using Rune stones can either help or ruin your life (pardon the pun).

Rune stones are normally flat shaped stones with carvings on them. These carvings were originally from the early Middle Ages but found to have been most prominently used during the Viking Age. While the symbols on stones are variations of an Old Norse language, they can differ in their inscriptions from numbers to artistic images. Those inscriptions can represent years, man, God, and such symbols as even the Christian cross. Used as memorial markers for a deceased person, much like our cemetery stones or memorial paving bricks today. I myself had memorial bricks inscribed and placed in a walkway in our local park for both my parents when they passed. The bricks show their name, dates and a brief remark for each. Perhaps you have done something similar for your deceased loved ones. Typically, representations of this old tradition of symbolic markers sell as mystical items in bookstores and gift shops.

It was in one of those mystical bookshops that my husband came across a bag of Rune stones. He was browsing the shop display case when he spotted the stones. However, it was not because they were Rune stones, but rather because they were made of bloodstone, which is his birthstone. The bloodstone is a green stone with a deep, blood color veining throughout and typically used as healing stone as well.

The shop was hosting a psychic fair that Saturday, offering brief psychic readings. My sister-in-law joined us that afternoon and we both decided to ask for a reading. After our obvious excitement over the psychic-medium's accuracy, my husband's curiosity was piqued. Mind you, he is not one for this sort of thing, the science buff that he is. Although he does keep an open mind when it comes to psychic phenomena, perhaps the influence of all those years of my readings and his own love of science fiction, especially the work of his favorite author, Andre' Norton.

I presumed he wanted a reading, as he quietly asked the girl behind the cashier how much a reading cost. I smiled at him and nodded to go ahead if he wanted to. Some minutes later, he emerged from the back room of the shop looking somewhat disturbed. I gathered the reading had not gone well. After we quietly walked outside the shop, he began to tell me what the psychic had mentioned a past life event, even though she normally did not do those types of readings at psychic fairs. However, she somehow felt the urge to tell him of an instance that would rock his world. Some say it is a typical psychic's tale of a past life, but my husband took the reading seriously. She explained that he had once been a Roman soldier during the crucifixion of Christ, and while he was supposedly not the one who speared Christ, he did not attempt to stop it either. The guilt from this possible experience carried over throughout his lives and that it might be part of his character today. This was extremely shocking to say the least, especially to a man who loves Christ and tries to follow in His teachings. After living in a strong Catholic household, the mere thought of possibly being involved in such a horrific moment in time troubled him greatly. We small-talked some as we waited for his sister to finish her reading and then decided to browse the shop. When he saw the Rune stones, he commented that he would like the stones just because they were bloodstones. Hoping they might pick up his spirit some, I bought them as a gift. His collection of rocks and minerals began years ago as a child, and quickly became a serious collection. The bloodstones were a gift he was happy to receive.

A few days passed before we talked of the reading again. However, he had been mulling it over in his mind a little each day. One evening in his den, he glanced over at the stones on the bookshelf and thought about their use as a psychic focusing tool. Since he had not yet overcome the psychic's remarks, he thought he would test himself with the stones. He read the booklet and instructions on their use, said a little prayer for clarity, and tossed the stones on his desk for the answers he sought. His prayer was to know if his supposed participation as a Roman soldier was purposeful under God's plan. He could not go on in life thinking he might have been part of something so horrific. The stones spread across his desk and he began to look at the meaning behind the symbols. It was surprisingly all good; they read much to his benefit. Finally, there was relief as he interpreted them to mean from such a negative came an awesome positive. From dying on the cross, Christ was able to rise again showing us all that there is eternal life. A greater good had come from an unbearable negative. Maybe he was there not only to witness the moment, but also to be thankful for the result of the soldier's actions. Maybe now, he could relax about the reading he had received.

However, a twist to this story came a few days later. I was in another room when my husband called out to me from his den. He noticed something odd about the Rune stones. He was thinking of sanding off the symbols and placing the stones in his rock collection when he realized that the stones had been incorrectly marked. The majority of the stones had the same symbol, one of a positive marking. He looked at me and said, "No wonder I got a good result with them the other day." The odds were favored for a positive outcome. Like the rolling of dice, it was all about the numbers and not some psychic interpretation after all. We laughed feeling foolish to have believed in them, even partly, and then talked about the experience. Yet, after much consideration, we had finally come to a completely different understanding of the whole experience. From the psychic reading to this moment of physical truth with the stones, the experience had taught us both a very valuable lesson. The experience had given my husband much reflection on his life now, particularly his interest and participation as a soldier and archer in the medieval reenactment club, The Society for Creative Anachronism, Inc. His hobbies have always reflected the collection of various weapons and hunting items, but he never really knew why. Typically, his hunting adventures involved a drink around the bonfire in lieu of actually hunting game. It was more of an excuse to be out in nature and enjoy camping with friends. His favorite times being those of conversation, song and merriment around a roaring campfire. Even so, collecting weapons is still one of his favorite hobbies.

We both thought the same thing about the experience, not the stones. The experience had lead us to believe that perhaps we were meant to not only see that things don't have power, but rather it is how we understand those events in our life which teach us about ourselves. The everlasting good that came from the crucifixion of Christ will far out way any heartbreaking imagery of his body's physical death. Perhaps this experience helped not only to remind us both of that very truth, but for others as well. Please remember to look for the good in things, events, and especially people, to the core of their very being. Look again for the good that can come from the most horrendous events, like the memorials that turn into causes from the loss of loved ones, or an event like the September 11th tragedy, and the great amount of good that came from it, unity and patriotism to name but only a couple. Think of all the people who came together in love and support that would not have otherwise even met. Think of the unity of neighbors that came from it. Think of the prejudices finally released with the understanding that such an action was not that of a whole nation or a whole people, but only a select few. Think of how you can make a positive out of a negative, a right from a wrong, and I promise, you will not need a bag of stones to help you do it either.

Clairsentience – Clear Sensing
Ma's Birthday Visit, March 26, 2005

I understand that animals, including our domesticated birds, cats, and dogs, have the ability to sense, if not see, the spirit world around us. Birds' feathers fly, cats arch their backs, and dogs bark to those things that not only go bump in the dark, but even to that which we cannot always see with our physical eyes. I had heard of many such instances from others about their own pets with similarly strange occurrences. However, I had never given it much thought until that Saturday night alone with Stitch, our Pomeranian puppy.

One of the happiest moments in our lives was the day we went to pick up our little Pomeranian puppy. We had been waiting for months for the next member of the family to be properly weaned by her mother. We were thrilled when the eight weeks passed and we would be able to take her home. We were all so excited that afternoon. Small enough to fit in the palm of our hands; so tiny it was almost scary. We were ready to leave when we asked about the last remaining puppy, the big boy. After we realized that no one had asked for the boy, we decided to bring him home as well, allowing both little sister and big brother to remain together. After all, two or one, it only meant more to love. We named them, Leelo and Stitch.

They have grown to be dearly loved and we have come to know their personalities very well. When you devote as much time and energy with your pets as we have, you can easily notice their habits and personality traits. Leelo was the little lion and Stitch her supporter from the rear, but both are pure, unconditional love. They have filled our hearts and home with great joy. We have gone through all the same things as with that of nurturing a child, and now watch proudly as they have become our beloved and trusted companions. They watch the house like security K-9, guarding the doors and windows and barking at the least sign of trespassers or unwelcome visitors, cats and squirrels included. Normally, its consistent barking until we investigate the matter. If all is well, however, they assume their normal positions each night, Leelo by the door and Stitch by my side.

The night of Ma's visit, Stitch was with me in my home office. I had been up late working on this book and adding some final changes to a particular paragraph when Stitch cried to be in my lap. I had just finished some editing and begun proofreading when he put his paws on my leg. Again, he begged me to pick him up. I let him on my lap and went back to proofing my work. It was nearing midnight and I was anxious to finish for the evening. However, Stitch still did not settle down. While in my lap, he continued to whine, and then soon started to growl. What was the matter with him? He was tense now, and all of his eleven pounds of muscle pushed against my chest and arms. He wanted me to hold him tighter. I stopped reading to pay closer attention to him. What is it big boy, what *is* the matter? He leaned in on me and cocked his head staring at the wall behind my chair. There is nothing on that wall but a picture hung high. Stitch was looking straight at the middle of a white wall and continued to give a low growl as if to warn me of a presence.

Perhaps there were insects or something in the wall that he could hear. Yet I knew there were no animals or insects in the walls as the house was new and it was an interior wall. There were no pipes or plumbing behind it, only drywall, insulation and wood, nothing else. He continued to give out a low growl, occasionally cocked his head, and whined. Remember, Stitch was not the fearsome Leelo, and something was obviously troubling him.

After all that I had recently experienced, seen and heard of in the last couple of years, particularly with regard to spirit communication, my thought was that it must be a spirit visitation. It was the only logical answer, which would explain his actions. It was nearly ten minutes of growling, head cocking and body twitching until Stitch finally settled down. Surprisingly, both Leelo and my husband never woke from their peaceful slumber. The whole time that Stitch was in my arms, I asked that the spirit be one of divine light, of God, rather than anything or anyone that could harm us (if that were even possible). I must admit at this point I was not yet as comfortable about acknowledging spirit as I have finally become. I was nervous and admittedly a little afraid of what kind of spirit it might be. I do not think I was ready yet to have had spirit materialize before my eyes. I most likely would have passed out or run screaming.

Finally, Stitch quieted down and lay still in my arms; he was now much more relaxed. He was finally okay with *the wall*. I assumed the spirit had left, and we once again were alone. I shut my computer down and let him off my lap onto the floor. I was curious as to what or who it could have been, but was extremely tired and went off to bed.

It was a few days later when I finally realized who the visitor might have been. Not paying close attention to the calendar, it had not dawned on me as to who it was. However, once I started to recall the date of the evening, I realized it was the eve of my mother's birthday. How slow of me, I thought. Why did I not I realize it that night? I wished I had noticed the date then; I would have been able to avoid giving my mother a belated happy birthday. It remains a special memory now to think that she was trying to communicate with me that evening. I am just sorry I did not recognize her efforts then, but hope she will try again. The next time, I will be sure to acknowledge her.

Clairfactory – Clear Smell
Heaven Scent, January 28, 2005

Just for a moment, try to recall the feeling you get when someone sends you flowers. Then, imagine that feeling multiplied by a hundred or two. Now, you might be able to understand how I felt the night I received flowers that were truly heaven sent.

It was the end of another long awaited Friday night. My husband and I were finally settling into our favorite spots in the living room. He was watching television and I had a good book. It was a cool winter night, so I grabbed a blanket and nestled in the corner of the couch. I was anxious to pick up where I had left off in my reading. Somehow, I was able to tune out the television and concentrate on the pages before me. It was a novel about the author's travels to Australia. Having been there myself some year's prior, I was reminiscing of my own trip as I read. I enjoyed my visit there. Australia's beautiful coastline and exciting cities had made it one of my favorite places; one that I hope to travel to again. Perhaps it was my relaxed state of mind or the late hour that led me to what happened next. Either way, it was to be a memorable night.

I was well into my reading whenever so subtly I noticed a beautiful flowery scent around me. I thought to myself, how lovely. It was as if the scent of a large bouquet of flowers suddenly filled the room. Then it dawned on me, I am actually, smelling flowers. I lifted my head in conscious recognition as my nose tried to locate the unseen scent. Knowing we had no flowers in the house, I looked at my husband and asked if he could smell anything. Distracted from his television show, he looked at me and instantly replied, "Like sugar; no it is gone now." I said, no, like flowers! I quickly got up, instinctively knowing what was happening. Yet, I had to prove it to myself that the scent was truly coming from spirit. Like a bloodhound on a mission, I put my nose in overdrive and started sniffing every inch of the house. The scent had faded away now, but I felt I had to know it was not from something or somewhere around the house.

The windows were tightly closed; the fireplace was burning only a small starter stick for ambience. The central heat had been on for some time. I sniffed every spot of the fireplace, around the vents, and every window and door. I covered every square foot possible inside. Then I went onto the patio, perhaps others would think the scent came from out of the house. I lingered for some time out under dormant trees, bushes and vines, but nothing was in bloom at that time of year. I checked the front of the house and then the fireplace once again, still nothing that would have given off such a flowery scent.

At this point, my husband asked me what I was doing. I told him that I had just recognized a scent of flowers, and I thought they were from spirit! He looked at me with his typical, okay dear smile and then went back to his television show. I sat back down in wonder and delight. Had someone sent me flowers? Were they for me, or someone else? Was I crazy? Had the smell come from the fireplace vents? Was the experience real or imagined? My logical mind continued to question, even though my soul could not have been happier. It remained a mystery, until just a short time later.

Several weeks had passed, and I was to see a psychic-medium, part research and part personal. It was not until the end of our conversation when she invited questions. One that came to mind, of course, was to ask, "Who were the flowers from?" I had not told her that they were from spirit, so she could not have known. She paused a moment and then replied, "The yellow ones?" I said, "No, those are what are in my kitchen now. (Still, it was awesome for her to have even known of those.) The flowers I received a couple months ago." She smiled and quickly said, "Oh, those were from a man in spirit who was thinking of you for a special occasion." Wow, I thought, "Really?" I was delightfully surprised that someone cared enough to manifest such a wonderful aroma for my benefit. Naturally, I was thrilled. It is not often one receives flowers, never mind such a special delivery of flowers that were quite simply, heaven *scent*.

Clairaudience – Clear Hearing
Wake-up Call, August 4, 2005

Psychic-mediums have told me of all the *clairs* that I am more *clairaudient*—clairaudient in ways I never understood until my journey began. Defined many ways, clairaudient is for the most part *clear hearing*. However, until I had experienced it myself, I could not honestly tell you that I believed in it. This whole book actually unfolded in that same way. As I experienced some psychic incident, I wrote it down. As I found answers to my questions, I wrote them down. I wrote to not only better understand such things myself, but for you, too. The things that happened to me were happening to and for others as well. I knew that from all the stories that friends and acquaintances would tell me of their own similar stories, some much more impressive than even my own.

Actually, once I began telling others of the work on psychic-phenomena, I came to hear of many more similar, paranormal occurrences. Some incidents ranged from hearing and seeing things not unlike something a Hollywood movie would create. In particular, there once was a woman in a seminar that I attended who asked the speaker why she was hearing her name called out each night. Nothing more, just her name shouted out, as if to say, hey, wake-up! Clearly, she was becoming more clairaudient, but it was obviously just as unnerving for her as it was for me the first time I ever experienced it. I knew my name was being called, but by whom? Until I knew it to be spirit, I wondered as that woman might have as to who or what was the cause, never mind the why. My own wake-up call came only weeks prior to the seminar.

After a psychic mentioned that I too was clairaudient, I was a little surprised. This psychic is really reaching if she thinks I hear people talking in my ear, never mind dead people. Nope, not me, and if I did, I am not sure I would admit to it anyway. They put people away for stuff like that. Although I will not lie to you, after some thought, I did find it a bit intriguing. I have always had a little *psychic envy* in the fact that mediums could so easily communicate with those in the spirit world. I thought it would be rather awesome to be able to directly speak with angels and spirits. Of course, if you can hear angels, spirits and deceased loved ones, why not saints, and Jesus.

How *do* psychics really hear anyway? Is it the mind's imagination or sweet little voices in your ear like whispers of a child? A famous psychic wrote in one of her books that it is more like a chirping sound in the ear. Yet others have explained it as anything from Morse code to someone speaking as clearly as we talk to one another. If you are a clairaudient reading this, you know the difficulty in explaining such a phenomenon. However, after my own wake up call one morning, I would like to offer at least one way that it might come across to the average person. Surprisingly, I have come to discover the same thing has happened to many others in the same way.

Somewhere in between the deep sleep of night and the lighter sleep of early morn', I heard someone clearly call my name out, Trinda! In an automatic reaction, I sat up in bed almost instantly and said, "Yes?" There was no reply. I thought it was my husband as he was not in the bed next to me. It was still before dawn. From our bedroom, I yelled out, "Yes, did you want me?" Again, there was no reply. I found him in his den and asked, "Did you call me?" "No, I did not." "Wow, I think I just heard someone in spirit say my name." My husband just shook his head. I knew he thought writing this book was beginning to get to me. Truthfully, the more I got into it, the more phenomena were occurring. Yet, I was awake now, and it came to me. This was just another example for me to write about, to share with others, as to what being *clairaudient* must be like.

It did not seem to be a dream or a thought in my mind, nor as if one spoke in my ear, either. It was more of a real voice *out there*. It was as if someone was speaking with my voice from the next room. Odd that I got up immediately as if a trumpeted, revelry woke me. I am truly not a morning person either, so it is going to have to be rather impressive to get me to move. While a few will say it was simply a dream, I *know* it was not. You know the difference between dreaming and something else, you just know. I gather that being clairvoyant is just that as well. You just know when something is not within your normal senses.

After that wake-up call, I had to add this little story because as I learn to *recognize the unseen world* and that of spirit, so can others. My impression is that they are teaching us. I know it may sound a little odd or perhaps even simply wishful thinking. However, if spirit is teaching us, what is it that they wish to say, exactly? Just saying my name is not much in the way of a message. Instead, I think that spirit was simply trying to explain how and what a psychic experience, such as what clairaudience, is really like, but especially that spirit is simply with us, that we are never ever, truly alone.

Through such experiences, I was beginning to understand that clairaudience might be more of an enhanced natural ability. While we all may have some degree of this ability within us, some can fine-tune their ability. They are able to know and sense much more than others. I would tend to think of the psychic senses as a part of us and not of something *outside* of us. I have asked many of the psychics that I have interviewed, "How do you do that?" Their replies are nearly all the same, *we just can*. They just *know*, they just *see*, or they just *hear*. It comes naturally, even though most do work at mastering and enhancing their natural abilities and skills as psychic-mediums.

Clairaudience may not necessarily mean audio *only*. In addition to meaning *clear hearing* as with audible sounds and voices, it can mean receiving messages as through writing. Having only *heard* my name thus far, my writing is where I most easily receive messages. I do believe that I receive thoughts or suggestions from spirit through both my drawing and writing. However, I must then do my part as well. I must then interpret what it is spirit may wish me to express. That is when *practice* is necessary. Obviously, some psychics may be more skilled than others, however, practice and development will improve any ability.

I know hearing only one brief word was not much, but it was enough. It was a demonstration by our teachers in spirit of just how psychics or laypeople like you or me might actually hear spirit. By lack of any other explanation, it was indeed a paranormal experience. I hope it gives you a better understanding of being *clairaudient*. Whether it is hearing your name or even through your own writing, when spirit wishes to communicate, I think you will just *know* it.

I also believe my experiences have occurred for a reason. They have a purpose bigger than for just my benefit. They have happened to show us all that there is more than what we see and understand from our known five senses. While it may seem like spiritual schooling at times, it is more of a journey of self-discovery. These things have happened so that you too can see how truly unique *you* are. I know there will be those who read this and see these experiences as similar to ones of their own. Having strong, natural psychic or intuitive abilities may not necessarily mean that you should be a psychic-medium, but rather that you might learn to recognize and acknowledge an unseen world and perhaps some of what that entails. I also have to wonder of the benefits of clairvoyance, especially clear seeing or hearing. Think of how those abilities could change the lives of the blind or deaf. Perhaps it is a future that we are only seeing glimpses of now.

Truly, it can be a wonderful journey of learning in this life and there is so much yet to learn. You exist to experience and in experience, you learn. Never get to the point in your life when you think you have reached full. I would imagine we never reach full on either the physical or the spiritual planes.

Clairvoyance – Clear Seeing
Indian Maiden, January 2005

In that deep sleep of night, I too would *see* things. I would travel to places that my conscious mind could only imagine. I would know of lives before this and dream of them as if entering a work of fiction. It was all so mysterious and wonderful at the same time. At times, the moments were clear and detailed, and at other times, it was as if I was looking at them from afar. Yet no matter how complex the scene appeared, I knew it was and *was not* me.

One cool night in January, with covers up to my chin, I fell into a deep sleep. Before waking, I saw the image of an Indian maiden and wondered who she might have been. She was off far into the dark, distance part of my mind. As if frozen in time, only the back of her was visible to me. She had long black hair in a single braid, a tan skinned dress and matching footwear. She was petite and I knew she was pretty. I wanted to see more, but could not. There were no other people, no animals and no scenery, just the dark of night surrounding her. I tried and tried to reach her, but she stayed at a distance as if to say, this is just a hint of what once was.

Why could I not see anything else? Who was she? I wanted to know more about this figure in the dark. What was it about this image that seemed so familiar to me; so real to me? Was this Indian one of my spirit guides or a past life? I eventually dismissed the thought of her, except for a brief notation in my journal. It was a couple months later when I would find out the answers to my questions.

Once my writing began, my meetings with psychics became a regular event. We would talk of spirit and reincarnation as if these things were common to all. However, personally, I was never truly, interested in knowing much of my own possible past lives. What was past is done and over with. I was more interested in what the future held. Nevertheless, three other psychics would reunite me with the Indian maiden.

The first psychic reading came shortly after my first image of her. I went for my first reading with Philomena, a wonderful medium in Cassadaga, Florida. She gave me an insightful reading, mostly about family members. However, at the end of it, she asked if I had any questions. I said, "Yes, I had a dream about an Indian once, can you tell me who she is?" She thought her name was Little Doe. She explained that when an Indian woman would give birth, she would often name the child after the first image that they saw at the time. Philomena had also seen an image of tall English man and listed the finer details of his wardrobe down to the ruffled shirt, long coat, and tall hat. Both of them were elusive to her as to who they might be in relationship to me. She thought, however, that the Indian was perhaps a past life or even maybe a guide of mine in that I had a strong sense of her, this unidentifiable Indian maiden. Either way, she satisfied my curiosity for the time, but new information would come about my past lives as an Indian more than a year later.

I was attending a psychic fair in another city when I would hear again of both the Indian and the English man. I was with another very talented psychic-medium who gave an astonishingly accurate reading. In our meeting, she asked if I had any questions and my dream came to mind. I asked if she knew who my main guide was, thinking she would confirm that she was an Indian. All the psychic could see was that it was a woman for sure, but that she had on a long flowing robe of some sort. Well, that did not sound like an Indian to me. I asked her if she was positive that it was not an Indian. The psychic said that the minute I said Indian, she heard a resounding, no! It was definitely a woman in a robe and not an Indian. Now I *was* puzzled. Who was the Indian, and who was the woman in the long flowing robe? The questions were on hold for only a brief time.

It had not been three months later when another opportunity would come to find out more about my guide and the Indian woman. Sitting with another very notable psychic, Sandy Anastasi, the answers came to my long-awaited questions. She paused during her reading and happily told me that my main guide was actually an angel. I was so surprised. I asked, "Are you sure?" She smiled and nodded, saying, "Yes, and she's very pretty with a fair complexion, light hair, and 'a long flowing robe.'" I could hardly believe what I was hearing, the exact words the previous medium had given. Finally, news of my guide, but what of the Indian; who was she? I had to ask. She told me that the Indian was a previous life of my own and not a guide at all. She just *knew* it. How interesting to think I might have been an Indian. It all made sense now, and the thought of one of God's angels by my side made me feel simply heavenly.

This was yet another validation of both the angel and Indians; yes, more than one past life as an Indian, as well as an Indian guide, would come long after the last reading with yet another wonderful psychic-medium, the Reverend Phyllis Dee Harrison, a notable medium from one of the nation's oldest spiritualist camps in America, Camp Chesterfield, Indiana. Phyllis and her spirit teacher graciously introduced me to my own spirit guides, teachers, and deceased loved ones in the spring of 2006. She was able to validate a few of my previous lives, and not one, but multiple lives as an American Indian. It was yet another validation of my own clairvoyance, my own *clear seeing*. There have been other confirmations of this, but now my conscious imagination could consider the thought of the lives as an Indian, and happily of an angel by my side.

What have you been in your previous lives? Were you once a doctor, lawyer or Indian Chief? Do you have a fondness for places or foods and wonder why? Do the children around you speak of strange people and foreign lands? Ask children to tell you their stories. It is the belief of many psychic-mediums that the very young, between two and five years of age especially, can remember bits and pieces of their past lives. If so, you may want to listen a little closer to the tales of children. It just may help to define them better in this life.

Listen closely to what you may hear,
as they speak of events and people held dear.
Recalling past lives and long-ago times,
ever so happily from subconscious minds.
Listen closely to what you may hear,
as dreams of past lives, become ever so clear.
With reasons for likes and dislikes you may find,
as well as, mysterious tales and signs.

I wish you clear and memorable dreams in your journey toward ultimately *seeing* and knowing more of the unseen world.

Spirit Text Messaging, March 30, 2005
I love today's technology. My phone can take photos, video, e-mail, surf the Internet, play music, and do all the things a phone today can do, as well as ring other phone numbers. It is all so amazing compared to only a few years past. If you can imagine the *days of old* (even as recent as my school days) when the thought of a cell phone was still science fiction, then you can image how I felt the night I received text messaging *without* the use of a phone at all.

I will admit the message was brief, very brief actually, almost not worth mentioning until you think of how and from whom it might have come. However, I knew it was simply a sample of something greater. Now more comfortable with spirit communication, I feel ready for nearly anything. However, some of the methods to attempt such communication with spirit are obviously, still being perfected. One such method is what I shall call *spirit text messaging*.

It was early one morning, shortly after a deep sleep and at the beginning of consciousness when the text messaging began. I knew someone was trying to get my attention. The dreams went away and the backdrop looked as if it were a huge blackboard on which to write. Then as if by magic, an alphabet pile of letters appeared against the blackboard. The letters were definitely Times New Roman font and bright white in color. Each letter clearly defined against the blackboard when the letters began to move about. Slowly the first letter moved away from the pile as if coming closer for me to see. It was the letter *M*. Once again, the pile moved some as if to get my attention in shuffling the letters. Then another letter, *y,* came to rest next to the *M* to form the word "My." I was focusing even harder to see what the next word might be when the dogs barked, breaking my silent concentration. They woke me out of my spiritual slumber. It was still hours from my normal wake-up time and for some reason, the dogs were awake and barking. My first thought was why, what did they hear or perhaps see? There was no noise, no sounds in the night, and no lights to bother their sleep. Yet, they bothered mine. I was just about to *see* that which was so carefully, placed as text on a blackboard when they interrupted spirit's *text messaging*.

I tried for days and days later to recapture the message, which began that evening, but had no luck. However, I will keep trying to perfect this form of communication and hope that spirit does too. Perhaps the dogs were frightened not by the moon or the passing of a cat that night, but by spirit simply attempting tomorrow's *text messaging*.

Birthday Bouquet, May 22, 2005

Surprise gifts can be so wonderful. Imagine how I felt when the surprise gift that I received was from the spirit world. Without any doubt, this was going to be a birthday to remember.

It was a week prior to my birthday. My husband and I had just finished dinner and we were at our respective computers when the doorbell rang. My husband answered the door and I heard him say, "Thank you!" I got up to see who it had been and I found him standing in the foyer holding a beautiful tropical flower arrangement. It was so impressive, decorated with seashells, a bird of paradise flower, palms, and miniature orchids. We were both stunned. When I asked him who sent them, he said it was hand-delivered by the neighbor across the street. Which neighbor, I asked? I only knew the woman directly next door to us. He said it was from the woman across the street, and she told him the note would explain everything. We placed the arrangement on the table and looked at the card. Almost ever neighbor on our street signed it. Still confused, I looked at the card again and it simply stated that they were happy to have us as neighbors. Now we were confused. Why would strangers send us flowers? What had we done that was so appreciated as to receive such a stunning arrangement? While we regularly mowed our lawn and put out the trash, we could not think of anything particularly special that we had done. She was on her way out for the evening and was not going to be available to ask. I promised my husband I would see her the next day to thank her and to find out why everyone thought of us. It was a beautiful arrangement, and the more I looked at it, the more familiar it seemed to me. Then it dawned on me.

Earlier that day, I had gone shopping. It was the first free day in ages. I wanted a dress outfit for work and thought I would browse the mall shops. Disappointment began to set in as I searched rack after rack for a style I liked. Hours later, I had still found nothing I liked or that fit properly. Then in a moment, I got an image in my mind of an outfit that I had looked good in some years prior. I remembered a photograph in which I wore a particular outfit while holding a flower arrangement. Then the thought came to me that the outfit was nothing special, just a plain skirt and nice top. I was just younger and somewhat smaller then. That is why I looked good in it. Why then would I have thought of that particular outfit? It had also been my birthday the day of the photo and my co-workers had given me a surprise party. In addition to photos of me in the office, someone had taken photos of the decorations, the cake, and the beautiful flower arrangement that I had received. My husband had sent them to the office that year. Normally, he would bring me flowers at home instead of the office. My husband's opinion is that bringing flowers home to me is more personal than having them sent to the office. However, this was a year to impress. Not only had he sent me flowers that year—and to the office no less—but also an exotic arrangement at that, a unique tropical theme with a bird of paradise in the center. I was stunned and kept the photos to both remember the day and the flowers.

I realized then that it was not the outfit that I was getting an image of, but rather the birthday bouquet I held. I had received a *clairvoyant* image while shopping. Yes, both flower arrangements were almost identical with tropical foliage and similar orchids. I searched my albums to find the photos to confirm it.

The next night I went over to see my neighbor about the flowers, but she was not home. Her next-door neighbor was sitting out on her front porch so I stopped to say hello and thank her for signing the card. As I introduced myself, I asked why she had signed the card. She told me that the woman occasionally does surprises like that for people in the community. She did not know why she wanted to give us flowers, but signed the card anyway. Besides, she said, "You always seemed like nice people." I smiled and thanked her again.

It was a several nights later when I finally found my thoughtful neighbor at home. We had met briefly sometime ago, but neither of us knew one another except for brief hellos and waves at the mailbox. When we met, I asked her why she brought us the flowers. She just smiled and said that I would not believe her. I told her that I had been experiencing many unusual things over the past few months and would believe almost anything at this point. She paused and then shyly said that *God had put it upon her heart* to do so. Spiritually guided to create the bouquet, she did not question God. She just made the arrangement, got the neighbors involved, and delivered it that night. I told her of the vision I had earlier that same day while shopping. I explained that it was similar to the birthday arrangement my husband had given me so many years ago. I had not realized it at the time, but the night we finally talked was the eve of my birthday. She had actually delivered birthday flowers as if personally sent from spirit. How amazing it all was. We both knew it was something special, and simply smiled and hugged as she wished me a happy birthday.

Birthday Bouquet
May 28, 1992

Birthday Bouquet
May 22, 2005

His Aura, June 2005

If you have never seen an aura, I would like to challenge your memory. Perhaps you have and you just did not know it. Only after witnessing this phenomenon myself have I discovered what an aura actually looks like. Additionally, with some concentration, I can now actually see auras around almost every living thing. It is an amazing skill to cultivate. If you do not initially become cross-eyed trying, you can interpret much from reading auras.

What is an aura anyway? Auras are a visual vibration, an energy or supernatural glow from any living thing. Whether a person, plant or animal aura, it emanates around the entity in many varying degrees of size, shape and color. An aura can be anything from a narrow hazy outline to a protruding rainbow of colors. While I have not seen the more colorful auras, I have finally begun to see auras much more easily. If seeing is believing, then I now believe in auras.

Even my husband, who initially thought it frivolous to bother trying at all will occasionally stop and point someone's aura out to me. I remember we were at a party one evening and he quietly leaned over to ask if I could see the performer's aura expand every time he played the recorder (a flute like instrument). I had not noticed it myself until he mentioned it. We could easily see his aura while he sang and played different instruments. However, it was not until he played the recorder that his aura impressively expanded out another two to three inches. You could literally *see* that he put his whole heart and soul into playing that particular instrument. It was as if it was a natural extension of him as his music effortlessly filled the room. It was wonderful to see and to make that connection. We both smiled and thought how special it was that we were finally at that place to share such a moment. This musician had obviously loved what he was doing and we were all the happier for it.

Yet, it was not always as easy as it was that night in seeing auras. My sister-in-law was the first person I ever met that could actually see auras, mostly around plants and trees, and especially at night or in low light. She said they just seemed to glow as if in moonlight. However, the first time I ever experienced it myself was rather unexpected. I had been relaxing by the pool, something I had not had much time for in a long while, and watched my husband making minor repairs to the deck. As he was bending over, I suddenly saw this white band around him. It was as if there was a foggy mist around his body. Nearly all white in color, the band appeared to be approximately three inches in width. At first, I was not sure what I was actually seeing. I blinked a few times and then rubbed my eyes trying to focus clearly. When the image did not vanish, I followed my husband's movements and realized that the white mist was actually his aura. Seeing it for myself made me a believer in this small but surprising paranormal occurrence. However, now I would tend to refer to such events as rather normal.

After seeing his aura, I began questioning and researching the whole concept. Much of how auras are explained involves the colors of our emotions emanating from someone's soul. Apparently, the various colors also have different interpretations. How you feel emotionally can be interpreted by the colors of your aura. The color blue, for example, is represents loving or nurturing; orange represents excitement; green indicates power or intelligent; red represents physical or sexual and lavender expresses fanciful or spiritual. Numerous people, psychic-mediums and laypeople alike have actually told me that they see a lot of white from and around my own body. Yet, supposedly, each aura is truly unique to that living entity and changes by their emotional or physical state at the time. Therefore, your aura at this moment may not be the aura of even just a few moments later.

One of the better references that I have found on auras is by a Dr. Tom J. Chalko, Ph.D., with the University of Melbourne, Australia.

Apparently, from his statements, most supposed auras shown in such photographs are using a photography trick called photomontage to create false imagery of auras. It is best to remind everyone, buyers beware, not all photographers claiming to use the Kirlian effect may indeed be doing so. Therefore, rather than spending money on the possibility that it might not be done correctly, why not use your own eyes to see auras. Start with yours.

Here is an exercise that you might try in order to see someone's aura or yes, even your own (with a mirror) and it will not cost you a cent. Choose a location in which you can relax and have a plain white or dark background. A colorful or confusing background may distract your aura interpretation. Select a focal point to look at, like a little left or right of the person's head for example, or at the center of their forehead, known as the third eye. Stare at that point for at least a minute or so. Afterward, use your peripheral vision to see the surroundings, all the while staring at the focal point. You should eventually see the background or border of the person becoming hazy, lighter or a different color than the background farther away. Remember, it takes both concentration and patience. Eventually, your sensitivity will discern the aura vibration reaching your eyes and you will see it. Remember, practice and patience, but try not to stare at others for too long, it may concern them somewhat when they finally notice your gaze. I try it in airports at times, but you must be careful that your stares are not noticed.

Psychometry, August 13, 2005

Psychometry is the psychic ability to perceive people, surroundings, images and/or events connected with a person by holding an object belonging to that person in ones hands, preferably close to the heart. Sounds simple enough; hold an object and you get an image, right? Well, for the most part, yes. While you might have thought I would offer some complicated and lengthy discussion about how to do it, I am happy to say there is no need. I believe the mysterious psychic phenomena known as *psychometry* can be accomplished by anyone with just a little patience and a very open mind. I feel comfortable telling you that after my own experience with it.

While I might have played around with it a couple times as a child, I never really noticed a special ability for it. Actually, I never really thought about it one way or the other, until one afternoon at The Association for Research and Enlightenment, Inc. (A.R.E. ®) in Virginia Beach. I was attending a conference there, *Exploring the Other Side*, and the main speaker for the conference was the famous, psychic-medium, James Van Praagh.

During his presentation, he asked each of us to pick a partner for some exercises. The woman to my right, who I shall call Karen, and I turned our chairs toward one another. Previously, we had only briefly exchanged hellos and small talk, but nothing of significance. Of course, you can assume a great deal about a person from their appearance. From Karen, I could assume she was a woman of comfortable means, possibly a professional, and from her wedding ring, married. Other than that, I would simply be guessing.

We exchanged jewelry items as James instructed us to use my ring and her bracelet. As he guided us through meditation, the lights dimmed slightly and a soft instrumental melody played overhead. It was a soothing background for my busy mind. I immediately began thinking about this woman as I cupped her bracelet in my hands. What images am I imagining on my own, and what images might be through psychic ability? How will I be able to tell whether I am not making it all up? As the questions quieted some, I told myself just let it all go, shake any thoughts from my mind, and leave a blank slate in which spirit might impress upon me of this woman. In that very instance, almost too quick and too subtle to notice, my thoughts went to a room surrounded by windows. My mind envisioned a large room with wood floors and lots of large windows or sliding glass doors. It was an open, airy feeling to the room and I *knew* that this was Karen's home. I held the thought for a moment, and then my mind began to wonder off as James led us out of meditation. The moment was over and we returned each other's items. That's it, I wondered, nothing else to this mysterious act? It was so easy, but the question remained, was I correct?

Now for the results; had Karen and I done well? It was time to exchange thoughts. I told her that I imagined a large room with wood floors and many windows, which gave the room a very airy and open feeling to it. "That is all I saw," I said. Her mouth opened in surprise, and she told me that I was correct in describing her home's living room. How wonderful, it actually worked. Now, her reading for me came. She said that she got a few images. First, that I had a daughter who sang, next, that we had a home surrounded by lots of trees, and lastly, that we were all quite simply happy. Her questioning look gave way to pure surprise and delight when I responded with excitement that she was indeed correct on all three counts. Her remarks were extremely accurate. First, we do have a daughter whose natural gift is being able to sing exceptionally well. Second, we had lived on five wooded acres and it was the best time as a family that I can remember. She was right; we were simply happy. I felt Karen hit 100% with her psychometry reading. We were both very impressed with the ability to pick up those details from only a few moments of meditation. Wow, I thought, just think of what you could do if you actually practiced.

After the experience, I wondered if it was not luck or great guesses. I tend to think, even today, that we really did succeed. The location was perfect, the mood was right, and the desire was there. All the best elements were in place and it happened. Remember, though, you may not always be as accurate as you would like, or as often as you like, but I really believe, it is possible. Try to remember that prayer or meditation can be a powerful tool in all endeavors, as well as your purpose in doing so. The heart, mind, and soul must work together, preferably for the good of others, for you to be successful. Many mediums warn that a frivolous attitude or wrong approach to the whole process of psychic development might even be harmful. I would suggest that you follow the advice of those professionals with the best of intentions to guide you in your exploration of this work. Ask for the ability itself, learn more about the exercises and purposes behind them and you should be successful. It worked for both Karen and me, and with practice, and it might work for you.

Spirit Messages at the Forest Temple, August 19, 2005

For better than a hundred years, psychic-mediums of Lily Dale, New York, have assembled to give free psychic readings for the general-public. Currently, every day at four o'clock, mediums promptly gather at the community's Forest Temple. Those visiting Lily Dale come from all over the nation, even the world, to participate in this rich tradition. The small, weathered building is a whitewashed wooden structure with an outdoor stage and dozens of benches under a magnificent green canopy of tall trees. It was a warm summer afternoon during my first visit to Lily Dale, but the breeze off the lake kept us all remarkably comfortable.

It had only been a few minutes after my arrival to this little psychic community when my Hostess, Rev. Barbara Sanson, a resident psychic-medium at Lily Dale, escorted me to one of the Temple benches. We did very little small talk as everyone that entered the sitting area became quiet with respect and anticipation. Quickly, each bench began to fill, one after another, until the audience grew to nearly 175 in attendance, women mostly, but men and children as well. We all anxiously awaited the first speaker.

Rev. Donna S. Riegel, psychic-medium, facilitated an hour of free readings. Her tiny voice barely heard over the sound of the leaves and branches moving gently above us. She introduced the first speaker, another resident psychic-medium and then another, another, and the time that followed seemed to fly by. Each medium would take their turn in front of the old wooden stage and address the audience with their polite introduction of "May I come to you?" As each medium took their turn to speak to the group, it reminded me of an old-fashioned town gathering. First, the medium would feel pulled to select someone and begin with, "May I come to you?" Yes. Thank you. From spirit, I have so-and-so coming through. Every introduction was respectfully presented to the visitor. Although that did not keep spirit from having fun with us with what came through. Their messages were usually loving and kind, but at times, silly and strange. Validations ranged from deceased loved ones acknowledging someone who had recently dyed hair or had poor baking skills to home plumbing problems. It was hard not to laugh at some of them and we all seemed to enjoy the fun way that spirit seemed to capture our full attention. Everyone was very receptive to the mediums relaying of messages and enjoyed the time together as a group, even if only a few were the recipient of a personal reading. This practice of free readings at Temple is a century old tradition that seems to have an even stronger appeal today. As they ended their remarks from spirit, they would close with either, "I'll leave you with that as I leave you with God's blessings" or simply, "God bless you." While their readings were approximately ten minutes each, the impact was immeasurable. Obviously, people were very moved by both the experience and the messages that spirit brought through. You could tell everyone wanted to receive a message. Everyone wanted to hear from his or her own loved ones. Yet, in a way, they did. I would have loved to have received a reading myself, but I knew I was there to work and after all, it was not necessary. I already knew spirit was with me. I hoped others would also come to the realization that spirit was inside them. Yet, little did I know what awaited me for my next visit to the Temple the following day.

Seeing Spirit, August 20, 2005

Saturday was the busiest day of my weekend in Lily Dale, with a full day of interviews scheduled. I was to meet with the resident mediums for hour sessions and the calendar was full from morning until night. I had a break for lunch and another planned for four o'clock. Great, I thought, I could revisit at the Temple once again. I had a marvelous first half of the day speaking with the mediums about their lives and the work they do. Then, at half past four, I realized I would be late for the meeting at Forest Temple. I had been busy with paperwork and not noticed the time. I hurried over from the Mediums League where I had been conducting the interviews. I wanted to be a part of the experience again, but also had hopes of finding one of the mediums (Patty) who had forgotten to sign some papers the day before. As I approached one of the rear benches, I noticed that there seemed to be fewer mediums present than the day before. However, Patty was *coincidently* there, and sitting next to another medium who I shall simply call the Reverend. I quietly approached the bench and joined them. Everyone sat quietly as the facilitator, Donna S. Riegel, began to introduce the Reverend as the next speaker. Patty quickly signed the papers and then we both gave our undivided attention to the Reverend's presentation.

After a few minutes into the Reverend's messages, Patty leaned over to me and whispered, "Spirit is with him." She took me somewhat by surprise and I replied back, "Really?" I had not noticed. I was busy looking at the audience to see their reactions to what the Reverend was relaying from spirit. She told me just to watch him. As he spoke, the Reverend rocked slightly, back and forth in his stance, from one foot to the other. It was a slow, almost hypnotic motion that I noticed immediately. However, I had not really seen the presence of spirit until Patty mentioned that I watch him. It was then that I realized the shadow to his left was not really a shadow at all. I had seen it, but did not notice all that was actually around him, even though it too was moving while the Reverend's swayed, I finally realized that *the shadow* had both a different form and variation in shades of gray and white. The inside appearance close to the Reverend was a darker shade of gray, like that of a shadow, but grew lighter more as it extended outward to a whiter, almost cloud-like substance in appearance. I was somewhat in disbelief when I leaned over to Patty and asked her if that was someone in spirit. She nodded yes, and quietly told me to keep looking. My eyes went back to the Reverend and I immediately saw two other spirits next to him. They stood to the Reverend's right with the one on the far end being a little shorter than the one closest to him. I began squinting and opening and closing my eyes to confirm what I was seeing, and when it did not change, I realized that they were indeed spirit. It was not his shadow or trickery with lights (remember we were outside in the light of day), but truly that of spirit without any doubt, and without any other explanation as to what I was witnessing. Surprisingly, as I write this, I realized that I reacted quite calm at the time. Even though my vocabulary has improved somewhat over the years, the only thing that I could utter back to Patty was, "Oh, cool." It was an inadequate response to such an incredible, if not miraculous moment. Yet it was my honest, first reaction to what had not felt at all like a surprise. It felt rather *normal* actually. Then, as if a deer caught in headlights, I remained perfectly still until the Reverend broke my concentration. His talk was over, and he began to walk back to our bench. While I heard little of his last messages from spirit, I saw everything I needed to know.

Yes, if seeing is believing, then I now believe and truly know that spirit is alive and with us. If this is either shocking or unbelievable to you, please stop if just for a moment and fully take in what I have just recounted for you. Amazingly enough, I have personally seen spirit, alive and with us all. I tear up just thinking about it as I recalled the moment once again for you. While I know I will always be a prove-it-to-me kinda' gal, those few moments at the Temple made me a true believer in life after death. Before then, I had only hoped for the day that I would be able to see spirit, especially my own guides and loved ones. Even though they were obviously the Reverend's spirit guides, I was just as delighted with the experience. Finally, there was the proof or validation of life after death that I always dreamed of experiencing.

Although I have experienced nearly all of my psychic or sixth senses, at the time of this writing, the only psychic sense I have not yet experienced is clairgustience, clear *taste*. Perhaps one day I will, but I am not sure I am actually anxious for that one. An excellent example of that is how a medium might describe their recognition of a gunshot, as they perceive of a metal taste in their mouth, like that of the gun itself.

Fortunately, throughout my journey, I have had experiences of hearing from spirit, smelling scents from spirit, and even feeling spirit, but none of them touched me like actually seeing spirit. Perhaps it has been the totality of the journey itself, which has lead me to the realization of spirit. Trust me when I say that the logical, analytical side of me has indeed been in shock, but I cannot dismiss all that I have recognized and now know of the unseen world around us. I have finally accepted all of the proof that spirit has been trying to give me over the past two decades. It has taken a long time to finally, believe in spirit communication and in life after death, but thankfully, spirit is patient with me.

With a full schedule, I was never able to interview the Reverend himself, but I hope through my writing he knows how forever grateful I am to both him and his spirit guides for the most amazing experience of my life. I will end here with the most memorable time of my visit, seeing spirit at the Forest Temple. Truly, they were all captivating moments at the Temple, ones that I will remember forever. If ever you get the chance to visit the spiritualist community of Lily Dale, be sure to stop by and sit among friends, both in flesh and in spirit, under the tall canopy of trees that shelter the blessed grounds of the Forest Temple.

Drawing of the Reverend and his Spirit Guides
Saturday, August 20, 2005
Lily Dale, New York USA

Remote Viewing, August 20, 2005

As you know, *clear seeing* is what many have described as seeing an image, like that of a photograph, of a deceased loved one or a scene through their mind's eye. For most, the image usually comes and goes quickly. The longer the individual can hold that image, the better they are able to notice more of the finer details contained within it. While psychics can be clairvoyant to some degree, the average person may not as easily see that of the unseen world around them, particularly spirit.

However, I have met and heard of those who can also perform *remote viewing* or as it was sometimes called, *distant point vision*, seeing people, places, or images from within the mind rather than with the eyes. While I have only ever heard of a few individuals who claim they can do so, some of whom used their abilities during war times to spy on the enemy. David A. Morehouse was one such individual. Resigned from military service in 1994, Dr. David A. Morehouse, former Army Major, was a remote viewer for twenty-five months from 1988 to 1990. David is now an international best-selling author and a leading teacher of remote viewing and spiritual transformation. Believing that, "Remote Viewing is truth! It is an empowering art and science that will open the possibilities within you, creating doorways to levels of understanding never thought attainable."

I never thought it was possible, until my husband unexpectedly proved remote viewing to both of us. Surprisingly, my husband has been able to do so occasionally and with great accuracy. He has demonstrated it a number of times, but as of yet not by his own will. The first of his newly recognized observances was while I was in New York for a few days doing research for this book. While I was having the experience of a lifetime seeing spirit, my husband was apparently having the experience of a lifetime, *seeing me* in New York, through remote viewing.

After my amazing trip from Lily Dale, New York, I returned home a changed and chattier (yes, possible) woman. Even after a full day of air travel, I arrived home with a great deal of energy and greeted my husband with a continuous stream of stories. My enthusiasm was apparent and my chatter went on for some time. Finally, after my tongue began to tire, I asked my husband how *his* time went without me. Before he began, however, he asked if I would like to hear something strange. Strange I could now handle. After speaking with and seeing spirit, nothing he could say would surprise me. However, my jaw dropped after he told me of that he was able to remote view or see from a distance.

It occurred when we had spoken by phone the night before while I was in a guest room at a private hotel in Lily Dale. Each room of the hotel is distinctly different in its décor and filled with a various angel images and figurines. It is a lovely place to lay one's head should you decide to visit. When my husband was speaking to me that night by cell phone, he was able to see me in the room and describe its every detail. Unlike clairvoyant sight, he was not seeing dead people, but rather seeing me from a distance, even more impressively, during his conversation with me. He never stopped to tell me that he could see me in the room, but rather waited until I arrived home to ask me if I indeed appeared as had seen me.

Now that I was home and looking into his eyes, I knew the experience was a little unnerving to him. He described my clothing and the details of the room with amazing accuracy. After he presented all the specifics of the scene, he asked if he was correct. Mind you he had not actually seen the outfits I had brought with me, nor been told what the room looked like. I had brought a number of outfits with me, so even if he knew I had six outfits and guessed the right one, he would still have had a one in six chance of getting it correct. Yet, he had.

I was shocked when he accurately described the room and its contents, even my outfit, beige slacks and white top. He continued to tell me of my exact sitting position on the bed with one leg up and my back not quite resting against the wall behind me. He also said that there was a small triangle shaped (tiffany style) lamp on the table beside me.

If that was not enough, I tested him even further. I told him the house had many rooms and six guest bedrooms. Then, I asked him about the six bedrooms, which one had I stayed in, again another one in six chance. Without much hesitation, he said six. I was stunned, he was right again. Not only did he know the right room number, but shortly afterward told me he saw that the actual number was a brass number 6 with two nail heads holding it on a white door. Correct again, but how could he know? What neither of us knew at the time was that he was able to see from a distance.

There are other similar instances, which took us both by surprise. If seeing me several states away was possible, then surely the next two occasions were just as real. A second instance was while I was at work one day. Again, we spoke on the phone together. While talking, he did it again and could see me at my desk. In the middle of our conversation, he stopped and asked if I was wearing my purple suit and leaning over my desk at my computer. I was surprised to say the least. Yes, but how did he know, I asked. I questioned him as to whether or not he could see anything else and then he proceeded to describe a co-worker's outfit. Stunned, I was still trying to decide if it was really happening. Could my husband actually see me twenty plus miles from home? It was all so exciting, but still another instance came a few months later.

We had met after work one evening to have dinner with his mother. Both of us had driven to the restaurant separately, his van and my car. In our drive home later that night, I took the lead and was eventually positioned several cars ahead of him in the same lane. We have a habit of chatting on our cell phones with the ease of earpieces during long drives and this night was no exception. While chatting away, I began to tire and started fiddling with my hair while holding the wheel with one hand. Then suddenly, my husband asked that I put my other hand on the wheel and drive more safely. I quickly responded and then I wondered how he could have possibly known one hand was not on the wheel. I looked to my right thinking he had changed lanes and was driving next to my car, but that was not the case. I asked him where he was with the van on the roads, behind me or had he already passed me and seen me while driving by? No, again, he was still several cars behind me. He started to describe seeing me through the passenger side window with the blue lights of the dash on my face and the position of my hands on and off the wheel. It was as it he was keeping pace with the car while looking in the window. He could see the movement of scenery through my driver's side window and me talking to him, but could not make out the words or the sound of my voice or any other noise in the car. He could actually see me. As quickly and uncontrollably as it happened, it stopped, but he was fully aware this time as to what was occurring to him. To both our amazement, he had proven repeatedly that he indeed had not only experienced this ability called *remote viewing*, but also that he was beginning to consciously, recognize his own clairvoyant abilities.

Virtuous clairvoyants are not those seeking fortune and fame, but insightful souls with a divine desire to serve for the betterment of others. They are those skilled psychics who have recognized both the unseen world and their role in it to be of service to their brothers and sisters. Psychic-mediums for the most part are usually not famous and with few exceptions, do not make millions of dollars in their profession. They live a relatively normal life trying to explain the paranormal to believers and non-believers alike. They earn less than one might think and must pay dearly in many ways, emotionally and financially. They take on much ridicule for simply trying to make sense out of their sixth sense.

Emotionally, they deal with frustrations and prejudices of seeing an unseen world and all that it may entail. Financially, they pay higher insurance rates and additional expenses while working out of their homes and small offices and shops. It is a lot to go through for such little monetary return. However, for most, I believe, they do it for a much greater reward, a purpose greater than themselves or for any fame or financial compensation. They do it out of love. It is as simply as that. They do it because they believe it to be the truth and the right thing to do. They do it because they believe the messages are from a divine intelligence. They do it because they know their thoughts, words, and actions are everlasting. They do it because they know that what they do here and now, will be with them forever, as life is indeed continuous. They do it for us.

Trust me when I say my husband is no psychic-medium. He has been a science teacher for nearly thirty years now and a technology coordinator for more than a decade. He is the least likely psychic candidate I know. Yet, he has moments that neither of us can otherwise explain. He uses his natural psychic abilities or intuitiveness as we can all do everyday. He uses his clairvoyance in ways that, until recently, he never even shared with me. It was not until my writing engulfed both our lives that he began to tell me of those things over the years known as supernatural, unusual, or as he put it, just plain strange.

Psychic-mediums and others are telling us that everyone has these natural abilities, strange as they may sound at first, if only we learned to recognize them. However, after some consultation with a notable medium, she explained to my husband that his initial experiences with remote viewing would remain sporadic until he learned to master it. Thus far, his ability to do so has only been with me. Perhaps our soul's connection with one another is so strong that it is just easier to see me rather than something else. Yet, I believe that with practice and development he could not only see me, but also our daughter, and eventually other individuals and places, if he wanted to. While amazingly real to both of us, an element of doubt lingered in him.

The other layer of doubt to his remote viewing was his ability to see the future. While he has not seen much in way of world predictions, he has seen some of what the future may hold for us, specifically, future retirement years, but only bits and pieces of events and places. Wishful thinking, I told him one morning while having coffee. You are just imagining a retirement home with your desire of what it could look like, I said. No, there is this place, this home that I see in my mind, and he went on to describe some of it to me. Then, if strange could not get stranger, I began to see it with him. Not in desire, but an actual place as if we had already seen the house and land. Like sharing a similar dream, we each told the other of numerous details to the inside of the home. We could each describe the same fireplace, the furniture, the layout of the home, even the dog, the lake, and the winding wooded entry into the property. Both our descriptions fit each other's perfectly. His matched mine, and visa versa, yet neither of us had consciously planned or had previously spoken of this vision. It was not even what I had hoped our retirement home might be like. How could he have described my vision of the house and property with such detailed accuracy? How could I have added to his image and been correct? Were we both remote viewing the same location or just in tune with one another after thirty plus years of living together? If he had not seen me in my room while I was in New York, or at the office in my purple outfit, or driving with one hand, or all the other times he has been so surprisingly accurate with remote viewing, then I would agree with the latter assumption, it was just a coincidence after years of being together. Yet, he was correct, he had seen me from near and far and neither of us knew it was truly possible until it actually happened. The phenomenon was validated; my husband had beyond a shadow of a doubt, truly experienced that of remote viewing. As Niels Bohr, one of the fathers of quantum mechanics, is quoted as saying, "No phenomenon is a phenomenon until it is an observed phenomenon."

Chapter 5 – Cassadaga

Meet the Psychic-Mediums of Cassadaga, Florida
Interviews, May 15, 2005

The town of Cassadaga, Florida, started from the founding of the Southern Cassadaga Spiritualist Camp Meeting Association. The Camp was founded by a very talented trance-medium, George P. Colby from Pike, New York. His spirit guide, Seneca, instructed him to establish a spiritualist community in the south. The location was chosen for its unique energy level. The word Cassadaga is a term used by the Seneca Indians meaning, "rocks beneath the water." The Camp was chartered in December of 1894.

It had been more than a year since I last visited the little psychic town, and even with the fast-paced growth of highways and cities that surround it, it had remained exactly as I remembered. The quaint and mystic town of Cassadaga, Florida, as most Floridians know, is the workplace for a number of psychic-mediums, as well as other talented individuals. Charming cottages, shops and cafes surround your first *must do* stop at the Cassadaga Hotel. I crossed the gravel driveway to the front steps, this time it was not for a psychic reading, but to meet with a few of the mediums who have made Cassadaga their permanent home. My heart began to beat faster with the anticipation of what my visit would reveal. Hopeful of simply just good interviews, I was surprisingly gifted with so much more.

I walked up the front steps and into the lobby thinking that this was going to be questionable at best, as most of the mediums at the hotel have become somewhat hesitant to say the least with interviewers and writers. Understandably enough as they had in the past been frequently haunted by, no, not ghosts, but by journalists and reporters, especially at every election year with unyielding persistence for predictions of presidential elections. They were, therefore, cautious at best with my visit. Yet, somehow, maybe my own intuition was reassuring me, this was going to be an especially memorable afternoon.

After my initial greeting with the receptionist in the hotel, I wondered around the gift shop where you will find everything from magnetic stones and crystal jewelry to books and incense. Afterward, I found a lovely Victorian chair next to a small, lace-covered table with an accompanying rocking chair. I was comfortable in the little corner of the lobby and ready to meet the first of several mediums. Quietly, I said a little prayer that all would go well. Some of the conversations that took place while we sat and chatted touched on such deeply personal and spiritual matters as their beliefs in God and reincarnation, as well as talking with the deceased. While some declined to be interviewed and one would only speak anonymously, I was able to assure a couple of wonderful women that they would be presented in an honest and respectable manner. The first psychic-medium that I would like to introduce you to is the Reverend Carol Ann Taylor, once a psychic-medium in Cassadaga; she has since relocated to Deland, Florida

Reverend Carol Ann Taylor
Psychic Medium
Deland, Florida USA

Meet Carol Ann Taylor, Psychic-Medium
Carol's experience includes her being a full-time reader at the Cassadaga Hotel, offering spirit zone tours and psychic discussions. Her work includes spirit contact, dream interpretation, and psychometry. She also uses tarot cards and crystals during her readings.

Carol began by telling me, "I specialize in angels, guides, teachers, healers, master guides, life on the other side, and teach paranormal workshops, as well as counsel those in the medical profession, through hospice and doctors. Especially with nurses, they want to know how to comfort their patients at the last moments. They want to give them insight as to what's going to happen and where they are going."

She went on to tell me of how she teaches workshops for caregivers so that they in turn feel comfortable and knowledgeable enough to console those who are physically dying with the message of life after death. "My heart goes out to them (the nurses)." She told me in earnest that she tries to make it as simple and easy as possible so that they might fully understand, and therefore, help their patients with a greater clarity of the transition from dying to living. She recalled that many nurses, whom she has worked with in the past, had actually seen the spirit rise from the body in operating rooms. Carol commented that, "Their insight is absolutely fantastic."

I asked her what exactly it is that *she* can see. She explained that she is both clairvoyant and clairsentience. She clearly knows and sees, but seldom hears things, and is trying to train her ears to be open, to be more clairaudient.

Remember, a clairvoyant is someone who perceives distant objects, persons, or events. They can also possess the ability to see through objects and recognize energy that is not normally perceptible to humans. A clairsentient is someone who is empathetic and senses energies, also known as psychometry, which is the ability to hold an object or touch someone and sense the energy surrounding that person, place or thing. Psychic-medium counselors use clairsentience to feel and sense information and thought-forms in energy fields, which can be revealed in color, light, or even emotion such as joy or sadness. Clairsentients can also experience a sense of movement. Clairsentience can manifest as a scent, sound, or sight; something I once experienced myself. The abilities of a clairsentient would be extremely beneficial for healers and counselors, but especially so for a psychic-medium. Carol put it more simply by saying, "Clairsentience is just 'clear knowing'; to feel and sense and know." She added, "I also see spirits, physically see them, as well as auras." All life— plant and animal—has an aura. She described it, as "Everything just seems to glow." I do not think she meant that she sees it all the time, but I had heard that same description before. A close relative of mine hesitantly told me on several occasions that she can literally see a glow, or light outline, around trees and plants, but not too much with people. It is not something that she would tell many others for fear of them thinking her odd. It is such a shame those with any exceptional abilities or gifts, would have to hide it from others out of fear of ridicule, or perhaps even worse. All the mediums I have ever spoken with have had some sense of that fear themselves.

As a little girl, Carol began seeing the dead walking and moving about the house, especially at night. Being only four years old, she did not quite understand why there always seemed to be so many people around. However, she was not too worried about all their company until as she put it, "It became scarier." She started seeing only parts of people, such as just the torso or just the head coming at her, even just the feet at times. Can you imagine trying to comfort a child that would see such visions? Then being told that it must only her imagination or a nightmare. It must have been a very unsettling existence for her. Unfortunately, it continued for many years later. It was not until she grew older, that she finally began to realize her visions were part of an ability they now call clairvoyant and clairsentient.

Carol explained that her parents were atheists and "a strict, police sergeant father" and her mother, "a sweet, country gal." Carol was the eldest of three children and had no one around who was able to counsel or to guide her during those critical years. The little girl who slept with the bed covers over her head was almost ten years old before she began seeking help. Her first attempts were visiting various churches to see if anyone could counsel her. Shunned, as no one understood what was going on with her. They all thought she was communing with the devil, or some other evil. She told me that it had made her close up even more and that it led to a rather secluded life. Not until she was a sophomore in high school when she met a teacher that understood ESP, did she have her first inkling of light, as she describes it. He knew what was happening to her, and helped her develop it. She happily commented that, "He gave me insight." After that, she studied Buddhism, and many other religions, as well as holistic healing with herbs. However, her real confirmation came around the age of seventeen. While most girls at that age were concerned with boyfriends and after school activities, Carol was working at an early age as an Air Traffic Control Simulation Operator for the government. From it, she was able to rent a little country cottage. The cottage was near a larger main house and a small dirt road. She began to tell me of that time in her life with excitement. She began her true story with joyful reflection. "I pulled up one day, and the owner came out. She was a delightful woman, bless her heart, and I was talking with her for a few moments. Then I looked back at the house and I saw this older man sitting on the step with a white shirt, black suspenders, and black pants. He had a bushel of apples and was pealing them." Carol told the woman that there was a man sitting on her front step and asked her who that was. As she described him to her, the woman quickly passed out. After Carol revived her, the woman told her that her father had passed away only three months prior, and that was what he used to do, peel apples. Carol had described him perfectly. Carol smiled widely and told me, "That was when it first became very, very clear." It had been a long time since the days of the little girl who hid under covers. Finally, the frightened child had become a young woman who was just beginning to discover her unique abilities. Those abilities would become a gift and not a nightmare.

I wondered why spirits are more easily seen at night. It seems to encourage nightmares. Carol reminded me that the mind is very busy during the day, constantly working, thinking, keeping schedules, and so forth. At night, most of us are more relaxed and quiet, and thus more receptive to receiving communication from spirits.

I asked her how we could better communicate with our deceased loved ones or other spirit. I know that the many times I had tried before bed only led to my falling asleep. Of course, the answer to that would obviously be not to meditate in bed, but rather sitting up and at another time perhaps earlier in the evening. Carol did suggest though that if I persisted it could gradually become easier. She also commented that, "Your right side is your psychic side, and your left side is perception. If you want to receive spirit, or if you wanted to use crystals or gem energy, you would hold them in your left hand. The left side is the structure and the conformity, the part that shuts us down when we are children. We were all wide-open receivers and when we started talking about imaginary friends, spirits and guides, our parents, grandparents and teachers would tell us to stop daydreaming and to stop this or that. So the right side starts shutting down which is your psychic side, the very open, very beautiful side." I interrupted to ask if it would stay shut down or could we change it? She nodded yes, "You can always open it back up again; at any age. That is what is so wonderful. It is never lost."

As far as seeing spirit, Carol did mention that we at times see spirit among us and do not even realize it. She said, "You know how you can be just going down the street or be in a crowded room people and someone catches your eye? Someone just catches your eye and you are like, hmmm. You may think, I don't know why I am looking at them, but

I am, and then you go on your way." She continued to say that, "Ninety percent of the time you're seeing a spirit or a ghost, 'cause they look like everyone else." I giggled and then thought of the many movies that have depicted that same type of occurrences. She recommended seeing the television movie, *The Sight* with Andrew McCarthy, as a form of reference. It is about a reluctant psychic that sees dead people in an old hotel that he has been hired to refurbish. I understand it aired sometime in 2000, but I have not yet seen it myself.

We moved on in our conversation to more divine matters with her understanding that there are many levels of entities too, as she says, "…the higher power, the source, and the universe." Depending on your faith and perception of God, the divine can be of various names and forms. However, if you were to imagine a pyramid of higher powers, according to Carol, there is a hierarchy from God, Jesus and Mary, Buddha and all the prophets, to saints, and then specialty guides. You have twelve rows of specialty guides, then angels, and cherubs and so on, and then your own guides and deceased loved ones above you in the plane above this existence. I asked her who her main guide was and she rather surprised me with the comment that he is a Zulu warrior. Carlo also has a set of twins, a little girl and boy named Isis and Jeremiah, from colonial days that act as guides for her, particularly with regard to her volunteer work with teens and children. Carol mentioned that she also had a man from India and a few others that also assist her from the spirit world.

Carol described someone that believes in spiritualism as a person who believes that there is no death and that life does continue. She believed it does not have anything to do with a specific religion or faith. I gathered that many of the mediums here at the hotel were from various backgrounds and religions, but that there was a common thread among them. They all expressed faith in not only life after death, but in a higher divine power, Jesus, Buddha, and the prophets, as well as spirits and angels. They also described a perfect heaven, one that we create to our own satisfaction, which is without earthly faults and imperfections. It is a heaven where everyone can live in his or her own reality and in his or her own way. However, unlike in the movie *What Dreams May Come*, even though a favorite among psychic-mediums, Carol said that she did not believe that we could change our appearance while on the other side as the movie depicted. Different from a few of the mediums that I had spoken with, she thought that we keep but only one appearance with our persona on the other side. When we go back, we stay in that form until we reincarnate once again, picking new physical features and attributes to meet the need of the next lifetime.

The next lifetime still sounded so strange to contemplate. Real or not, the thought can encourage one to look at his or her life more objectively. Yet, no matter how you are seen, remember that you do have purpose and value. Your worth and purpose is validated each and every day and by many. Not just in how you interact with family members either. It can be in what you mean to your neighbor, your co-worker, or the stranger, who perhaps needed a helping hand. A psychic once told an acquaintance of mine that this was her last life, so she might want to get it right. Why wait for that last life? Make this one count like no other. Approach life as if it was your last go-around and at least *try* to get it right. Remember the effort is just as important as the result. Many things and people can get between the goal of soul and us. However, it is the positive energy put forth, which makes the difference. Remember, when you have lived a life of good intent and effort, there can be little regret whenever you contemplate this life or in the hereafter.

I could have spoken with Carol for hours, but our time had ended. She had somehow made an uncomfortable topic seem comfortable. She had shown us all a side of the psychic that few see. It was the human side. She had given us all a look into the private life of a psychic-medium. She had shown us a glimpse of how she became the person she is today. While she may be a clairvoyant to a sitter, she will just be Carol to the rest. If you would like to meet Carol, you may visit with her in Deland, Florida.

While the next psychic-counselor wished to remain anonymous, I would like to include some of her comments for you. Partly because she so willing gave of her time, but mostly because she hoped that her interview might help others.

We began by talking of the symbolism within a reading, such as what an apple means to one psychic might mean something completely different to another. In addition, her own symbolism for things changes by the sitter she is reading. She told me, "It depends on who you are reading as to what the symbolic meaning is." Depending on the reading, she might also see a photo or a scene of something in which spirit wished to communicate about. She explained, "You have to hold it (the image) there, in your mind, long enough to get whatever details they want you to pull out of it. Everything in that photo may not be necessary." Then I asked her if she *hears* (clairaudient) as well?

PSYCHIC: Yes, I hear.

TRINDA: How? Is it a voice in your ear?

PSYCHIC: I don't hear a voice out of one particular ear, it is just…around.

TRINDA: Is it clear?

PSYCHIC: Yes, very clear.

TRINDA: Really, no muffling or distortion of any kind?

PSYCHIC: Mmm-hmm.

TRINDA: Do we have only one guide that communicates directly to us or do many come together to relay messages?

PSYCHIC: There is more than one. You have a doorkeeper, and a protector. The doorkeeper screens people. For example, if she were reading for someone who needed a legal counselor, she said, "They will bring in the proper lawyer that had passed on."

TRINDA: The individual that could best assist?

PSYCHIC: Yes, and to make sure it is the right one.

TRINDA: Is our main guide the doorkeeper?

PSYCHIC: I feel so, yes.

TRINDA: Do you know all your own guides?

PSYCHIC: No, because they change. As your needs change and you grow spiritually, they will change.

TRINDA: Do we have one main guide that stays with us throughout our life?

PSYCHIC: We have one that stays with us.

We spoke about our guides. While her names for various positions of those in the spirit varied, their purposes were similar to what other psychics have said.

TRINDA: It seems to me that we only get limited information during a psychic reading, whatever is relevant to us at that time, and not a whole lot more. Is there a reason for this?

PSYCHIC: You could not handle it. It would be too much, especially with the tragedies. So, we have to have it spoon-fed to us. For instance, if they (spirit) sat you down at birth and showed you everything that was going to happen in your life, would you do it?

TRINDA: "No, probably not."

PSYCHIC: No, so, isn't it wonderful that they do not let us know? How could you deal with it all?

TRINDA: Will we ever be able to easily see and communicate with those on the other side (heaven), or not?
PSYCHIC: One day.

She went on to explain that time is of man and not of spirit, but that there is a type of quickening to our time now, which we are slowly becoming able to recognize. Like in our acknowledging of so few holidays left in a year, or the few remaining years to our life.

TRINDA: Will we approach this spiritual awareness within the next, say, one hundred years or so? Without hesitation, she quickly responded back to me.
PSYCHIC: Oh, yes. Oh, yes.

It was odd to think that we might really be ready for such awareness. So many of us are unable to live peacefully now; I could barely imagine it. Even though a day of enlightenment may one day be upon us, I truly hope that it will be sooner rather than later.

My next and last interview was with a psychic-medium that I had actually met once before. I remembered our meeting very well and desperately wanted to interview her. I recalled thinking she was so accurate with my reading that perhaps she would have even more answers in an interview. Therefore, it is my pleasure to introduce you to the next medium from Cassadaga, Philomena.

Meet Philomena, Psychic-Medium
Her Work: Clairvoyance, Soul Development and Purpose, Clairaudience, Past Life Karmic Awareness, Clairsentience, Relationship and Career Issues, Psychometry, Business Consultant, Palmistry, Message Circles, Tarot and Guided Meditation.

Philomena was born with her psychic ability to English and Irish parents in London, England. During the bombing of England during the war, Philomena was sent away from the city to safety. With her childhood spent in the countryside of Surrey, Philomena became known for her ability to communicate with spirit. Noticed by the Queen's dressmaker, Philomena was taken under her wing, and encouraged to continue her abilities. Eventually her curiosity and desire for more knowledge led to her current home in Cassadaga, Florida. After more than a decade as one of the town's best psychic-mediums, she finally consented to do an interview. Philomena is an ordained, licensed and certified, psychic-counselor. She has toured, lectured, and appeared on radio and television, and for several years was the head of the Spiritual Awareness Center (ULCO) in Orlando, Florida. Philomena's name means *strong with God.*

Philomena and I had met only once, more than a year prior to my interview with her that Sunday afternoon, and I remembered her fairly well, even though she politely had to ask what my name was when I walked up to her in the hotel lobby. She stood there paused in the moment, hesitant to approach, a petite woman with blond hair to the shoulders. Interviews had apparently not always gone well for several of the psychic-mediums at Cassadaga. It was obvious in her stance that she, like the other psychics, was at the very least cautious about another writer wanting a story. With that in mind, I hope to present a slightly different, but honest and fair look at those intuitive women that both live and work at Cassadaga. I would like to give you some of what Philomena and I spoke of that afternoon. First, however, my sincere thanks go out to that down-to-earth woman who so graciously gave of her time, and more importantly, her trust in me.

Philomena is a professional psychic-medium that says she can see images in a flash and then recall them. She can hear and sense the presence of spirit. When seeing spirit, she is using her third eye. Philomena gestured with her index finger by pointing to the center of her forehead and said, "I see images here."

When she was only in her twenties, she would conduct her earlier readings while seeing her father standing next to the sitter. She could accurately describe the sitter's deceased loved one from the way that she saw her father's appearance. She admitted that, "For a while I did not know why he kept showing up all the time." After she made the connection, she realized he was actually helping her with her messages. He was helping her by giving her someone comfortable to connect with and in describing her father's outfit, for example, it would match to the sitter's deceased loved one's appearance. However, she told me that as her confidence grew, the image of her father slowly turned to that of finally seeing the actual loved one. I gather it was a progressively learned skill, eased into it with a little help from her dad. Now, she tells me she can also see spirit as if in the flesh.

Even though Philomena sees and talks to the dead, she still described herself in her own words as an apple-pie, no frills, kinda' gal, who is straight talkin', and one who does not need to use those ten dollar words to tell you what she thinks and believes. Actually, it was rather refreshing to meet someone who was so confident, who was holding true to herself in the mysterious world of psychic phenomena. However, the revelations were more of what she said, than how she said it.

In spirit, Philomena is apparently just as busy as she is in the flesh as a medium. Not only would she tell me that she has traveled the universe in spirit during unconscious states known as astral travel, but also that she is a soul rescuer, helping lost souls find their way home toward the light. "I once took a little girl home," she said. Describing to me how she found a little lost girl in her travels and then guided her back toward the light "…toward a large round, pipe-like entrance." She stated another instance with two Civil War soldiers "…one in gray and one in blue" who had perhaps not yet realized where they were even dead, until Philomena guided them both home toward the light. It was all so amazing, but somehow believable as she softly spoke of spirit. Even her most amazing comments sounded convincing, like when she mentioned, "I played with Jesus, the child…when I have been in spirit." However, it was her use of the words, "the child," which took me by surprise. She just explained that she knew Jesus in spirit, recognized Him clearly as being Jesus, but that the image was not of an adult man, but that of a child like herself while on the other side. I loved the idea that she could do that.

Besides being able to interact with the dead, Philomena also tries to communicate with the living and guide them toward living better lives in the here and now. We talked about that for some time, and how we can all help each other in the process of becoming better human beings, to be more spiritual or more Christ-like, if you prefer.

One of the simplest ways, and yet one of the most powerful, was an example she told me about. She began, "You know when someone cuts you off in traffic, and you say, '*bleep*' it!" That is a negative thought and it comes right back to you; if not then, later on." She continued with even if you say it, feel and mean it, you should try to acknowledge the error, and simply say something like, "Cancel that and bless you." It may sound like a silly little suggestion at first, but think about the deeper purpose behind her suggestion. Re-program yourself, from a negative pattern of thinking, to that of a more positive behavior. There is some lack of control to our thoughts today. People seem to be able to say and do whatever they want, but what are the consequences of those words and actions? After we have said something enough times, does it eventually become a habit or pattern of reality? After giving time and energy into those thoughts and words, do they not manifest into form?

Consistent anger, for example, would most assuredly begin to create a real and harmful effect on someone or something. What Philomena was alluding to was that we could change that negative pattern of thought, or anger, by beginning to recognize when and how we express it to others, even so freely and easily as swearing at someone in traffic. Sure, you can get upset at such things as reckless driving now and again, and perhaps not cause an obvious or immediate harm to someone else, but why not instead try to let it go and turn the other cheek as Jesus taught? How many of us actually practice that on a daily basis, even in the smallest of incidents? As busy as our roadways are now becoming, letting it go could be of great help to both parties, at least with one's blood pressure anyway. I would hope that we could begin to pay attention to not only what we do, but what we *think* and *say*, and that we might overcome any *negative programming* in order to reverse those too common reactions. My mind flashes to the movie, *Sister Act* (1992), when the character, Sister Mary Clarence is upset at her ex-lover and rather than swear at him while dressed as a nun, she says, *bless you.*

So much of what we talked about was simply common sense and just plain human courtesies that I grew to like Philomena, that down-to-earth gal, who just happens to talk to the dead. I felt there are just some people you like, or do not like, and then wondered why. Philomena believed that it was because our soul can recognize, in her words, "a good spirit when it knows one." Behind the physical is our soul, and it is either going to be white (good, of love and the light), gray or black (dislike and negativity) and we intuitively recognize the type of soul or person behind the flesh of the body. She gave me an example and said, "You know how everyone liked Princess Diana. They all mourned for her and flowers came from everywhere." I replied, "Yes, why was that?" I remember being deeply, touched by her death, and yet I never understood why. Even though I really did not know that much about her except what the media told us, her death deeply touched me. Was it just because she was a young and beautiful princess, and we all wished for the happy fairy tale story? The more I thought about it I realized that many young, beautiful people pass away every day, and yet this type of global outpouring of emotion did not occur for those individuals, famous or not, as it did for Princess Diana.

As you know, the Princess of Wales died on Sunday, August 31 of 1997, in Paris. In the Queen's message to the world shortly after the passing of Princess Diana, she commented on the great expression of grief and condolences, not only throughout Britain, but also around the world. Those who knew of Princess Diana would never forget her; literally millions were greatly, moved by her death, as I was.

Philomena said that we all felt that great loss of someone very special. "She was one of the White Sisterhood." To Philomena, white means of love and light. Supposedly, we all recognized that within ourselves, from deep within our souls, and we mourned the loss of such a loving spirit here on earth. It is just her physical presence that is missed. Therefore, could she still have an effect on us, and what of the barrier between the spirit world and this reality? Would there ever be a possibility of that barrier lessening? Philomena did not think that the time would be soon, but explained that while the barrier may be difficult for spirit to communicate through for several reasons, one being our polluted planet, it is not impossible for them to come through either. Philomena had proven that hundreds upon hundreds of times with spirit messages for sitters who find their way to her in Cassadaga, Florida.

However, if all that this interview time together did was to help me analyze my own actions toward others, in and out of traffic, then it was worth the drive to meet and speak with her. Philomena and the others give us all the validation of a continuous life with messages from the dead nearly every day. Messages that are serious or silly, important or frivolous, it matters not. Her messages to one sitter after another are spreading the word of life after death, as well as help to thin the barrier between two realities, as we learn to recognize and validate that of an unseen world around us. I walked away from this little psychic town with much more than I realized at the time, and only hope now to remember Philomena's suggestion when those lessons of life, both large and small, occur again.

Personal Reading, January 10, 2004

Before my conception of writing ever began, I met with Philomena at the Cassadaga Hotel for my own personal reading. Somehow, I must have known that I was destined to know this woman and what it is she has devoted her life to do. However, my last meeting with her was about the experience of receiving messages from spirit. What would our time together allow me to know? My memorable meeting follows next.

Philomena's first and foremost comments were that the information given might deal with either the past, present, or possible futures. Therefore, she told me that I might want to listen to the tape recording of the reading a little later on for perhaps a better understanding of what was said. Conveniently, most psychic-mediums will supply a tape recording for you of the session, normally included in the cost. Her fee was reasonable for a half-hour of counseling.

The first thing that Philomena did was a simple palm reading of my hand to examine the heart, head and lifelines. I am not sure how much of it was her reading my palm rather than it was her taking a moment to focus her psychic attention. As with tarot cards, some psychics do palm or numerology merely as a tool to help themselves focus as they seem to tune-in psychically. Most psychics will agree that their tarot cards will hold onto their personal energy, helping to illuminate their own natural ability. Understandably, there might be a brief paused moment or two before a medium would then begin the reading. While holding my hand, palm up, Philomena began.

> PHILOMENA: I see that you were very close with family as a child. You had to work hard to be independent. Why are you still worrying so much? I see some depression; are you okay; are you okay now?
>
> TRINDA: I am much better, thank you.
>
> PHILOMENA: You worry about things of tomorrow; do not, as it is a negative emotion, so do not worry about things that have not yet happened. You have traveled to other countries.
>
> TRINDA: Yes.
>
> PHILOMENA: There is travel designated within your own country, as well.
>
> TRINDA: Oh, okay, good.
>
> PHILOMENA: I have a lot of creativity around you; do you do anything with it?
>
> TRINDA: Yes.
>
> PHILOMENA: You have a lot of color around you. Do you like interior decorating?
>
> TRINDA: Yes, very much, but I have many interests.
>
> PHILOMENA: Oh, okay. You have had one child, a daughter. Is she in a marriage, or in a relationship?
>
> TRINDA: Yes.
>
> PHILOMENA: This is fairly, new.
>
> TRINDA: Yes.
>
> PHILOMENA: Okay, because it is in the first card.

A few other details followed about my daughter, and then some more talk of work and finances.

PHILOMENA: Stop worrying about money. No, no, it is not your husband that is worrying about money, is it? No, is that right; or is it you?

TRINDA: No, me, I am always worrying about something.

PHILOMENA: You are not looking at what you have. You are looking at what you do not have. Yeah, so, when you worry about money, you stop the natural flow. Tell yourself you have more money than you could possibly ever spend. Now, I do not get the word *in-law*, I only get the word *mother*.

TRINDA: It is my mother-in-law, but we all call her Mother.

PHILOMENA: She is elderly. She has had a lot of stress lately. Where does she live?

TRINDA: Close to us.

PHILOMENA: Did her husband die quite recently?

TRINDA: Yes.

PHILOMENA: There has been a lot of confusion here. She is…yes, she does not know quite what to do, and I do not know why they did not talk this out; it was just the way it was. I know it is not anything you want to talk about, but things should have been settled. There is a lot of confusion. It is almost as if she does not know whether to stay in the house or not.

TRINDA: Exactly.

PHILOMENA: Did he have a lot of problems around the throat area? (She gestured about the chest, neck and face area.) I went to the chest, but with a breathing issue. I was in the chest area, but then it is as if I could not breathe.

TRINDA: Yes. (She was exactly right as my mother-in-law's husband recently passed away and he did have several issues in all of the areas she described.)

PHILOMENA: He is here. He is the one telling me this. Has she got confused about some policies?

TRINDA: Yes.

PHILOMENA: He is saying it is not that confusing and that your husband will be able to work it out.

TRINDA: Okay.

PHILOMENA: She has to get where the policies are. She has to remember where they are; there is more than one. There is more than the large one found. Let me see. I cannot be a hundred percent, but you have found the biggest one, yes? There should be two smaller ones, which could easily be over looked. I do not know what it is with your mother-in-law, but she did not know they existed, I think. I am pretty, sure, let me check again...the large one is pretty big; is not it?

TRINDA: Yes.

PHILOMENA: I want to say the other two are like a quarter of it. He says that he does not know how you missed it because it was supposedly by the large one. Keep looking. He is talking about envelopes. Make sure they are in the right envelopes. Two of them might be together in the same envelope. So tell her, do not go throwing things out without going through them thoroughly.

TRINDA: Okay, we will try.

PHILOMENA: She looked after him for sometime.

TRINDA: Yes.

PHILOMENA: She knew he was going to go, but it was still a shock. Anyway, she will never be quite the same, the depression that she is experiencing is natural, but it is not natural for it to continue as if I think it is going to. Where does she live?

TRINDA: The house they have had for many years.

PHILOMENA: It is too big. Somebody is going to talk her into selling it.

TRINDA: Would that be good for her?

PHILOMENA: Well, let us put it this way, not yet, but it is too big for her. It was okay when he was there and she was busy and taking care of him, but it is as if someone pulled the rug from under her feet, and now it is as if she does not know what to do, as if she is not needed.

TRINDA: I understand.

PHILOMENA: It is almost like later on when things settle down, I do not know who is going to suggest it, and nobody is going to push her, but just ask if she would like a smaller place. Perhaps an assisted living place where she can be independent, but there is help if she wants it. She is an independent woman, very much so. It will go the way it is suppose to. We cannot push people, but if she is left alone too long, she will go into severe depression. Are you around?

TRINDA: Not as often as we would like.

PHILOMENA: Well, that is why his father is telling me not to feel guilty about it. No negativity, but do not be surprised if she does not want to stay on this earth plane much longer.

TRINDA: I understand.

PHILOMENA: I am not going to say when, but she might get to that point, where it is not worth it. So, when she gets to a certain time…there are times when your soul will give you a chance (meaning to exit). Do you understand?

TRINDA: I understand that she will take it if she wants it.

PHILOMENA: Yes.

TRINDA: She went on to other matters and then came back with a question as to who was trying to communicate with me next.

PHILOMENA: Has your own mother been having problems with her legs? I just got Mother and problems with legs. Not sure who. She is coming in to say hello. Did she knit or did your mother knit?

TRINDA: My grandmother lost her legs to diabetes, and she crocheted.

PHILOMENA: Did you know anybody that sewed beads together?

TRINDA: The same grandmother often had rosary beads with her.

PHILOMENA: Oh, I just see beads.

Do you know anyone that plays a mouth organ?

TRINDA: Possibly, on my husband's side of the family, but I do not know. (I did not know it at the time, but it was my father-in-law once again that she was referring to.)

PHILOMENA: Oh, okay, because I have someone showing me a mouth organ here.

TRINDA: Could you give me something else to be able to associate it with someone?

PHILOMENA: He tried smoking a pipe once, and did, but I don't think he like it.

Again, it was my father-in-law, but I had not realized it yet. Amazingly, another psychic-medium would also give me the exact same message some time later on. Only after that second message would I finally get to validate Philomena's message that my father-in-law had come through. Too bad it took a couple readings and more than a year later to do so. While some messages may be immediately validated, others may take more time. Incredibly enough, Philomena was once again correct in her statement, even if I did not know it at the time.

Our conversation ran over the length of the tape in her recorder, but concluded with a conversation as to whom my personal guides might actually be. It was an impressive reading, and all that she brought up was true. Quietly walking down the stairs back into the lobby of the hotel, we spoke some of a spiritual awakening that seemed to be occurring to so many people these days. It is odd now when I recall that I was actually questioning such matters over a year prior to my research for this book. She explained that it began sometime in the late 1980s (1987 or so), and that we are indeed headed for a time of spiritualism in the world. What a wonderful thought it was to end our time together.

Chapter 6 - Father's Day

Reading, Saturday, January 15, 2005

Starchild Books out of Port Charlotte, Florida, is a quaint and mystical bookstore that offers various works by spiritual and new age authors, a great deal of which is astrologically influenced, astrology being a passion of the owner and author, Sandy Anastasi. The shop offers her work on psychic-development, jewelry, and unique gift ideas. It is also the home of several very talented psychic-mediums, who periodically hold brief psychic readings during the shop's monthly Psychic Fair. It was at one of those fairs that I met a very talented psychic-medium, who I shall call Ann. The minute I met this woman I knew the reading was going to be genuine. My impression of her was that she could easily be someone's mom or confidant. Her confidence showed as she escorted me to the back room where several of the other mediums were conducting their readings. I wondered how I would be able to hear her over the others and our privacy came into question. Yet, somehow, even with all the simultaneous conversations, we were able to speak easily enough. It was just the two of us, and spirit of course, for a little over fifteen minutes.

Without wasting a moment, she began. She clairvoyantly knew that I had a daughter. She talked of her, her boyfriend, and their possible future together. She was amazing and definitely caught my attention. After several personal comments, she was happy to tell me that I was receiving a loving squeeze on the shoulder by someone in spirit. I asked who it might be, and she said that she saw a father figure. How wonderful, but which Dad was with us?

She thought it was my deceased father-in-law present, and described him as a very jovial man. He was happy that I was into this stuff so that he could come and connect. She smiled and said, "He thinks of himself as quite handsome now". I laughed. Dad was the sweetest man I ever met, but handsome was not a word I would use to describe him toward his later years. From little to no hair and missing several toes,

Dad's big and burly physic was showing definite signs of hard use after 86 years. He was a Pennsylvania ironworker whose career in engineering and construction spanned over a half century. The gentle giant that he was, however, made him handsome to all that knew and loved him. She said that he has been trying everything but actually materializing before his wife, but that she was not catching on, even though she wanders around the house talking to him. Ann explained to me that they were still very much in love and that Dad wished Mother could sense him. He thought about materializing, but figured she would probably pass out and hurt herself, or worse. I told him he could materialize before me with no worry, but has not done so yet. She went on to validate that it was indeed Dad by telling me that while using an odd "Mmmm" sounding name for her, everyone else calls her Mother. True enough as Dad used to call her Mumma with everyone else calling her Mother. The psychic also mentioned that he is delighted with watching the youngest in the family who was under seven years of age. Again, true, one of his granddaughter's is indeed a character and will probably be in the theater as an adult. However, the clincher did not come until the end of Dad's visit. She mentioned that he "…played a mouth piece, (a harmonica) but not very well," and smoked a pipe. I knew he had smoked pipes sometime ago, but I never knew him to have played a harmonica. I dismissed it thinking she might be reaching a little. However, it was not until weeks later when, under very unusual circumstances that Ann's comments were validated. I had also not remembered Philomena giving me nearly the same message a year prior.

My visit with the first Dad ended just as the other began. "I have another father here." He was my father, and it had been less than a year since his passing. Ann said that he was trying to communicate through her that he takes partial responsibility for his actions. I knew what she meant immediately, but she kept trying to relay his message in different ways, several times. I tried not to show how I felt. Then she told me that he would leave us now as I was becoming quite, bothered by the conversation. Yet, she wanted me to know that he was in healing for it over there. She simply suggested that I keep him in my prayers.

Our time was up and I walked away knowing that she was correct on all counts, except for the harmonica playing, or so I thought. When I asked my husband about it later, he said he did not recall his father having ever having played one and thought the psychic had made a mistake. As I mentioned earlier, I was able to validate it later on at, of all places, a Marti Gras party.

A few weeks had passed and my sister-in-law called to ask me if I was available to go to a party with her. I was curious, why me? Apparently, no one else was able to go with her. She was to attend a Marti Gras party as a fundraiser for her work and she did not want to go alone. Normally, I would have turned her down, the party-girl that I am not, but for some reason, I quickly agreed. After I hung up, I told my husband that I just agreed to go out with his sister to some fundraiser and did not even know why. The next week flew by, and I soon found myself driving us to the party. It was in a beautiful, large pink and white hall festively decorated with a Marti Gras theme of balloons and streamers, even champagne on every table. This party was becoming promising. The live band on stage was a great amateur jazz band playing a wide variety of music. Everyone seemed to feel the music and danced on the wood floor next to our table. We were sitting rather close to the stage, so small talk was not really, possible. Hours later, the evening had almost ended and I found myself surprisingly enjoying the party. We had eaten, shared the champagne, and listened to great music. I was glad I came after all. However, the best part of the evening came in last few moments before leaving. I was watching the lead singer play his harmonica when my sister-in-law leaned over and said, "You know, Dad played the harmonica, but not very well." Almost word for word, she repeated that which the psychics had mentioned. I nearly fell out of my chair. I had been watching this singer use a harmonica all night long and I never made a connection. I had not even thought to ask her about it either. Her eyes opened wide as I told her about the readings, the one recently, and another one a year prior. She told me Dad was rather young when he played the harmonica, and that my husband might not have ever known. To both our delight, she had validated his message without even knowing of it. Still, here we were, as if it were an invitation from spirit to receive yet another validation through music and fellowship. We smiled, and in the midst of all the noise, quietly toasted Dad. We only hope he enjoyed the party, too.

Sandy Anastasi
Psychic-Channel, Astrologist, Author,
Owner and Operator of Starchild New Age Books & Gifts
Port Charlotte, Florida USA

Chapter 7 – Starchild

Meet Sandy Anastasi, The Psychic's Psychic
Interview, May 28, 2005

Sandy began with, "We all have psychic abilities. The more you pay attention to them, the more frequently it happens." As she explained further, "The difference between a psychic and a lay person is the psychic recognizes the information from the other side."

Sandy sees and knows spirit as an experienced psychic and channel. She has been a professional psychic and teacher of metaphysical studies since 1979. In 1983, she founded the Astrological Institute of Integrated Studies (AIIS). AIIS has by now trained hundreds of students who have gone on to become successful psychic readers and teachers. Most notable among these, of course, is the famous psychic-medium of today, John Edward. In 1995, she went on to open Starchild New Age Books & Gifts. While Starchild initially functioned as a support to AIIS, it has long since grown to be its own successful retail business. Later offshoots of Starchild were the Constellations Coffee Shop and Internet websites: http://www.starchildbooks.com and http://www.sandyanastasi.com.

As a psychic, Sandy blends her ability to channel both her and your guides by using her gifts of empathy and clairvoyance when she reads the tarot cards or does astrology. She is also known to have a real gift for foretelling the future. In fact, one of her early challenges was pulling her predictions in. Projections were often so far in the future, clients could simply not relate to them. Sandy firmly believes that we create our own futures. Finding out where things are probably going will help us to get a better handle on them. Perhaps it may even enable us to change the things we want to avoid.

Sandy also does special past-life readings, using the tarot cards and her natural psychic skills. Although she is not a spirit medium, she can often obtain information about deceased loved ones, and sometimes can make contact with them in her readings. This she did for me during both a personal reading and during my interview of her. She is also a Reiki Master, and her interest in healing has led her to study herbs and aromatherapy, which she teaches.

Although she realizes now she was always psychic, Sandy's early background was in technical fields. She graduated magna cum laude from Adelphi University with a B.S., and a certificate in Corrective Therapy. She then taught school (Biology, Chemistry, Health, and P.E.) and worked as a safety engineer for eleven years. Eventually, her ability as a psychic blossomed. The residue of that early technical background is now obvious to both her students and clients in her common sense approach and in her ability to make the complex seem simple.

Sandy has appeared on radio and television and has written many books, which she utilizes in her classes. Her most important work being The Anastasi System of Psychic Development, a series of manuals that accompany the Psychic Development and Spirit Communication series taught at Starchild. Originally intended as support for her classes, all of her books are wonderfully informative and make for a great read. *Astrology for Beginners* and *Intermediate Astrology* together give a great foundation in astrology for students of any level. Sandy wrote *The Tarot Reader's Workbook* because there was simply no other book available that covered what she was teaching in her beginning level class. *Kabbalah Pathworking* is a compilation of paths both channeled by Sandy and adapted from past students work. It is a way to learn about the *Kabbalah* by living it from the inside out. To traverse these paths is to truly, experience a life-altering journey. Additionally, as of the date of this writing, the book she wrote many years ago, *The Old Religion*, is being edited for future release while she is working on yet another.

Writing, teaching, and helping others through her talents, experience, and psychic abilities, Sandy has touched many lives with a positive impact. After my own psychic reading from her several months prior to this interview, I am like the many others most assuredly forever grateful for meeting her. I can honestly tell you that through my meetings and getting to know Sandy that she is indeed, the real deal, but more importantly, a genuinely compassionate soul. It was a delight to have had the opportunity to meet her on several occasions, but also now to bring you one of the most enlightening interviews yet.

We began by sitting together in her small private office at Starchild New Age Books & Gifts. It just happened to be my birthday that day, so spending the day doing something I enjoyed was a gift in itself, never mind spending it Sandy. This notable psychic was graciously giving me a bit of her valuable time to answer some of my most pressing of questions, and I had lots of them. I wanted to know a great deal, and I believed Sandy could deliver.

After some reacquainting, she intuitively knew what was on my mind and began pouring out her explanation of what a psychic is and does, modestly stating that, "The difference between a lay person and the psychic is simply that we become aware while we're getting the information." Of course, recognizing rudimentary psychic skills is the first step to developing your own potential psychic abilities. She continued to explain that somewhere down the road, there are other skills that must be developed. As an example she said, "When I was first starting out as a reader, I can remember driving to someone else's house to do a party, and getting a sharp pain in the back of my neck, which was not mine, and realized that something was going on where I was going for that party. Of course, I immediately thought maybe this lady had just become battered or some major fight was going on there. When I got there, I found out that the mother of the woman who was giving the party had had a fight with her husband and called her on the phone and complained to her. It really was not a big deal. You see?"

Sandy went on to explain that over the years of trying to interpret those physical reactions and getting the same results for the same situations and things, she gradually developed a language to more fully, understand what spirit was trying to communicate to her. However, she said, "When you develop your third eye and your crown, you start to have more of a direct connection," a direct knowing verses an indirect method through symbols and signs. A more fully developed psychic may no longer have to look to symbols and interpret them. Apparently, they would be able to have a direct connection and simply know, see, or hear what it is that spirit is communicating to them.

Sandy continued to explain that she will actually see dead people in a session for someone now and no longer needs those earlier symbols or signs. She said, "They are physically there, and I am hearing what they are saying. Sometimes I see them out there, literally like a shadowy form. Other times I am seeing a projection of what's in my mind, but out there." I asked her if she ever saw them in the flesh like seeing my body before her. She said, "There were very few times when I actually saw them as real as you are, very, very few. Most of the times, I will see them…almost see-through, if I see them with my physical eyes, but even that is rare. More common is a mental projection. I'll look around and I'll seem them there next to you, but I am aware that it is coming from out of my own mind." Clarifying for me further, she said, "The image would be in my mind, but projected out."

Sometimes, however, there is the possibility of trans-mediumship, which she really does not like to do. There are several types of mediumship; clairvoyance, clairaudience, clairsentience to name but a few, as well as transmediumship, which is when a medium just steps aside and allows a spirit to come into them. Transmediumship is a type of physical manifestation that is rather rare, and while Sandy adamantly stated that you would never catch her doing it, allowing an entity to enter her body to communicate, she did state that, "We all have the ability for that."

Thoughts of the film, *Ghost* (1990) came to my own mind for the moment. She emphatically stated, "I don't like it; I have an aversion to it; I think its self-destructive and so forth." When a spirit comes through, therefore, she likes for them to be on the sitter's side of the table, even though occasionally, she gets the touchy-feely ones, who want to be right next to her where she has actually felt their touch or even felt their breath in her ear. She can feel things from them. Sandy wanted me to fully understand that the energy is there and not just in her mind. Even though Sandy said she could see, hear, and feel a spirit's presence, I asked if she used all of her physical senses during a reading for someone. She explained that while it is possible, as all of our physical senses have a mirrored psychic sense, it might depend on the spirit coming through. If, for instance, a spirit has a visual or audio ability in their persona, then that is how that person will most likely project himself or herself; it is *their* ability. "So that will enhance the skills that I have," she added. She believed that all psychic-mediums are using their client's abilities and those of the deceased loved ones for the enhancement of their own. For example, with me, whom she perceived to have a better audio ability, she might become more clairaudient, and with another perhaps more clairsentient, and so forth.

Since everyone has different strengths in their own psychic abilities, Sandy tries to remind her students of mediumship that they should try to enhance all of their psychic senses, especially if they wanted to read someone, for example, who may not communicate as well on their particular ability; be it clairaudient or otherwise. As an instructor, Sandy tells them, "Just because you may come in with a very good ability to intellectually interpret symbols and be able to respond to them and get physical results, and while that might be your strongest way of connecting, it cannot be your only way. Suppose you are working with someone who does not communicate on that level at all, to you, that person would be like reading a brick wall and you would be missing out on the message all together."

Therefore, all the senses must be trained in order to notice both the sitter and the deceased person's strongest abilities. What she has found is that the best psychics are those who have developed all of their abilities. Of course, not all may be perfect, but they should indeed have some ability with each of the senses, thereby being clairaudient, clairsentient, and so on.

Now that I better understood how Sandy uses her abilities, I was curious as to how she began her career and asked her to tell us about it. But before I tell you of both those times, yes, both, I must tell you that in the process of the interview, somewhere in between the specifics of transmediumship and psychic senses, she stopped briefly to matter-of-factly state, "By the way is your Mom gone, 'cause I am getting a mother figure over there."

I will tell you that it was a true test of my professionalism, and I am proud to say I believe I passed with flying colors. I just nodded and smiled as she went on with details of my mother standing there to my left, and then, without even a breath afterwards, Sandy went on with her explanations. The conversation kept going and we never skipped a beat. It was not until I was in my car some several hours later after our meeting when it finally hit me emotionally. Ma had been there and she helped with the interview. How awesome was that. Sure, I believed her. After all these years of hearing the same thing, I was, finally becoming a believer. It was just one more time that my mother and I have been together since her passing. Of course, I realize not everyone's mother may become one of their spirit guides, and even though I never really ever expected that in the beginning, I am very glad to have finally recognized that yes, she is, and yes, I feel blessed for it. We did and still do have a very special friendship, it is one that I am both deeply thankful for and at times, still impressed with having.

Sandy continued by telling me, "First of all, I have always been psychic, but I probably only realized it when I was in my late twenties. I remember astral traveling when I was kid, as well as looking through walls, literally, with my eyes closed, and seeing through to the beams and then to outside the wall. It was as if I had x-ray vision. I was a tiny tot when I had those experiences, but you know, after a while, you shut that stuff off."

I asked her if anyone in particular had ever shunned her for such things, or discouraged her by saying it was just her imagination. She said that it was typical, of course, and that she stopped talking about it because no one else did, and she was told to not tell lies or make stuff up. While she said that she was never really put down or chastised for her abilities, they simply were not encouraged either. Sandy reflected on that and said, "Probably my strongest ability as a kid was empathy. I was the kid who would hide in the corner of the room. If there was an argument in the house, I was shivering under the covers because I could feel the energy. I was afraid of what was under the bed because I could feel the energy collect under the bed."

Thinking back now to those things and understanding psychic ability, she believes she was always psychic, but just never knew it. Therefore, the next time your young child comes to you with visions of people and places, you may wish to ask them just a few questions, rather than dismiss them as the carefree, imaginative thoughts of a child at play. However, I would doubt that every single incident of imagination is that of spirit connection.

Sandy was just fourteen when she got her first astrology book and began to study it. At fifteen, she began palmistry, but soon dismissed them both until nearly a decade later. It was ten years later when, one night at dinner, a previous teacher had questioned Sandy as to whether or not she was still giving readings as she remembered her being very good at it. Sandy had not only stopped those many years prior, but had forgotten all together that she was indeed any good at it because of a bad experience. She recalled that she had given a woman a negative reading and when it came true, she must have blocked out her memory of the whole matter, as well as her ability to read others so accurately. It was many years later that she would recall those moments of her childhood that allowed her to do those things and rekindle her interest in them. While in her mid twenties, Sandy first got involved in a form of martial arts, Tai Kwon Doe, which then led to meditation, where she began to see and feel auras. However, it was also at that same time that she had gotten married, and for a few years had to have a full stop to those interests. Finally, a few years later, after her divorce, she was able to go full-time into both astrology and psychic development, and never looked back.

Even though the first year or so in her career was a difficult one, she grew wiser from the experience. She had met up with someone who had misguided her during her time of psychic discovery and growth, and only after breaking free from that situation was she able to come to understand the foundation of all the abilities that she had. As a result one of the things that she now teaches in her psychic development classes is how to build up protection in all things. Sandy elaborated, "To try and make my students totally self-responsible and totally in control and have them understand, scientifically, everything that they are doing, to the best of my ability, so that they can recognize what is being done to them against their will. More importantly she commented, "And, to have the ethics to not do any of those things to another person."

Psychic ethics were obviously important to Sandy, and it came across in her tone and manner as well as her words of continued emphasis on the importance of what you do with your psychic skills, for good or ill. For example, if she picked up that a couple was having martial problems, and said they should get a divorce, that would be a negative use of the information coming through. Instead, she could suggest they might seek counseling to help them.

I asked her where she thought her information was coming from, her own guides or from other sources. She emphasized, "Definitely, way more." She told me that was why she chose to become a channel as apposed to a medium. Mediumship is by far in her opinion the most difficult of all the psychic abilities, but you have to be a channel before you can be a medium. She also added, "Not all mediums can channel from the higher level of beings."

Yes, she said *beings*. While I promised myself that this book would not broach the realm of science fiction, it does at times come to that likeness. Yet, for many, it seems harder to believe in higher beings helping to guide us through life than it is to believe in bible stories of winged angels and so on, although I do not know why. Perhaps it is just more comfortable to stay with those stories most familiar to us. Are we really, afraid of unknown worlds, higher entities, and the infinite possibilities, which may actually exist?

There were many more questions remaining for Sandy. We simply continued to take them one at a time. Not that Sandy or any one person has all the answers, but I wondered if too many answers came to us at once, or if they came from but only one source, would we simply dismiss them in their entirety as one's fabrication. Perhaps that is why we are only just now getting bits and pieces of the puzzle to our existence. It would most likely be too much for us to accept all at once while in this presumably limited human form. Only when we are in our original state of being might we fully comprehend the vastness and complexities of it all. I would like to think I could handle anything coming my way, be it ET, or seeing my mother standing next to me again. Maybe it is better this way, one piece of the puzzle at a time. It may all seem too great or too unreal for us to grasp. Then again, do we really know what is real anyway? I explore our reality, our existence, and much more with Sandy and others in my next few books. Please remember to join me then as I continue my interview with her and a number of other intriguing souls, not only of our reality, but also the afterlife and spirituality, which, I am sure, will fascinate and captivate you as it did me. Yet, for now, I thought I would share some of a personal reading that I received from her in our first meeting only months prior to this interview.

Psychic Reading, March 5, 2005

Finally, the morning came when I would travel to Port Charlotte to see the prominent psychic-channel, Sandy Anastasi. I was anxious to meet this woman and grateful for the chance to not only receive a reading from her, but hopefully, to get to ask her a few questions. As a psychic, Sandy uses her abilities to channel both her and your guides with a unique clairvoyance as she reads the tarot cards or does astrology for sitters. As a future oriented channel, Sandy can see far into the future. As we sat together for the first time, I wondered what she might see in my future. Sandy started by telling me some of the basics of giving a reading.

SANDY: I am going to be getting my guides and your guides throughout the reading. They will have a more accurate answer if you ask questions. You have to interrupt me if you want to speak with those guides. Then we will have the answer rather than waiting, as they may be gone later. That means that the guide that can answer that question is there then. It is like changing the channel on your television, and you come right back to the reading, even if it is in the middle of a sentence. Guides come in and out. If I see bad stuff, I am going to tell you. It is because you can change it. If I hold it back, it would prevent you from fixing something. Think about it, it is purely logical. Why would your guides tell you about something bad if they did not want you to change it? Since I have realized this, I have been able to save a few lives. I do the 'psychic' stuff, but I am also into science very much, and quantum physics is now showing that the instant the observer interacts with the experiment, the outcome has changed. The act of my telling you has changed the outcome. Psychics really cannot hold back on what they get. What I believe is that before you come into life, you have certain things (not everything) along the way that are here for your growth and that you must experience. However, between those things, your free will reigns; you can do whatever you want. Even when it comes to those things, you can veer off some, of course. They are junctures in your life that you will have to deal with, whether you like it or not. They are there because you choose them before you came in and nobody tells you how to handle them. You have your own free will on how you go through it. Again, the only reason to get a futurist psychic reading is if you're looking at the now and seeing where it goes, you have a better handle on how you're going to take care of it. A psychic reading should never tell you what to do; it should give you an idea of what is coming. If you are at a juncture in your life and you need to see alternate possibilities, you can choose among them. It is really, neat.

TRINDA: Very nice. You know, I have always wanted to interview one of you (psychics). There is so much more I want to know. I want to learn not only how you do what it is that you do, but also what else is possible.

Little did I know, I was intuitively hearing what spirit would lead Sandy to know and tell me about in our interview together after this psychic reading.

SANDY: There is so much more. This is what I loved about *Crossing Over*. John Edward is going to be back on TV because the guys upstairs aren't done with him yet. You can count on that. However, what he wanted to get into on his show was more things that would educate the public in the exact way that you are talking about, and I think that it was removed at that point because people were not ready for that yet. People are still at the wow, show me what you can do stage, but soon they are going to be at the, I want to know how and why stage. That is when you are going to see him back out there again.

Yes, he was out there again with another new show less than a year later.

I thought of what Sandy was telling me when I was at one of John's seminars sometime back. The audience was asking about personal things, of course, rather than how the process worked. I wanted to know more about how it works, why it works, and so forth.

SANDY: When you do interviewing, when you get into interviewing...because you are going to do that, you realize.

TRINDA: Really?

SANDY: Yeah, you will and when you do, you will be building a pyramid of some sort and the interviewing process is the bottom level. I don't know if that is a pyramid toward forming (pause). It does not feel like it is *just* writing a book or doing a radio show or something like that; it has to do with something you are creating a structure for.

TRINDA: Is that the spiritual push that I feel?

SANDY: Yeah, but when you do, it may very well be that this stuff has to come out and it may come out in a book, but it will come out in different interviews first. Do not just interview me, interview as many different psychics as you possibly can. Then, integrate it into a book; this one says this and this one says that; here is an alternate possibility, because everyone has a different slant on things. For example, you know who Sylvia Browne is. She is a famous medium and I have read some of her books. The thing is, however, I absolutely do not agree with probably 80 percent of what she says about what is on the other side. I just do not agree. On the other hand, it does not mean that she is wrong either; it is simply *her perception*. That is why you have to interview a whole lot of different people. I am not going to shoot down her perspective because for her, that is what is going to work.

TRINDA: Do all mediums each see the afterlife differently?

SANDY: Two movies you need to see are *What The Bleep Do We Know!?* and *What Dreams May Come*, which talk about the afterlife and heaven very accurately.

TRINDA: I have already seen *What Dreams May Come*, and remember the graphics most of all. They almost seem to overshadow the story itself.

SANDY: See it again, for what is beyond the imagery, and look at the rendition of heaven. The reason I say that and why I do not totally agree with Sylvia Browne (about the afterlife) is because I astral travel. Do you know what that is?

TRINDA: Yes.

SANDY: I have always done it, since I was a kid, and I astral travel a lot.

TRINDA: I remember a couple of times very vividly.

SANDY: Okay, then you know; well, guess what? When you astral travel, you can go on the other side to actually meet dead people. They are in their own place or places. You can go to the Catholic heaven and you can go to the Jewish place, and so forth. Are you beginning to see what I am saying?

TRINDA: Yes.

SANDY: You know we really do not just create our own reality here; we also create our own reality there. What you believe is what you are going to get. That is what I believe. The reason I believe it is because I have had my own direct experience with it, which remember, is also colored by my own beliefs. It is fascinating. Along the way, you will realize that if you are going to follow that line of thought, you also do need to see those two movies, and look at them from more of a scientific perspective. Then you are going to have to go and interview some of the people that designed those movies because they are the scientists. What you really want to do is to take quantum physics and integrate it with the psychic world.

TRINDA: It seems like there is currently a lot of material that shows us that, but we only have bits and pieces of a bigger picture.

SANDY: It is a gradual process of education. We are experiencing what you can only call a *quickening of the planet* right now. I do not know if you have heard of this, but we are getting ready to go through what is called a *dimensional shift* and nobody on the planet is even going to know they went through it; it is that subtle. However, that dimensional shift will mean a change in consciousness and one of the things that will happen is, we will *evolve*. The whole planet and everyone on it is getting ready to evolve. One of the things that will happen when we evolve is that we are going to become more aware of the unseen world around us because as we evolve we become closer to it. So right now, you are seeing this major education of all these people on the planet, so that they are ready for it. It is one of the *big purposes*, which we are here for, including you.

TRINDA: Do you believe astrology is connected to all of this?

SANDY: Oh, absolutely. You would not believe how strongly I believe in it. I have been in astrology for thirty-five years. I was in astrology before anything else. John, my business partner, and I are both very well versed in Alice Bailey's work, which many astrologers are not. Not only are we well versed in it, but we also understand it. There was a book by Norelli-Bachelet called *The Gnostic Circle* (1978), which talks about our solar system literally moving around some central sun; that whole thing takes over twenty-five thousand years. Yet, each time we make a change in signs, as we go around that central sun, we make a leap in consciousness.

SANDY: What I usually do in my readings…by the way, they want you to write, are you aware of that?

TRINDA: Oh, yes, yes. (The minute she said that, her words echoed a truth from deep within me.) However, I am not sure what direction to take.

SANDY: This might be the primary reason that you are here. You might want to think of them all as small books. Think of it as a series of small books and then you can put your series of books on different thoughts and arrange them into a bigger book if you wish, or a series of bigger books. The reason I said to you that they want you to write something, and as I said, there is going to be more than writing because you are going to have a lot more to do, is that part of the pyramid that I see behind you is a pyramid of your guides. You have many guides and you do see some of your guides; you are very connected. You have many of your guides who are very close with the physical plane. Some of them you have known, some of them are in the physical flesh and do not even know they are giving you information. You get that kind of guidance, okay, that is your lower level guidance.

In the pyramid structure, you have tons of guides behind you and you are very much under (if you were to study the Bailey material) the second ray, the teaching ray. The ray that deals with love and devotion is a Christ ray and you have that too, that is there, but that is more of a personal ray. The other energy that is coming in for you has to do with teaching and instruction. You do that…you seem to do that with everybody you meet. It is not that you gather information, but you also dispense information. On a physical plane, there is going to end up being some kind of an organization or foundation or something.

TRINDA: I have been looking for something, but I have not found it yet.

SANDY: No, you are going to *create* it. Like I said, and it may be that it is a central something that is going to coordinate many other organizations; you see? You may just be a hub. It is hard for me to describe exactly what I am seeing, but it is like a hub that will have many different focuses that do not connect with each other except through you. Again, I get the feeling as if it is almost all virtual. So it is either all on the computer or it is all just not physical, talks or connections or letters or books or whatever. As far as the actual data that you are talking about, it is as if you are being fed information, fed information, fed information and you are going to be both writing and talking about it. Your feeling is, I could have a lecturer come in…you could have a lecturer support you, but you are going to be lecturing on your own. That may not happen immediately, but that will be along the way, okay. There

will come a time when you will be spearheading your own organization. Mind you, I have to tell you that I am talking about all the *possibilities*. You do not have to do a single one of them because what we are talking about here not only has to do with your own growth and the world's growth, but it has to do with personal choice as well, and it would involve a lot of personal sacrifices to be able to do what you're thinking about doing. If you do that, remember, you are never *made* to it. That is totally your own choice.

TRINDA: I just want to be happy at it. I know that I would be better at it then.

SANDY: It is because you are seeing the bigger picture. Yeah, you know it is funny because you are at the age when you are feeling. I don't mean your chronological age, I mean age in the developmental stage where I am learning, I am learning, I need more, more, more, but you're very quickly approaching when you have gotta' turn it around. By the way, when you turn it around, it does not mean you cannot keep learning; you love learning. It is going to keep coming in and going out, coming in, going out, that is just the way it has to be.

Now you know your sun sign is Gemini. It should not come as a surprise for you that your south node of the moon is where you are coming from another life that is also a Gemini. Now when I see a past life as a Gemini and this life also in Gemini, this is what you are learning to be. I mean that if you have done it before, you are not learning to be it again; you are taking it to a higher level. You are not your average run the mill, typical Gemini.

Now, again, it says that whatever journey you are on, you have already begun it in another lifetime. In this lifetime, you are continuing it. Your Mercury is also in Gemini and Mercury rules Gemini. Mercury has a great deal to do with communication. You are born to communicate your knowledge.

You also have your moon in Capricorn and I have something I need to tell you here. You went through a hell of a time growing up and not just growing up, but after you grew up. Life for a very, very long time was a desperate situation where things almost fell apart.

I had not said a word yet. Sandy just kept going without even asking if it was true or not, but it was. I sat quiet as she continued.

SANDY: Now the reason that happened is this. What happened *astrologically* to you is that Uranus went into an aspect of your Cardinal signs when you were in your twenties. Neptune went into Uranus when you were in your late twenties and early thirties, and what little foundation you had left, Neptune totally stole away and ripped apart by the time you went into your thirties. This was astrological transits. However, there was a reason for it. Number one, you are a much stronger person. You know what you are capable of doing and not capable of doing. There is another thing too. The Capricorn moon also talks about a lot of Capricorn energy that you came in with from another lifetime. The good part of that is that you are an entrepreneur, you know how to make money at things, and you are someone who has a very practical, down to earth, single-minded focus on things. These are all good things that come from Capricorn. You are a natural born administrator. You are someone who is very responsible. You are not afraid of taking that responsibility on. These are all good qualities. You built on those good qualities during those hard times, but Capricorn also has bad qualities like impatience; remember it is a past life drag. Capricorn moon has this feeling like, well, heck, I will just take it over and do it because it is easy for me, so you leave, which is of course, a negative quality. It is hard for you to share the power. However, I will tell you that during that period when everything in your world was collapsing, you learned to release and let go, and you learned that it was not always going to be about the things that *you* wanted to create, it was about something higher. You found your spirituality during that time. I know it was a hard, hard time, but if you look back and wonder why it had to happen, it is because you have balanced out those Capricorn qualities within you. How can I put it…you do not get rid of or cap those qualities that are negative, what you did was transmute them into a positive. So your tendency to take control has turned out to be an absolutely phenomenal administrator.

TRINDA: I am better than I was.

SANDY: Yeah, it is great because it is now transmuted to an ability to look at all the pieces and say, okay, we can use this, that works, this we have to throw out, and so on. You see what has happened is that you changed these qualities to what works. Just look back at it and say I could not be where I am without having gone through that rough time. Incidentally, you also developed a lot of psychic ability during that time and that is still with you. I think that the reason you do not see it as clearly as you could is that the psychic ability that goes with Capricorn is very hands on, very earth-oriented. It is being at the right place at the right time; it is meeting the right person exactly when you need to meet them. That is Capricorn psychic; it is being able to recognize, yeah, this money deal works and this does not; it's earth oriented. You have really developed that to a very fine pitch because you have found if you do not listen to your intuition, nothing works; it is very intuitive of you.

That I felt was very true, things would happen without the conscious effort and I had always wondered how. Sandy went on with even more astrological interpretations, but I wanted to mention that while all of this may seem rather personal, I have included it as an example for hope and encouragement to others. My hope is that from my experiences and Sandy's explanations, you will see that healing is possible. Even after someone has gone through a tough time in life, be it depression or addictions or otherwise, things *can* get better. You can get through it. You are stronger than you know, and you can become even greater than you ever thought you could be. Trust me in this only because I have been there. Sandy went on with a few more strokes that were of a positive nature.

SANDY: You have a lot of energy. You are a high-energy lady. You come into a situation, and you uplift it, if only because you bring energy into it. You have always done that. That is something you can give yourself credit for. Meanwhile though, this Pluto transit has already changed your life's direction. It has changed whom you are with, it has changed where you are physically living, and it has changed your professional direction. I think that right now, you are doing a lot of looking back at the changes you have made, reassessing and saying, am I happy with this or not? Which things do I want to take on with me and which things do I really want to get rid of? The reason for that is Saturn has retrograded; Saturn retrograded in mid October, so you found a lot of old issues in your life coming back at that point. It is still retrograde now, but you have about four more weeks and it goes direct. Once it goes direct, it is going to race out of the sign it is in and move into the next sign, which is happens to be Pluto. Pluto and Leo are opposing your Mars and Aquarius, so your changes and transformations are not done yet. Relative to the stuff you are dealing with right now, you have to have the foundation laid first. You have to go through all the closets, decide what you keep and what you get rid of, and what your direction is, and you got have that decided by the end of this month, okay? Once Saturn goes direct, you are going to be racing ahead into this new time and you are going to have all these career-oriented things crashing in on you. Decisions have to be made and action has to be taken immediately or you are not really going to have the time to be ready to go back and address the things around you right now.

Do you have a daughter?

TRINDA: Yes.

SANDY: One of the problems that you have to deal with in your life is that...you know you were born responsible. You were born feeling that whether your family's life is a success or a failure is totally, dependent on whether or not you were there for them. It is a hard nut to crack. Especially because of a lot of the stuff that happened through your thirties and forties. Now that you are at this point in your life, you are saying you cannot let go of her for a minute. Guess what, yes, there are major changes happening with her and you have to stay out of them. You are like this (she places her thumb on the table). Give her her freedom. If you try to hold on, if you try to control, try to tell her what to do, eventually you would have a face-off and there could be a big break. However, she would eventually come back because you both are very close. There is a lot of love and lot of caring there. I will tell you, your daughter is every bit as strong as you are. If you try to tell her what to do, it ain't goin' to work.

TRINDA: Let her go and she will be fine?

SANDY: Well, let me ask you this, your Mom had to let you go, did she not? Are you fine? (Yes) Okay, point made. You need to be able to step back and realize some things have to run themselves. Things that have to run themselves around you are the people you love. The things you have to run are the things that you are involved with, like your book, your organization, your job, and the things that are out there in your *own* learning experiences. Those are the things you have to grab hold of and control the hell out of them. Put your energy into them because those things need that kinda' control. You see, it is just a matter of reorienting yourself.

However, what I see for your daughter is that she will get married and she will have kids. She is a good solid person, you know. This is interesting, you have no grandchildren yet, but I am seeing little kids with buckets of sand. Isn't that interesting? She is telling me that there will be kids coming, unless that is *her desire*. I saw that a couple of times already.

Sandy went on to talk more of my daughter, of our relationship, and of what our futures *might* be like. She reminded me that the observer has already changed the outcome of what is being observed. By simply sitting there, listening to Sandy, I have already affected that of which she spoke. Only if nothing at all were to change from our thoughts and actions might those outcomes remain as she said they would, as *free will* plays a key role in our lives.

Then, after much conversation and wonderful compassionate advice, Sandy asked if I had any questions of her. One of the minor questions that I had was what my spirit guide's name was. I know it means little to spirit, but somehow I wanted to connect with her, and a name helps to do that. I knew my guide to be a female energy, but very little else.

SANDY: The one that is giving most of the information *for this reading* is your Mom.

TRINDA: Is there only one *main* guide?

SANDY: Well, actually, you have many guides and you have many guides in different areas. However, the one that I think you get most of your information from is an angel. There is a lot of white that comes in from her. It is a she, and yes, she is an angel. Angels were never people, remember? She comes in, and again, I am not very good at names, but I am hearing an "S" sound, a really, odd name.

TRINDA: Another psychic said there was a female energy that was very important to me.

SANDY: Well then that would make sense.

TRINDA: She always felt like a family member though.

SANDY: Well, it would be like a family member as she could have been there since you were a young child, would have been there as your life-guide. This one is a guide, so you actually have an angel who is a guide.

TRINDA: That is so surprising.

SANDY: Yep, light hair, very fair, very soft, and very pretty.

TRINDA: Oh, thanks, that is so nice to hear.

SANDY: Also, there is another person with an Mmm sound; mur or mar?

TRINDA: My grandmother's name was Mary and I have been told she is with my mother.

SANDY: Okay, but your Mom is with you all the time and you do talk to her.

TRINDA: Yes, I do.

SANDY: Yeah, she hears you.

TRINDA: Oh, I have another question. I got flowers a while back and I would like to know who might have sent them?

SANDY: Were they the yellow ones? I am getting yellow flowers.

TRINDA: No, I got those recently for someone who was never able to receive them, so I kept them and they are in my kitchen now.

SANDY: Well, I was getting yellow flowers. She is showing me yellow flowers.

TRINDA: I recently had a *clairfactory scent of flowers* one night this past January, and would like to know who sent them.

SANDY: It was a man, a guy who died who is on the other side whose birthday perhaps was around that time. I am getting a name with a strong "T" name or in the name. It is someone who died, was going through some kind of a celebration at that time and that is when you picked it up. (Much later, I learned from another medium about one of my guides, a doctor/chemist, and his name is Dr. Thomas.)

TRINDA: One last question, Sandy. Am I ever going to have a visual experience with any of my guides?

SANDY: Oh, yes, and you have already.

TRINDA: So far, only in my dreams.

SANDY: That is when you can see them the best.

Our conversation had ended, but as you now know, it would not be the last time that we would speak. Sandy had much more to share and I wanted to learn more about how her ability came to be, and what she is capable of doing with it. I knew that we would meet again and I looked forward to that time. She was indeed a very good psychic. She had captured all that I was and was dealing with to help give me a clearer picture of my possible future, and even encouraged me to trust in my own intuition. I was delighted to have someone like Sandy recognize my desire to seek more out of my life, to do something even more meaningful with it, and perhaps begin it by writing. Whether it would be through books or other avenues, I was thrilled that she was able to bring my inner most secrets to the forefront. I was excited about *all the possibilities*, and hopefully, the ability to make a difference with my life, whatever that might come to be.

If the only purpose to our meeting was to encourage me and give me hope for a brighter, more meaningful future, then I was happy with our time together. I was happy too, that she was doing what she loved to do, helping others with her own gift and natural abilities. From her ability to connect with spirit, I finally realized that it *is* possible for all of us to connect with loved ones, and to create the future of our dreams. It is possible to create a reality that yields whatever we wish it to be. However, it is up to us to put those thoughts into motion. We can begin to see all the possibilities with the help of wonderful souls like Sandy. If you ever get the chance to travel to Port Charlotte, you may wish to stop by Starchild New Age Books & Gifts and ask to speak with Sandy Anastasi, or any of the other gifted psychic-mediums. I promise you, it will be well worth the trip.

In the meantime, however, I would like to introduce you now to another spiritual soul who just may be one of the most candid and down-to-earth spokespersons on the paranormal that I have had the pleasure of meeting. She tells it like it is and holds nothing back. With blunt talk about life, sex, love, God, spirit guides, and her gifted psychic abilities, she is America's number one radio psychic counselor, Allene Cunningham.

Allene Cunningham
America's No. 1 Radio Psychic Counselor
Wichita, Kansas USA

Chapter 8 – America's No. 1 Radio Psychic Counselor

Meet Allene Cunningham
America's No. 1 Radio Psychic Counselor

    A true pioneer in the field of psychic counseling, Allene Cunningham has simply been doing what she loves best, helping people. For over thirty-five years, Allene has touched the lives of thousands upon thousands of people. Why is it that people flock to Allene? What is it about her that keeps people coming back to her? What do these people experience with her? First, they find a friend in Allene. They find a compassionate, sensible counselor with a wonderful gift. Her unique *intuitiveness* helps give others clarity of purpose and direction in their life. She is there for us with a soft voice, a kind heart, and an inner knowing unlike anyone I have ever met.

    Allene Cunningham, this popular radio broadcast psychic-counselor, was in the middle of a live interview on a Tampa Bay radio station when I first heard of her. She tries to make Tampa, Florida, one of her many annual stops, and in 2004, I was very glad she did.

    As I listened to the caller and Allene, I could tell this was a no-nonsense woman with a lot of common sense and intuition. She was simply enjoyable to listen to. She sounded more like a psychiatrist with a sense of humor, but she had that little something else, too. That something else was her psychic ability, which seemed to be more of a subtle intuitiveness that just happened to be remarkably right-on. My first thought was I just had to meet this woman. I was able to schedule an appointment while she was in town and received a personal reading like no other. If you get the chance to meet someone as wonderful as Allene, you should count yourself lucky. Until then, I am pleased to introduce you to Allene Cunningham, truly America's sweetheart and No. 1 Radio Psychic Counselor.

    A Hollywood starlet at seventeen, Allene Cunningham was destined for fame. Allene started singing at the age of nine as a shoeshine girl in her hometown of Wichita, Kansas. By the time she was seventeen, she had auditioned for major Hollywood studios and had signed contracts with Paramount, RKO, and NBC. She even received a scholarship from the Chicago Light Opera Company. However, she left it all to return home and marry a Baptist minister. Allene finally came to realize her psychic abilities and from it was able to help her family financially. However, something was missing. Money does not always buy happiness. With a rollercoaster childhood and later a tragic marriage behind her, she continued to search for answers. Like we all want to at some point in our life, Allene wanted to know her life's purpose. With the acknowledgement of her sixth sense, her destiny began to unfold. Allene's unique perspectives of the human condition and highly developed sensitivity enabled her to do what she did best…help people.

Now, DJ's across the country call Allene Cunningham "America's number one radio psychic." She is adored by thousands, myself included, and rightly so. My first meeting with Allene came almost a year prior to my interview with her. I heard Allene Cunningham giving psychic counseling on a local radio show and very much wanted to meet with her. I should say I *knew* I needed to meet with her. Initially, I really did not have a strong desire for a psychic reading. Instead, I simply wanted to talk with her. I wanted to know how this woman could do what she did. It was all becoming so fascinating to me. I was searching for a greater understanding of psychic phenomena and thought Allene could help.

When I first met with Allene, a year prior, she was like a combination of my mom and an earthly angel in one huggable woman. She was all that I imagined her to be and so much more. While brief, in our time together she had answered some of what was on my mind, and allowed me to actually see and touch one of God's messengers. She made me feel comfortable, and I could have stayed and talked for hours. In the instant, we said our good-byes; I knew we would meet again in the not so distant future.

Personal Reading, June 26, 2004

"Allene's highly-developed sensitivity and involuntary psychic abilities have enabled her to help people of all ages and backgrounds define and deal with their personal problems. Allene receives her information through voice vibrations; therefore, telephone counseling provides the purest readings. No visual images consciously or subconsciously can affect her impressions and opinions." That was what

I was about to find out in my first meeting with the famous radio psychic counselor, Allene Cunningham.

As I stood at her hotel room doorway, she welcomed me in with a warm greeting and I sat down next to her. How nice, I thought, she is just as she seemed on radio, very open and inviting. She let me into *her space* without any hesitation at all. She started immediately into her sense about my disposition, mental attitude, and physical health. She confirmed that I was indeed for the most part healthy, and mentioned that I would live to be an old woman. She assured me that I would age well, keeping my wits about me with no worry of mental loss. She simply stated that I would remain witty, very alert, and able to enjoy my life. I was thrilled, of course. All of that made me feel great right off, but then she asked a question that told me her intuitiveness was at work. She asked, "Why then the moments of depression?" Before I could answer her, she answered back telling me that I worried un-necessarily about things. She added that I needed to think more positively, saying, "Always think of the glass as half-full and not half-empty." Then commented, "What we think…will be!"

Allene looked at me with a little smile and said, "You are a very old soul, dear. You have had many lives." Yet, here is where it gets good; she said that I knew it when I was very young, say around seven or eight years old. Well, I almost fell out of my chair. She was literally telling me of something that only *I knew*. While I had never told anyone about that time of *knowing* in my life, I remember those thoughts clearly to this day. Even at that young age, I distinctly remember thinking to myself that I had done this (life) before, and many times. There were moments that were very specific when I recall knowing it, which I had never told anyone. Yet, here I was sitting with someone who casually mentions one of my childhood memories of reincarnation, as if speaking of something as common as the weather. She now had my full and complete attention.

Allene commented on how my own psychic awareness was being validated by the recent phenomena that I was experiencing. Most recently were those times after my father passed away were validated with signs and unusual occurrences. She confirmed those validations. They were real and not imagined. I felt much better by this time. Some of those occurrences, or signs as they are often called, were beginning to be a little unsettling. After so many of them, you begin to think either you have gone completely mad or perhaps you are making them up because of grief. However, some of them were fairly, obvious signs.

Allene continued on to matters that were more current and stated that my job would continue to go well. She stated that they are very fair people, and I had no disagreements thus far with anything she had mentioned. She also stated that I was talented at what I do, and that I should never worry about loosing my job. All I ever needed to do was occasionally ask how I could help even more. Psychic or not, it was all good advise.

After some talk of the job, she began to discuss my husband and our family. Allene, the psychic *counselor*, started to give details, one after the other. One I can share with you now, which might be of help to others, was her mention of my husband's enjoyment of late night snacking. True enough, a lot of us like snacks, especially while watching television in the evenings. After her suggestion to switch the treats from ice cream to fruits and other healthier choices, she continued her counseling. She positioned herself so confidently and offered advice that actually made me blush. She described how our evenings should go after television, and added, "If it leads to the bedroom, dear, that's even better." Once again, the chair and I were on unstable ground. According to my husband, that was the best part of the whole reading. Now, even he liked her.

Allene went on to speak more of our health, and what we were doing with our home. At the time, we were having problems with our bed, not us, the bed. Of course, my husband told me I had to make that perfectly clear to everyone. We had an older bed and not been sleeping well. Allene mentioned that right away. She recommended for now that we just buy a pad for the top of it. We did not like the idea of getting a pad and did not think it would help much. We were already considering buying a new bed, and had actually started shopping for one that same week. However, Allene was insistent on our getting a pad for now. We thought it might be a good idea for our budget to try her idea since we were not *anxious* to spend thousands of dollars on a new bed. It was a good thing for us that we waited. Allene saved us a great deal of money with her advice. Because the bed was rather old, we were simply ready to replace it. However, for the time being, we bought the pad on her recommendation. Shortly afterward, we had a bit of a surprise, come our way. We were out looking for living room furniture over the next few weeks and while talking to a salesperson, we found out that there was still a warranty remaining on our bed. We could not believe what we were hearing. Replacement of our bed was possible under the warranty. It was something we had not even considered because the bed was so old. Yet, when all was said and done, we were able to save nearly half the cost of purchasing a new bed. If we had bought a new bed earlier as planned, we would have missed the warranty savings. We are very glad we listened to Allene's advice. We have been sleeping soundly ever since.

Allene went on to talk of our daughter, what she was like, and of her dreams and plans. Again, she was correct with all her comments about her boyfriend and her career path. I had not told Allene anything about having a child, let alone a daughter. I was very impressed that a woman I had never met before was telling me about my daughter with such exact details.

Details continued, one after another. "I see a trip out west," True again as our daughter was living in California and we made the trip later that year. She went on to say, "I see a cruise for you in the future." She advised us to plan and save up for it first, however. She kept giving details, advice, all with the best of intentions. She really seemed to care about what she was telling me. She went on and on with information about family members and health concerns. Her remarks included, "He will stay on the path already in progress, and you cannot change him in that regard." Another intuitive comment, "She's not doing well without him." Both family members described with complete accuracy. Allene truly is psychically gifted.

Before our time had ended, Allene was kind enough to ask me if I had any questions. Of course, I had many to ask. While you might think to ask what the winning lotto numbers are, most people tend to ask about the well-being of others. Is it not all that truly matters? I had mentioned that my niece was recovering from cancer, and I wanted to know how she would be. Allene's first response was in her immediately placing her hands on her own stomach to say, "I see the cancer here." She then asked, "How's the baby doing?" Well, if that did not tell me she was psychic, nothing would. My niece had indeed had a cancerous tumor removed during the birth of their third child, a baby girl. Both mother and daughter had been doing well. Allene thought that she would continue to get well, but recommended that she treat her cancer by eating healthy foods such as raw vegetables, taking vitamins, and drinking fresh juices, including carrot juice. She also smiled and said, "Tell her not to worry about the skin turning orange from too much carrot juice; it wouldn't do that." Once again, all sound advice from a very caring woman who just happens to be psychic.

I wondered how individuals like Allene see the matters of strangers so clearly. It was all so fascinating to try to comprehend.

Psychic-mediums tell us that we all have psychic abilities. Yet, some like Allene have perfected that ability. I do not doubt she has taken this natural talent and perfected it from years of practical exercise. A talented psychic counselor, Allene has proven her accuracy on *many* occasions and with *thousands* of people, and I am proud to say I am one of them. Little did I know then that it would only be thirteen months later when we would speak again, but this time in one of the most candid interviews with a psychic. It is an interview left mostly in its original question and answer format. I wanted to make absolutely, sure that I not color Allene's words in any way. My hope is that you will better understand not only the messages in her answers, but also get to know the wonderful soul behind the fame and glamour of the Hollywood starlet, Allene Cunningham. Counselor and friend to all of who know her, Allene *is* truly America's sweetheart and number one radio psychic counselor.

Interview, July 15, 2005
TRINDA: First of all, thank you, Allene, for speaking with me and allowing others to meet with you in this way. Some of what I would like to talk about is of your psychic ability.
ALLENE: All right.
TRINDA: On your Internet website address at www.esphelp.com, it states that you are able to receive your information through voice vibrations. Are you clairaudient?
ALLENE: Yes, I do hear, and I do feel people greatly.
TRINDA: Is there any psychic phenomenon that you can tell us about?
ALLENE: Sometimes, I have what most people would think of as abnormal experiences with things that happen. I don't have them often, but I have them every now and then.
TRINDA: Like an occurrence?
ALLENE: Yes, an occurrence. I believe that being psychic is being spiritual. It is a gift, and it is spiritual. It is not something I can cultivate or train for. It is something that you're born with.
TRINDA: Can you perfect it to a certain level?
ALLENE: Well, I can use it at a certain level. However, when it is with me, I cannot force it do anything. I cannot make it do anything; it just does it.
TRINDA: Do you train yourself in certain ways, through meditations or anything like that?

ALLENE: I meditate a lot and will meditate on certain points or things ever day.

TRINDA: A lot of your ability is clairaudient, correct, what else can occur?

ALLENE: Yes, I sometimes hear things and I sometimes feel things. I'll sometimes see something. I'll see a picture, but it does not last very long. I wish I could hold it still for a moment and then take it apart. I'll try to dissect it.

TRINDA: You may see an image or photograph in your mind as well as hear things, but it comes and goes quickly?

ALLENE: Yes, they go very quickly. If I am looking for somebody, sometimes I'll see a certain thing. You know I had a person the other day—we were talking about somebody who had passed over, and I said that I saw a pumpkin pie. He said that it was his Dad's favorite pie. Now, his Dad is not up in heaven eating pie, but I was seeing what he did when he was here. That identifies him.

TRINDA: Do they ever give you images of what we should not do?

ALLENE: Yes, I get that many times. One of the most unusual things was that I had a man come in and he did not want to tell me what his problem was. Then he said, "I pin a diaper on my girlfriend." I said, "You what?" He said, "I pin a diaper on my girlfriend. That turns me on." All of a sudden, it came to me. I said, "I see you at 4 years old. You used to help Mama pin the diaper on your baby sister. Mama would pat the baby and say, 'There, there, all nice and dry.'" Suddenly baby soiled the diaper again, and I saw him giggling. That had become a response, which he has carried over into adulthood. By my being able to see that and show him where that began, he could stop it.

TRINDA: If you believe in reincarnation, do a lot of those types of things you have described come over from life-to-life? That man's issue was from his childhood. Could something like that be from a previous life?

ALLENE: Sometimes I get things from a previous life, where somebody has been there, or done that and once in a while, we can call it karmic. When you meet somebody that you feel you have always known, for example, but we don't have many of those experiences, just a few.

Also, I believe that people are at various soul levels. I find that older souls, those that have incarnated many times, have a psychic ability. I find that young souls do not. Now, when psychics teach that everybody is born with it and then they have to cultivate it and study it to make it do something, I do not accept that. I have not studied something to become psychic. When I know something, I cannot study to know it, like knowing about the pumpkin pie.

TRINDA: Allene, do you also see auras?

ALLENE: Yes, I do. The first thing I ever saw was an aura and I thought I had eye trouble.

TRINDA: What does it look like to you? Is it clear, cloudy, or have color definition?

ALLENE: Well, most times it is pretty clear. It is like a hazy, misty-like substance if I were to try to describe what I am seeing. It may also have more pastel colors than dominant colors.

TRINDA: One of the first times I ever saw an aura was around my husband while he was working. It was as if there was a two or three-inch fog around him, but there was no color.

ALLENE: That is the way it will look. People sometimes talk about a black aura, but I have never seen anything like that. I have seen auras that are grayish looking, but that is when people are not very well.

TRINDA: You have not seen anyone with a black aura, someone having perhaps a negative energy.

ALLENE: No. No.

TRINDA: Allene, how did you first know you were psychic?

ALLENE: I believe that people that are old, old energies that have lived before who come back into life seem to be blessed with some psychic ability. When I was a child, I was always in church. It was a southern Baptist church. Of course, they don't accept any of this. They teach about the devil and all that crazy stuff. I would have it occur in my dreams. I dreamt my father died, and he was not sick a day. Then, when I went the next day to his home, he was dead with a heart attack.

TRINDA: That must have been very difficult for you. Allene, do you have a psychic *knowing* without seeing or hearing things?

ALLENE: Yes, I do.

TRINDA: Do you prefer to do readings with people by phone?

ALLENE: I do a lot of them by phone, but I like to read for them and see them in person. They certainly like to see me in person.

TRINDA: I did too. I saw you about a year ago.

ALLENE: Most of them say, "May I give you a hug; may I touch you?" It is really strange. Once a little girl came and she did the reading and came back ten minutes later (we generally book back to back) to ask, "Is there any time left? I just want to come and sit with you. It is not too often you get to sit in the presence of a live angel." That is what she told the secretary.

TRINDA: Isn't that wonderful. Allene, do you believe we have angels, spirit guides, and all of that?

ALLENE: Yes, we do. I have seen them. The first one I ever saw was when I woke up one morning and it was standing at the foot of my bed.

TRINDA: An angel image?

ALLENE: There was just a form. It scared me to death. I jumped out of bed and ran for the doorknob. That is out of this reality; that is what it was.

TRINDA: How did you see it? Was the spirit as if it were in the flesh, or as if see-through?

ALLENE: It was just a form. I did not see a body; it was a form, and I knew it was not flesh.

TRINDA: Who do you think is guiding you now? Do you have certain guides?

ALLENE: I believe I do. I think some of them are like that guide who was from the fifteenth century. Maybe I have lived in that century. He did not give me a name or anything.

TRINDA: Do you know any of them specifically?

ALLENE: No, no, I don't know who they are, but I feel sure I have guides around me all the time.

TRINDA: You can feel their presence.

ALLENE: Yes, I feel their presence and too many wonderful things happen that are *extraordinary*. They just cannot happen without somebody doing something.

TRINDA: Can you remember any things in particular?

ALLENE: All kinds of things. I was in show business when I was a child. Things would happen even then that were just too unusual. I always had front-page publicity my whole life, since I have been nine years old and not just once. It would be constant publicity. In Chicago, I would be front-page news, the whole page. The Mirror gave me front page, the whole page. Colonel McCormack owned the Tribune and he would write editorials about me and would give all kinds of stuff. Everybody would open up and pour out their pocket books to me. They did that all the time.

TRINDA: Do you think the psychic senses mirror our regular senses?

ALLENE: Our psychic senses go beyond our regular senses. I don't think everybody's born with it. I think those that have it have evolved through many lifetimes, and they come in with it.

TRINDA: They have evolved into this person who has an ability that could be much more than the five senses.

ALLENE: Yes, my father was very, very perceptive and psychic. He never called it that, however. He called it lucky like with ball game endings and such. He would always know the numbers. He never missed on any of that. I was never tuned into the sports world. I don't like it very much, so I don't tune into that, but he always knew. I do not think being psychic is hereditary. Some people will say it runs in my family because my grandmother was psychic. It might be that you were put into a family where you have got older souls there and they have it all right, but it is not a hereditary thing. I think it is a gift. Like people with music occasionally, you may have two or three in a family that like music. In my family, I sang and was a child prodigy, but there was nobody who sang in my family.

TRINDA: Do you think child prodigies that come in who able to sing or play an instrument exceptionally well are given it as a gift.

ALLENE: Yes, definitely a gift.

TRINDA: What would you like the readers to know about how you work as a professional psychic counselor?

ALLENE: What I try to do is help people. I found out that just to give a yes or no answer to people was not satisfactory. I have one girl who calls me all the time. I have named her boat. I have named the husband's new address for his office. They adopted a child, and I have named the child. I have named the dog, the cat, everything. She will call me and say I need to know this or that. Another time, I had a doctor's wife who used to call me. I am sure he did not even believe in it. They had a two-year-old. The child had a twitch in the shoulder. She asked me where that came from. The child was about eight when I told the woman that at the age of two the child had taken some medication she had given it and that was a side effect. She told the doctor and they looked it up and sure enough, that was the side effect. The doctor calls me now and then. I told him, "Hey, doc, you have the degree. I don't."

TRINDA: You do not give out medical advice, but you can tell people of health concerns.

ALLENE: When people come here in person and they ask me certain things, I will answer them, but if they ask me when so-and-so is going to die, I will never do that. A lot of wives, for example, wish their husbands were dead and would like a time on that. Sometimes I see loads of sex problems too. I have seen every single problem in the book. I do not think there is anything else I could see. An interesting thing regarding sex concerns happened when I saw a woman who came in years ago about her husband. They owned a lot of things in the town and were church people. She came home one day and found him having sex with the family dog. She said, "I have never mentioned it." Well, of course, not. Whom would you mention that to, I thought?

TRINDA: When you do see the negative, do you tell them all the time?

ALLENE: Yes, I do.

TRINDA: Do you think the fact that they hear it from you might influence an outcome?

ALLENE: Yes, if you cannot see the truth you cannot correct anything. A woman called me the other day and said that her husband had a best friend. He has her in bed with the best friend and he watches them have sex. I said, "Does not that seem abnormal to you?" She said at first it did to the man, but now we are all getting used to it. I said, "Come on lady, wake up! You know that is not right. You cannot believe that is love. You don't even know what love is." That is what I told her. Love is honesty, loyalty, generosity, communication, and they did not have that. They had lust; that is what they had.

TRINDA: Do you have any advice for young people? I think there needs to be an outlet for young people, which we do not always have in our communities. How can we help them?

ALLENE: We put *thou shall not* on so many things that may or may not be wrong that young people do not know what to do. Therefore, they become either fanatics, troubled, or nothing at all. However, through their own trial and error in their lifetime they will begin to see that there are consequences to everything they do. If I would have done it a different way, then what would have been the outcome? People have to decide that on their own and that is what makes you grow. You grow by pain. Pain is there that it may teach us.

TRINDA: What about better parenting?

ALLENE: Yes, better parenting, but the parents have to become aware first. You cannot teach somebody something if you are not that yourself.

TRINDA: Yes, they are leading by example. Allene, we seem to be in a kind of *prove it to me stage* as far as psychics. Do you think that it is going to change, and will we finally get into *why* they can do it, start getting into all of the reasons for individuals like yourself?

ALLENE: I think most people think of it as a fun thing; they see a psychic as a tea reader. "What's my future? Am I going to meet a man and so on?" They do not see it as something that is a gift at all, a spiritual gift, because we have had too many people make merchandise of it; it is just been crazy.

TRINDA: Yes, very true, Allene, and they ruin it for those who are genuinely, moved by spirit to do this work. Do you ever fear any negative energy influencing us?

ALLENE: You mean that maybe negative will influence me?

TRINDA: Should we be afraid of any negative energy coming in and influencing us in any way?

ALLENE: No, that is impossible. I have people that come to me and say, "I have got a curse on me. Somebody's got a black cloud over me." I tell them, "Only in your mind, my dear. It does not happen, they cannot do that." They do not do it *unless you accept it as something*, and *the way you think is the way it brings it to pass*.

TRINDA: I have met people who ask about that all the time. They will say, "I see visions and I am worried it is either evil or a bad entity."

ALLENE: A bad omen or something; they think they are going to die. That is the first thing they think. It is scary. I won't tell somebody that is not scary, that is reality. If I saw that every day and every day of my life I was encountering that, I would be afraid too. It makes you afraid.

TRINDA: If you know it is not a bad entity, but rather one that is trying to help us become more aware perhaps, will they help us?

ALLENE: It will come about. They come to help. They pick us; we don't pick them.

TRINDA: So you can pray for visitations all the time, but if it is not meant to be, it is not going to happen.

ALLENE: No, they know those with whom they can communicate. Do you go out and communicate with some guy on the street that never heard of a psychic, never heard about anything you're talking about. What do you have in common there? You cannot communicate with them.

TRINDA: They will know if we are willing, open, and able to receive them.

ALLENE: Exactly. If they see you cannot receive that higher input, they are not going to waste their time and go to someone that they are going to keep hitting on to try and get you to receive. Remember, they pick us; we don't pick them.

TRINDA: Is there anything else that you would like to tell us?

ALLENE: I will tell you one interesting thing. A man came back the other day and he said, "I saw you seventeen years ago. You told me at the time that I would be married to a dark haired woman, I would have one child, and I would work with light bulbs. I was married to a blonde and she could not have children. We got divorced, and I married a (dark haired) Cajun woman. I now have one child, and I work with light bulbs."

TRINDA: Your prediction was much was later for him.

ALLENE: Timing, I do not always have the timing. I did not say you were going to go right out and do this, but that is what I see.

TRINDA: Do you see quite a bit into the future?

ALLENE: No, I can see whatever I see. I do not know the timing on it exactly, but I will see something. A woman called me on the air the other day. She said, "I have been to every doctor in town to see if I could have a baby. They all said no. You said I could have one and now we've got one."

TRINDA: Eventually it was to happen whenever the time was right.

ALLENE: She said, "We have a baby now."

TRINDA: You do not ever know when it is going to happen.

ALLENE: Sometimes I do know on the timing, but most times, I just will hear the event, or see the event, and I do not know where that goes, but it is going to come to pass pretty soon or I wouldn't be seeing it.

TRINDA: What about your marriage counseling ability, did that just come naturally to you?

ALLENE: When I talk to people who are in deep, deep trouble in their marriage, I cannot say, "Yes you're going to get a divorce" because they do not know why. I had one the other day, and I said, "Your husband is a borderline homosexual." She did not know what that meant. I had to explain that he is not a gay guy out there doing gay stuff, but he does the kinky stuff with her that he would do with a gay man.

TRINDA: Did that just come to you?

ALLENE: No, *psychically* that is how I see it and get it.

TRINDA: I know that when you did my reading it was a combination of psychic intuitiveness and counseling, which was very helpful.

ALLENE: I try to use it like that because people are so desperate for some help. They come for some help and for some psychic reading. To *only* tell them, for example, "Yes you're going to have cake and ice-cream on Sunday." What good does that do? They need the help as well. People come to me with some severe problems and need help.

TRINDA: It is amazing why they are coming to you with all this. I guess they understand intuitively on their own that you can help them.

ALLENE: I have a doctor in England that calls me all the time. I have somebody from Brazil that calls me, and I have people from around the world that will call because they have problems. Just a yes and a no will not do. They want to know what do I do and how to fix it. Therefore, that is what I will do and I have saved many people a lot of money, too. A woman called and she was getting ready to buy a candle shop in a mall. She would have lost her britches over that. I told her, "They are lying to you. You don't want it under any condition."

TRINDA: Do you want to continue to do this for quite some time, Allene?

ALLENE: Yes, I will do it probably to the end of my life because I like what I do. I have been very happy doing it. I have been very blessed. They call me America's number one radio psychic; the DJ's did that.

TRINDA: They all like you, Allene, as well as the DJ and radio audience here in Tampa, Florida.

ALLENE: Yes, Mason is a sweetheart.

TRINDA: And so are you, Allene. Thank you.

Chapter 9 – Near Death and Astral Traveling

CNN Larry King Live, May 23, 2005

Astral travel is having as an out-of-body experience. It occurs as an altered state of consciousness when there is separation from the astral and physical bodies. The astral body connects to the physical body by a silver cord, an etheric umbilical cord.

The Holy Bible speaks of the silver cord in numerous versions. The New International Version of the Bible (NIV) appears to speak of astral travel and the silver cord in the passage from Ecclesiastes 12:6: *"Remember him—before the 'silver cord' is severed, or the golden bowl is broken; before the pitcher is shattered at the spring, or the wheel broken at the well..."* In the King James Version of 12:6-7, it reads, *"Or ever the silver cord is loosed, or the golden bowl be broken...then shall the dust return to the earth as it was; and the spirit shall return unto God who gave it."*

Many of those who claim to astral travel, say they do so by way of the silver cord that can seem to stretch endlessly to far off places in this world and beyond. Their techniques for astral traveling include meditation and trance states. They describe seeing their body from high above looking down and not being able to control any part of it. Most, who have reported astral travel, do so particularly in near-death experiences. Some claim they have even seen their body being operated on and could actually recall the conversations of doctors and nurses during that time.

In May of 2005, celebrity, Jane Seymour, while on CNN's Larry King Live spoke of her own out-of-body experience in that same way. His television show was on near-death experiences and their conversation went something like this:

LARRY KING: What happened, Jane?

JANE SEYMOUR: Well, I was in the middle of a film. I was playing Maria Callas in *The Onassis Story*. I had a bad bronchitis. A doctor was brought in. I was given antibiotics by injection in Madrid, in Spain.

Immediately, on getting the injection, I knew something was wrong. I felt like my throat was closing. I tried to speak up, but I didn't speak.

The next thing I remember, I was panicking, and then I was not panicking. I was very calm, but I was not—I was looking down at my body. I saw this man screaming, yelling, "Emergency, Emergency!" I was now rolled over. I was half-naked. I had two huge syringes in my backside, and I was watching from the corner of the room. I saw this white light. I had no pain, I had no tension, and I just kind of looked, and then went "That is very strange. That is me, but that cannot be me if I am here." Then I realized that I was out of my body and that I was, you know, going to die.

LARRY KING: You were changed. What happened?

JANE SEYMOUR: Well, what happened is I remembered—all of a sudden, I just looked, and I went, no, no, I am not ready to go away. I want to get back in that body. I have children. I want to raise them. There is so much I want to do. I want to give back. I want to do so much in the world, and I am just—I am not ready to go. And so I asked whoever was up there, God, a higher power, whatever one wants to call it, I just said, whoever you are, I will never deny your existence, just please let me get back in that body and I won't let you down. I will never let you down. I am not going to waste one minute of my life if I have it back.

LARRY KING: Did you feel yourself go back in?

JANE SEYMOUR: No, the next thing I knew, I was in my body, and my body was out of control. So, it is very interesting, because I was in control, but my body was not. My arms were flying, my legs were flying…There were two or three people there trying to hold me down and coming up with a million excuses for why this has happened or what has happened. What has actually happened medically was that I had anaphylactic shock. What they had done, the injections, were cortisone and adrenaline. The reason I had anaphylactic shock was that when they—the injection site was the wrong site. They put it into—instead of a muscle, they put it into a vein or an artery, and so that is what happened. My system was shocked.

LARRY KING: Had nothing —had nobody come to your attention, you would have died?"

JANE SEYMOUR: Oh, absolutely. In fact, I made them get my American doctor on the phone immediately, and he told me that I almost died and that had I not been given the cortisone and adrenaline, I would have gone.

While I have not had a near-death experience in this life, I can recall, as I am sure many of you can, the joy of astral traveling during sleep. We have nearly all had the dream of flying at one time or another. It is a common dream. Flying dreams are often associated with rising above the mundane aspects of life, triumph over life's difficulties, and breaking free from limitations. Then again, it could very well have been really flying as spirit can in astral travel. Astral traveling is much more than just dreaming. While awake in a relaxed state or during sleep, it is the sensation of having separated from one's physical body. The experience can simply be your awareness of being able to exist outside of the body. You may have an awareness of the silver cord, or you may not notice it at all. You might be aware of others and them of you. You may be able to recognize other locations here on earth or elsewhere. You may see deceased loved ones, and you may see and do much more.

The experience can even be proven. Sometimes the traveler can retain information during an out-of-body experience to prove that is was indeed real. It is understandable that without that verification, one would think it only a dream. Yet, one of the things that can make a dream different from astral travel is the clarity of the memory. If quickly forgotten after wakening, then most likely it was a dream or the mind's way of playing with or making sense of recent experiences. If retained with full clarity and memory over time, then it was your spirit in astral travel.

Allene Cunningham, Psychic-Counselor
Astral Travel (Interview, July 15, 2005)

In my interview with the psychic-counselor, Allene Cunningham, I asked her if she ever had a paranormal experience such as *astral travel*. Allene shared her startling story with me and said, "One of the most interesting experiences I had was in New York, while reading a book one night. I went to turn off the nightlight, and suddenly I was lifted out of bed and hung against the wall." I asked her if she just *felt* that way. She quickly replied, "No, I could look down and I was in the middle of the wall. I could see I had this old orange robe on and grease (night cream) all over my face. Oh, God, I thought, I look a mess and I am in levity. I could 'absolutely' not move and was just hanging there. Suddenly, a big crashing sound went through the room, the room lit up, and became super bright. On the opposite wall was a spirit form, a man with the biggest shoulders I have ever seen. He had a silver metal thing in front of him. I started to say something, but I could not get anything out. Soon I was lying back in bed. What in the world was that all about? I wondered. I heard something say, "Fifteenth century." It had said that I lived in New York and it was dangerous, some of the places I had to go sometimes. He was apparently a guide, and I heard him say that is what he was. A guide from the fifteenth century had taken care of me the whole time I was in New York. I wanted to see it again in the physical. We want to dissect everything. Well, it did not let me do that. I never did see it again. I only saw it that one time.

As amazing as Allene's experience was I could empathize with her desire to experience it again. We want to know as much as we can of life's mysteries. As I have experienced astral travel myself, I can only say it appears to be a very *real* experience. Even though I have not floated to the ceiling or nearly died in an out-of-body experience, I do believe my sleep has led me to astral travel to many a far off place.

To this day, I remember a couple of trips very vividly after a great many years. However, one of my most recent and memorable trips was coincidentally the night before drafting this writing. I wondered if was meant to be yet another example to share with you. I had been figure skating on water, without skis or other devices to stay afloat. I know it may sound crazy to most, but there it is. I knew I was somehow miraculously playing on top of the water. It was a wonderful experience, but at the same time, I knew it to be something different, something unique. I knew I was not in my body, as my body could not do such things. It was as if I knew better, but did those things never the less. I know what I experienced was not a dream; I experienced the act of astral travel. I only hope to do more as I learn how to perfect this amazingly act of the spirit.

Chapter 10 – Blue Feather

Séance and Channeling with Blue Feather

For most, the word séance conjures up images of dark, candlelit rooms, floating ghosts, and a little table tipping. However, I can tell you from experience that is not always so. The method in which a medium conducts a séance depends greatly on their teachings and experiences. From spiritual circles to trumpet séances, these gatherings are a reflection of the medium conducting them. Know the medium and you will know what type of séance to expect.

The thought of attending a séance had somewhat concerned me. I really had no idea of what to expect except what Hollywood had always depicted. Cautious with the thought of attending a séance, I hesitated when someone invited me to my first séance. Yet, as in all other aspects to my life, I have looked toward the light of God in my exploration of the paranormal. It is only in those places where the divine light shines that I have researched the supernatural. After all, you attract what you seek. If you are searching for the truth, you *will* find it. I have always kept an open mind while seeking answers to some of life's greatest of mysteries, communication with spirit being one of them. Who is to say that the information cannot come from divine entities? Only *you* can determine that and no one person should ever force their opinions upon you.

Like everything with regard to my writing, I have let spirit guide me in such matters. They have shown me much that has strengthened my faith and spirituality. I have learned to trust their guidance and direction. With that in mind, I decided to accept a relative's request to join her at a local shop downtown that was presenting a spirit medium for a séance with Blue Feather. Blue Feather's instrument, a psychic-medium, regularly conducts séances in local establishments, this time in a quaint gift store, mostly containing reading material, home décor, and jewelry. Somehow, I *knew* I should go and scheduled my attendance for her next séance.

Scheduled during the bright light of day, it was actually held on a Saturday afternoon in May of 2005. As I entered the gift shop, I found no floating furniture and the only candle was a white, votive candle. I signed in and took a seat on a small folding chair in the center of the shop. Others continued to trickle in one after another until we had a nice size group of about ten or so, mostly women and no children.

We all sat anxiously in a large circle and waited for the medium to begin. She was a petite woman, freckles and reddish, brown hair with an expressed desire to be the John Edward of our day. I found several of the mediums over the years who felt that same desire. Some knew that they were as skilled as John Edward, Sylvia Browne, or James Van Praagh, but have not yet risen to that level of fame. Yet, of all their secret desires, they primarily wanted to serve. This was also Janet's desire, to serve humanity along side Blue Feather. She boasted of his wisdom and told us of their special relationship from past lives together, once even as a father and daughter. It was a unique bond, this strong warrior and petite woman with an infectious giggle. She was not at all what most would expect a spirit medium might be. Therefore, I am pleased to introduce you now to the spirit medium and channel for Blue Feather, the Reverend Janet M. Reynolds.

Reverend Janet M. Reynolds
Certified Spirit Medium
Tampa, Florida USA

Meet Reverend Janet M. Reynolds, Psychic-Medium

The Reverend Janet M. Reynolds is a Certified Spirit Medium who offers practical channeled guidance from the spirit world with intuitive consultations, séance gatherings, and home parties, as well as corporate events, and fundraisers. I could think of many a staff meeting that would have benefited by Janet's presence. Janet Reynolds' intuitive consultations are unique and much sought after. She works very closely with her spirit guide, Blue Feather, a Cherokee Indian teacher who speaks through her and also brings through the client's relatives and loved ones from the other side. Blue Feather's messages always come from the heart and touch the lives of those who seek spiritual answers. The guidance is always pertinent and practical.

Rev. Janet M. Reynolds is also an ordained minister with a private practice in Tampa, Florida. She is a graduate of the mediumship certification program of the College of Metaphysical Studies in Clearwater, Florida. She studied at the Metaphysical Academy in Tampa, and the Arthur Finlay College of Psychic and Mediumship in England. Janet was ordained as a minister through Harmony Church in Tampa, and currently serves at People's Spiritualist Church in St. Petersburg, Florida. Certified in clinical hypnotherapy by the American Institute of Hypnotherapy, Janet obtained advanced instruction in hypnosis and past-life regression at the Edgar Cayce Foundation in Virginia Beach, VA. In addition, her studies include medical intuition with Caroline Myss and Dr. Norman Shealy. Rev. Reynolds is also a certified Reiki Master. Reiki is a type of alternative medicine or healing practice.

Janet Reynolds had previously owned a successful data processing business. She understands the business world as well as the spiritual world. Her intuitive readings and trance channeling sessions are a reflection of her ability to span both worlds. Her specialty is bringing guidance from the perspective of spirit into the world of form and function and the wisdom with practical directions for using it. Her work is valued for the concreteness of the information offered, and her ability to put esoteric knowledge into ideas everyone can use.

Janet specializes in séance gatherings during which in-depth messages are given by Janet's guide, Blue Feather, or by relatives of loved ones. The messages could be about life direction, inspirational guidance and practical information for resolving problems, or giving peace of mind to family members from those in spirit. She has said that participants in the séance circles always come away with a sense of more meaning, closure, or a better idea of how their loved one wanted something handled after their departure from the earth plane.

As we all sat in a circle and waited for Janet to begin, some appeared slightly nervous. A number had traveled quite a distance to participate in this séance, and I gathered they were worried whether it was worth the trip. Janet began by introducing herself and her master spirit guide and teacher, Blue Feather. Blue Feather had come to her when she was very young and now Janet makes her living as a certified spirit medium. Janet states that she and Blue Feather have been together during many lifetimes. In this particular life experience, Janet serves on the earth plane with Blue Feather guiding her and speaking through her from the spirit world. With his direction, she can offer others her unique channeled guidance from the spirit world.

With the shop door now closed and the lights still on, Janet stood center circle with a votive candle and asked that we begin with a prayer and a song, stating that *spirit loves music*. We followed along with sheet music and then said the *Our Father* prayer while holding hands. Thus far, it felt more like a small church service than a séance. As Janet led us in song, her voice dramatically changed at times and we all wondered why. She saw our confusion and later explained that Blue Feather likes to sing along with her at times. After that, she had my full attention.

We had all put our name on a piece of folded paper and placed it into a bowl for Janet to select. She reached in, pulled the first name out and began a reading for the first woman, which led to our next two full hours together. Janet would read each of us in this manner, pulling a name and then giving a psychic reading for that individual, all with the help of Blue Feather. As personal as readings can sometimes be, I would prefer a private reading rather than this type of gathering. However, in a group, Janet is able to offer each a reduced fee compared to that of a private reading. I thought a séance meant something different from a public reading. Perhaps for other mediums that might be so, but for Janet, it was nearly the same, only with sitters openly sharing in the experience with others. Had I known more of what to expect, I might not have gone. However, Janet approached the more *personal* information in a very careful and respectful manner for each one of us and I enjoyed this sharing of information. My name was one of the last ones selected. Therefore, I had time to sit back and observe Blue Feather's messages and the sitter's reactions while I waited my turn.

I had come with a relative, whom I shall call Jan, and we sat next to each other in the circle. When Janet pulled *Jan's* name out of the bowl,

I did not know *I* would be next. As Janet started to read Jan, nothing was connecting for her and I started to realize the information coming through sounded as if it were for me instead. Then the confirmation with specific details for each of us, led us all to believe we were simultaneously, being read. The reading that followed went something like this:

JANET: "Who draws?"

I raised my hand.

JANET: "Who has the nurse for a daughter?"

Jan raised her hand.

JANET: "Whose daughter lives out west?"

I raised my hand.

JANET: "Who has a son?"

Jan raised her hand.

It was the funniest fifteen minutes. Back and forth, Janet addressed us like a ping-pong ball in continuous play. While the reading continued with details for both of us, it seemed confusing at moments for Janet. She was trying hard to distinguish which was for whom, but the messages were apparently coming through as fast as she could relay them. As frustrating as it must have been for her, Janet was a real trooper about it and brought through much information for both of us. Everything she said was completely accurate, but I must tell you of one detail that actually changed from just my receiving the information.

At one point in the ping-pong play, Janet directed her attention to me and said that there would be a different job in the next month. I told her I did not think so as I was not actively looking. She insisted and said that a definite job change would present itself within the month of June. Actually, she said, "It would be different, but the same kind of work." I assumed she was wrong, but wondered about it nevertheless. By the middle of the following month, however, I received a phone call from a local city human resource director asking if I was interested in coming in for an interview. After some conversation, I realized I had submitted a resume some time ago and forgotten about it. She came across the resume and wanted to meet with me about a recent position that had become available. I went to the interview out of curiosity, and found that the position was the same type of work I was already doing, but as a manager instead. I could not believe Janet's accuracy. While I am confident that I would have been offered the position, I decided to decline even before being offered. I know now that I chose the best path by staying where I was. Janet did state, however, that *the opportunity would present itself*, only I choose not to accept it.

Another reminder is that while a psychic may tell you of a possible future event, it is, of course, only one possible path for you to choose. *You* are the only one who should decide what to do with the information you are given. It is an important point to remember that no psychic should ever tell you what to do, only what the possibilities might be, if given any predictions at all. By the time the séance had ended that afternoon, we all felt like friends from our time together, perhaps because we had gotten to know each other from the readings.

That is the positive side to a group gathering of any kind; getting to know one another better. Sharing in each other's lives can indeed bring people, whole communities, or even countries closer to one another. As world peace committees have done for the world, so can any gathering of people. Whether it is in a church group, business meeting, house party, or even a séance, it is a great way for individuals to get to know one another, and hopefully for the better.

It was a wonderful afternoon together and I did feel as though I came away with a greater awareness of the unseen, particularly a warrior spirit called Blue Feather, and a likable, little woman who just happens to talk to the dead.

Channeling Blue Feather, March 14, 2006

Author Note: The following is the actual, detailed dialogue recorded from an evening with the Reverend Janet M. Reynolds while in trance, channeling her spirit guide, Blue Feather. The notations of coughs are of Janet with a dry mouth from having too little water to drink before channeling Blue Feather. The names of those participating have been changed to protect their privacy. Lastly, Blue Feather has lovingly nicknamed Janet his "Mistress," rather than his "instrument" for this communication.

JANET: He's here. I am gettin' hyper'. I think maybe now.

The red velveteen armed chair was placed in front of the candle-lit altar. Janet's small frame rested against its high back as she placed her feet flat on the floor and closed her eyes. Her breathing became more noticeable and her left hand was showing signs of Blue Feather's presence with the twitching of her forefinger. As I glanced around the room, nearly all those present were already in quiet prayer. Janet had asked that we all say a prayer before his arrival and the Lord's Prayer after his exit. I was becoming aware of my own heartbeat and a jittery feeling of anticipation. I, too, anxiously awaited Blue Feather's arrival. Would he *really* be able to come through? The others were sure he would as they had met Blue Feather in this way several times before. Yet, my skeptical side doubts until proven otherwise. I hoped the experience to be *real*, but kept a clear and cautious mindset as I watched Janet slowly go under. Her left eye closed tighter and her facial features seemed unusually different. I tried observing her aura to watch for any change, but it only seemed closer to her body and void of any color. Then without further signs, we heard Blue Feather speak.

BLUE FEATHER: Good-eve-ning-every-one.

Blue Feather began with the deepened and raspy voice of his Mistress. We excitedly answered him back, and he replied with, "And...how...are...you?"

We choired with wonderful, fine, and good.

BLUE FEATHER: I feel all of the energy in this room and I want you to know that it is a very nice feeling. I know that you have come with love and you know that love is important in today's (Janet coughs) world. My Mistress will learn one of these days to drink more water (soft giggles) but, between now and then, she will just have to work with me being here and her mouth being dry. Do you understand that?

In unison, we quickly replied, "yes."

BLUE FEATHER: So, you must once more tell her, even though all of you know she will not listen. (soft giggles) Now, you do understand that everything must be done in order. When you can, and I am sure that it will be done correctly. You will do one question at a time for me. I can answer whatever it is that you need to know. So, *please*, whoever it is that needs to start, please, *do it now*. Remember to tell me your name and remember to be quick.

The first of us began immediately.

CB: Blue Feather, this is C.B. I have lots of questions, but I'm going to wait to hear the answers that I need to know right now.

BLUE FEATHER: You want for me to answer for you, questions that you are not giving me. Is that what you said, C.B.?

C.B.: I am sorry, Blue Feather. Please, would you tell me what I need to know?

BLUE FEATHER: I...will...tell...you...this. *Patience* is very hard for you and for quite a few of us. (cough) You must have patience with what you are learning. (Janet coughs hard several times as a few tears run down through the freckles on her cheek.) I hope that my Mistress can work with this. She is having a hard time. I am sorry for that, but what she thinks she is doing and what she is doing are two different things so, we must tell her that. Now, back to you, C.B. I want for you to know that, yes, *patience is the answer!* You need more patience. (cough) I also want to say to you, travel around the world. You will do more traveling than you think. There is much for you to learn and there is much for you to see. You must take one-step at a time, and be patient! Your house will sell soon, as soon as you put it on the market, it will go. Now, is there more for now that you need to know, C.B.?

C.B.: No, thank you.

C.B.'s house sold only weeks after he placed it on the market.

THE REVEREND: Hi, Blue Feather, this is the Reverend and I wanted to know if I will be able to manage the job that I want?

BLUE FEATHER: Reverend, you are a very capable individual. When you set your mind to something, *you do it!* You have set your mind to what it is that you want, so know that your capabilities will be able to handle whatever situation you are in. *I want for you to be exceptionally careful this week with people that you are working with.* I want to say to you, and please, listen, I want for you to, please, for this week only, *to watch your back.* Do you understand me?

THE REVEREND: Yes, I do, thank you.

JULIE: (softly spoken) Hi, Blue Feather, this is Julie. I wanted to know about Robert in the spirit world.

BLUE FEATHER: Robert is a loved one of yours. Is that correct?

JULIE: Yes.

BLUE FEATHER: Would you once more, please, tell me your name?

Julie gave Blue Feather her full name.

BLUE FEATHER: Julie, much is going on around you. Robert *is* around you. Robert sends you all his love, but what he says is…you must take better care of yourself. You are not doing that. Do you understand me?

JULIE: Yes.

BLUE FEATHER: He says for you to be more careful with what you are eating also. He is also saying that you need to take any and all medication if that is the case. He is also saying for you to see the doctor. Have you been to the doctor?

Julie replies with a simple no.

BLUE FEATHER: Do you need to go?

JULIE: Yes.

BLUE FEATHER: Okay. He is saying for you to do this. There is much love coming from him for you. He also says he understands *financial*, but he says you have always managed and you can manage again. Do you understand that?

JULIE: Yes.

BLUE FEATHER: He says take care and that he loves you very much. He is around you more than you think he is. He tries to be with you as much as possible. Please take care of yourself.

JULIE: Thank you.

TRINDA: Hi, Blue Feather, this is Trinda and my question is with regard to my understanding of the levels of existence as has been explained it to me. Is my understanding of it correct?

BLUE FEATHER: *Most* of what she has said to you, Trinda, is very, very true. There could be maybe one or two exceptions, but it goes according to how each one sees things. She does much studying. I feel that what has been said to you can be used. Do not concern yourself with it. It is of good taste.

TRINDA: Thank you.

I had *not* asked if it could be used in my writing, but it *was* my unspoken intention and the main reason for asking Blue Feather. In receiving Blue Feather's validation, I feel more than comfortable now in sharing that knowledge with you in my next books, which are an in-depth look at the reality of life, death and ultimate existence. I seek truths and in Blue Feather's one brief answer, his confirmation of an existence that could mirror the best of any science fiction novel awaits you in my third volume on *the afterlife and infinite beyond*. It is there that we explore such mysteries as the reality of heaven and what lies beyond it. I hope you will join me and the many other gifted souls, both in and out of flesh, who share their understandings of that which acknowledges and explains the unseen world around us.

In the meantime, I would like to take you back to the afternoon with Blue Feather and his Mistress, the Reverend Janet M. Reynolds, with more messages from beyond the grave, for both the world and especially to those in attendance, including my reluctant husband, Richard, who was next to receive one of the most encouraging messages of his life.

RICHARD: Hello, Blue Feather, my name is Richard. Could you give me a message, please, that I need to hear?

BLUE FEATHER: Richard is it very good to see you here tonight. I do not think that was easy for you, was it?

RICHARD: No.

Blue Feather's voice was softer now, as if he were trying to ease his Mistress' obvious discomfort. Tears continued to trickle down Janet's face as Blue Feather spoke to Richard.

BLUE FEATHER: There is much strange things going on around you and you do not always understand them, but know that you are on the right path. Always question what you think and always question what you feel. It is okay to do that. Do you understand me? You work also with your heart, you have a big heart, and that is a good thing. It would be good for you to learn more spiritual, so continue to do (cough) what you are doing (more coughing). I am trying to speak with you at a low voice so that I do not pull on her throat chords. That is a good thing; but, continue with what you are doing, Richard. You are doing well. I also would like to say to you that I feel in your business world things will be better.

RICHARD: Thank you.

Before Blue Feather had finished with his message, Richard and I were tightly holding hands. I was having a hard time keeping tears of my own from flowing. Richard had needed to hear that and being from spirit made it even more meaningful. He had never been to this church before and I had never told Reverend Reynolds, or anyone else, about my husband or his recent supernatural experiences. My writing had consumed *my* life, while subtlety had begun affecting my husband's life. Over the past year especially, his own natural abilities as strange as they had seemed, were emerging and taking us both by surprise. Our left-brained, logical, rationally, and analytical thinking, was quickly being influenced by the right, intuitive side and I could not have been happier. My analytical husband was finally hearing from spirit what seemed to matter most to him, that he *was* on a good path. He had always worried about doing what was right in this life, especially being a *positive* influence to others. Was his teaching over the years actually making a difference for the young men and women in his classes? That responsibility was always present in his efforts at leading them to successful lives by presenting the best in higher education. Leading by example and doing well by others were high moral standards to live by. Yet, in my opinion, he had always done just that for nearly thirty years. I mention it not only out of pride, but also as an encouragement to most who may only hear of negative news with regard to today's educators. For the most part, teachers are doing an outstanding job with our youth and truly want the best for *their kids*. Please remember to thank a teacher, community, or youth leader that is a *positive* influence to a child, the few goods words you say but once may sustain them for a lifetime.

As it was from Blue Feather for Richard, sometimes we just need to hear that we are not only doing things correctly in life, *on the right path* as it is said, but also that it is also okay to question things in life. After all, we are still human in this existence. Ask those questions you need answers to and when the answers come from God, the divine, or an infinite intelligence if you wish, you *will* know it. Ask questions of the highest and best that the divine offers and you will receive that which is of love. The God within will tell you clearly and quickly what it is you wish to know. You will not need to hear it from Blue Feather, a psychic-medium, or anyone else. However, I must admit, it is an amazing experience nonetheless. As our time together came to a close, Blue Feather asked if we had answered everyone's questions and added a few of his own comments before leaving us.

BLUE FEATHER: Have we answered everyone's questions?
EVERYONE: Yes.
BLUE FEATHER: Is there any more to be answered or is everyone satisfied?
C.B.: Is there anything you would like to add?
BLUE FEATHER: *Yes, C.B.,* how did you guess? (soft laughter) Of course, I cannot leave here without saying some things that you need to know. There is much, of course, that all of you know, I'm sure, about what is going on, in and out of the country, but also with the planets. There is much havoc coming once more in the next two to three weeks, there is also bad weather on the way, so everyone brace themselves for what is coming. Please take care of yourself.

I would like to note here that the weather for that March included significant drought across the United States, especially in Florida, and throughout such distant areas as Ethiopia, Somalia and Kenya. Yet, Australia saw heavy rainfall along the east coast, which stranded thousands. Thousands in New South Wales experienced river flooding. Thunderstorms affected six villages in Bangladesh and in the Democratic Republic of Congo. Australia also saw tropical cyclones of the Coral Sea and Timor Sea wipe out 90 percent of banana crops and close oil fields. The global temperature anomaly was the seventh warmest March since 1880 (the beginning of instrumental records). Warm land surface temperatures covered central Asia and northern Africa, while cooler than average temperatures were widespread across much of Europe. It was definitely a time of climate extremes and hazards for many on the planet.

BLUE FEATHER: The Blessed Mother is also here. I would like for you to know that...all of you. She sends much love to all. She would like for all of you, as well as me, to stay on the path that you are on. *Love is so important.* I must leave now, but I go with all my blessings. As you can tell, my Mistress' voice is better, but it was just a matter of her getting over it. Please inform her of what I have said. Bless each and every one of you. I must go now.
EVERYONE: Thank you, Blue Feather.

Everyone had heard what he or she needed to hear that evening, if only for a few brief moments. Blue Feather may be from *a long time ago*, but he is still *a strong and good warrior,* a warrior of strength, yes, but also one of hope and of love, which as he said, is "...*most important in today's world.*"

Blue Feather and the rest of us had been asked by the Blessed Mother to stay on our paths, and to remember that all-important natural law of the universe, love. It was a goal we all felt divinely driven to. The Reverend and the rest of us had all gathered that evening, not only to help Janet become stronger in her channeling, but also to help one another with our own efforts at reaching the same goal, to help bring about more love. It is a daunting task in today's world, but we all have faith that we can accomplish much, both individually and collectively. Therefore, we agreed to meet again the following week and if possible, for another channeling session with Blue Feather.

The next time that we gathered, we all shared in our efforts at aiding others throughout our workweek. As we spoke of work relationships and moments of counseling, Janet mentioned that several people had come to her for advice, fearful of negative influences approaching them from the spirit world. She tried to reassure them that *like attracts like*, and if you wish only that of love and light from the divine and spirit, then that would be what you would receive.

However, if you at any time feel uncomfortable with spirit contact in your meditation, dreams, or thoughts, you should simply request them to leave you alone. It is as simple as that, Janet reminded us. However, it was something we could consult with Blue Feather about for certainty. Many of us have had dreams that seemed scary or dark at times, which had occurred to my husband earlier that same week. While trying to meditate one evening, to open up more to the word of God, he drifted off to sleep with prayers of enlightenment and wisdom. Before his waking that morning, he felt as if his body was somehow energized, but without his permission, and it bothered him greatly. He asked that it stop and then immediately woke up. His concern over the incident had led us all into discussion about how one would know in meditation and prayer if approached by either a loving or harmful spirit. Janet thought it was time once again to seek Blue Feather's advice. In the next channeling session, my husband asked his concern of Blue Feather.

RICHARD: Blue Feather, this is Richard. While I have been advised to develop my own natural psychic skills and spirituality through meditation, I experienced something that bothered me. Could you explain this?

BLUE FEATHER: Sometimes in our dream world things happen to us, sometimes we become concerned. Yes, it is very possible that if it is as we call *an entity* or it is as we call a *spirit* getting our attention, all that is necessary is that you ask for them to leave you be. Sometimes entities need our attention as we need their attention and that is why you have many family members around you that are trying to, let us say, communicate to you one way or another. If at any time you do not feel good about a situation, all you need to do is ask them to leave you. They need to do that when the request is put in. Do you understand? Did that answer your question?

RICHARD: Yes, thank you.

BLUE FEATHER: It went rather quick tonight. I see that not everyone is here and when I say I see, I do see, but not like you see. I am making myself clear on that. It seems that my Mistress has done well tonight, but of course, I am sure it is because of what you had to say to her. So, I would ask you once more to continue to explain to her the necessity of water and I am sure she will listen to you.

There are many spirits in this room or shall I say there are many family members here tonight for each and every one of you. Reverend, I must tell you that your son is here too with much love. I also need for Trinda to know that her mother is here, and Pat, your mother is here. There are many more family members, just know that. Each and every one of you, please continue with the good work. I must leave you now, but let my instrument know, my Mistress, as I so say, let her know please that she is getting stronger and that she will do well when she goes to England. Also, please let her know to do many classes. It will also help her and please let her know, financially, things are going to get better. Now I say to you, God Bless and take care of yourself.

EVERYONE: Thank you Blue Feather and God bless *you*.

Yes, Richard and the rest of us understood Blue Feather to mean that while our loved ones are trying to communicate with us, we may not always understand their attempts, perhaps may even fear. We fear what we do not always understand and can think the worse when in fact it may be a blessing instead. Like Richard and the rest of us, I am sure there are many family members and loved ones around you who long to communicate with you. You see it every time you watch a medium connect with a loved one when their messages of love and personal validations come through. It is a growing phenomenon, which is quickly becoming a normal occurrence. Remember to ask your loved ones to approach you subtly and clearly in your dreams or meditative time together and you may find the experience a much more rewarding one.

For more on Blue Feather and Reverend Janet M. Reynolds, to make an appointment with her, you may visit her in the Tampa Bay area of Florida, or at her website at http://www.bluefeather.net.

Next, it is my great pleasure to present a world famous survival evidence medium of our time, James Van Praagh.

James Van Praagh
Survival Evidence Medium,
Speaker, Author and Producer
Pasadena, California USA

Chapter 11 – World Famous Psychic

James Van Praagh, Survival Evidence Medium
Interview, August 13, 2005

His very natural, easy-going style would lead you to believe that James Van Praagh is chatting with a friend on the telephone, not communicating messages from the grave. James is a survival evidence medium, meaning that he is able to bridge the gap between two planes of existence, that of the living and that of the dead by providing evidential proof of life after death via detailed messages. "I am clairsentient," he explains, "which simply means clear feeling. I feel the emotions and personalities of the deceased. I am also clairvoyant," he adds, clarifying that, "the first is feeling, the second is seeing, very much like Whoopi Goldberg in the movie, *Ghost*" (1990).

The true essences of the messages are the feelings behind the words. James is an expert on this subject, since he has been in touch with those feelings most of his adult life. "The spirits communicate by their emotions. No words exist in the English language, or any other for that matter, which can describe the intense sensations."

Personality traits come in as well. If a person was talkative while alive, he will come through with plenty to say. James also relays physical traits and death conditions as evidence. "If I convey recognizable evidence along with even a fraction of the loving energy behind the message, I consider the reading successful."

James' public popularity began during his appearances on the NBC talk show *The Other Side*. The show concentrated on paranormal issues, and James became the favorite guest and resident expert on the subject of life after death. Even Howard Rosenberg, the Los Angeles Times distinguished television critic, dubbed James "spectacular".

Through the years, his message of hope has touched a great many more people due to his television appearances on such shows as Oprah, Larry King Live, Maury Povich, 20/20, and 48 Hours. His unique paranormal experiences during the past sixteen years have seen him author best-selling books, create meditation programs and development videos, teach mediumship classes, conduct seminars to sold-out audiences, and produce successful television projects.

James was born in Bayside, New York, and is the youngest of four children. An average child, he remembers having a tremendous fascination with death. He was raised Catholic and served as an altar boy, entering the seminary at the age of fourteen. It was there that his interest in Catholicism ended and his sense of spirituality began.

There are no schools or training that could prepare James for his unusual vocation. Indeed, his ability to communicate with the dead arose out of his...well...life. This belief was affirmed by an astonishing encounter that he had when he was only eight-years-old. The young boy was praying for God to reveal Himself to him, when an open hand appeared through the ceiling of James' room emitting radiant beams of light. Incredibly, he recounts, "I was not scared. It was actually very peaceful."

Graduating from public high school, he continued to pursue his studies and later graduated from San Francisco State University with a degree in Broadcasting and Communications. You could say that he ended up working in Communications, just in a different capacity. After graduation, he moved to Los Angeles where he became involved in metaphysics and psychic phenomena. At twenty-four, the promise of that outstretched palm so many years before was fulfilled.

During his early days in Los Angeles, James was invited to attend a session with a medium, although he did not even know at that time what a medium was. Given that, he was understandably dubious when the medium informed James that he would be doing the same work within two years. "My first reaction was, "I have enough trouble dealing with the living; why do I want to talk to the dead?"

As James' sensitivity increased, he began doing psychic readings for friends. During these readings, he began receiving detailed messages from the beyond. Though at first this seemed bizarre, the more he learned, the more he could not deny the fact that he had the gift to reach beyond the familiar plane of existence we call life. Today, James is recognized as one of the foremost mediums in the world.

Naturally, there remain skeptics about his abilities. James, however, is the first to say that he welcomes healthy skepticism, declaring, in fact, that he is a skeptic himself. "I believe that I am doing this, but I don't believe that just anyone can do this. All mediums are psychics, but not all psychics are mediums."

A psychic senses energy around the living people or objects. A medium not only senses energy, but is able to interface between the slower vibrations of the physical world and the much faster ones of the spirit world.

Though James is quick to point out that his gift does not provide insights into the future, he is able to provide detailed evidential proof that a loved one survived death. Surviving death may seem to be the supreme oxymoron, but he has a firm belief that we are all spirit beings, and that there is far more to our life than our life span.

Ultimately, James feels extremely fortunate to be a conduit of comfort, healing, and most importantly, love. "As a medium, I have never experienced anything but love and compassion and healing in my work," he avows. "It is the love bond between people which allows me to make the connection between the living and the dead."

James' unique paranormal experiences during the past twenty-two years have been recorded in his best-selling books *Talking To Heaven*, *Reaching To Heaven* and *Healing Grief*, all published by Dutton Books. His fourth book, published by Simon and Schuster, is the proclaimed *Heaven and Earth - Making the Psychic Connection*.

In September 2003, teens were introduced to *Looking Beyond: A Teen's Guide to the Spiritual World*. In November of that same year, his book, *Meditations with James Van Praagh*, brought a new awareness to the meditation experience.

James shared his extraordinary gift on television with a daytime talk show of his own entitled *Beyond With James Van Praagh*. The show aired in the U.S. from September 2002 through September 2003, and is still showing in syndication in Europe, Australia and Latin America.

In April 2002, James began an ongoing relationship with the CBS network and produced an incredibly successful mini-series *Living With The Dead*, inspired by his first book *Talking To Heaven*. This mini-series starred Ted Danson and Mary Steenburgen and was the highest rated show for CBS in two years. In October 2004, his second successful CBS project aired entitled, *The Dead Will Tell* starring Anne Heche.

Currently James is developing another CBS movie titled *The Haunting of Bleaker Place* and is Co-Executive Producing his first CBS primetime series *The Ghost Whisperer* starring Jennifer Love Hewitt to begin airing in September 2005.

To assist others in spiritual awareness and fulfillment, James has produced four (4) meditation programs featuring music by the world's leading composer of sound healing Steven Halpern. The titles include

Divine Love, Spirit Speaks, Soul Discoveries and Meditation Tools. Each program includes two CDs and two cassettes and a workbook with meditations and conversations with James.

His single CD meditations are also great teaching tools and include *Tuning Into: Intuition/Abundance* and *Tuning Into: Healing / Forgiveness.* In his instructional video, *Develop Your Psychic-Self,* James shares his personal techniques to develop your own innate abilities.

"The books, CDs, video and television projects are ways to share my abilities and the message that our personalities do indeed survive death. My greatest satisfaction in doing this work is witnessing an instantaneous change in people," states James about his work.

"When someone is alone and overwhelmed by grief, life seems over. But, when someone is able to make contact with a loved one, their grief and loneliness disappears and proper closure can take place." And, so..."When a bright smile overcomes tears, it becomes a smile that can light up the world!"

James Van Praagh is what he calls a survival evidence medium, meaning that he is providing proof of life after death from communicating with the deceased. He has said that he is clairvoyant, meaning that he can see the dead. He is also clairsentient, meaning clear feeling. He *feels* the emotions and personalities of the dead. If he can successfully convey a recognizable personality or some evidence of the life of a loved one behind any messages, significant or not, then he considers the reading he gives successful.

While that is a professional and brief personal introduction, I would like to present a more in depth look at the insightful soul behind the world famous psychic-medium, James Van Praagh. I had wanted to know more about the famous psychic who says he can literally speak to the dead. Can he *truly* communicate with spirit? How is James able to sense spirit while others cannot? What does he know from being able to communicate with spirit? Those questions and many more came to mind as I prepared my list for James. I was thrilled that he had granted me an interview, but wondered of all the hundreds of questions, which few I would select to ask of him.

We were in Virginia Beach, home to another well-known psychic of earlier days, Edgar Cayce, the famous *sleeping psychic* who would give readings while in a trance. James was in Virginia to do a seminar later that same day at The Association for Research and Enlightenment, Inc. (A.R.E. ®), an Edgar Cayce foundation.

In my conversation with James, we spoke of spirit communication, his understanding of God, the afterlife, our consciousness and this reality, and especially love. Believing that *unconditional love* is the key to every locked door, James told me that when he does messages for people, the amount of love, the energy of love that comes through is simply immeasurable. James stated, "You know it is so limiting to describe in just a word, love. It is so limiting. People do not get the full conception about what love is, but I get a sense, an inkling of that love, of that light, that pureness of light when I do my readings. It is just a loving feeling, and that is why I started doing this work, years and years ago, because that energy is so strong."

It took a big leap of faith for James to begin his career as a psychic-medium over two decades ago. In leaving the security of a *real job* to that of doing personal readings, he trusted that energy of love to guide him in his work. James remarked that, "When I just started doing this 24-25 years ago, you could not even talk about dead people and communication."

"People would probably think you were out of your right mind if you did," I said.

James replied, "Yeah, they'd think you were crazy and now it's mainstream. So it takes a little while, but it'll get there eventually." I told him that I hope so, but asked if we are doing any good now. "Yeah, definitely," he quickly remarked. "Now everybody has had experiences. Before, you could not even talk about psychic experiences because everybody would be like, ooh, that is weird. Now, everybody talks about it. It is okay to talk about psychic experiences. It is like yoga, its okay. It is like Feng Shui, its okay to meditate."

True, yet while times have definitely changed, we still seem to have a long way to go. James and those like him have made it their life's work to help others realize that life does continue after physical death and that we can indeed *talk to the dead*. Perhaps that is the reason psychic-mediums exist to begin with, so that people may know life *is* continuous. He told me that, "It is something of an understanding and awareness, but it'll happen. Slowly, *slowly* it will happen with movies like that (*What Dreams May Come* and *What The Bleep Do We Know!?*), books like mine, books like yours, and people going out to lectures. It'll happen."

When a psychic-medium like James Van Praagh, or other popular mediums offer a lecture or seminar to the masses, the odds are fairly high that you will not get a personal reading. At minimum, there are usually hundreds in attendance at these types of events and not everyone can be read. I know that much from being one of them myself on many occasions. I always thought I might be read at a seminar, but as of yet never have been. The same realization came over me as I sat in the audience later that afternoon for the seminar with James at A.R.E.

Even though I had just spoken to him that morning, I still would not have minded a reading. I would like to remind you of something that may be of comfort when you attend events like his, which I have reminded myself of many times. There is a basic principal within the Edgar Cayce material found at A.R.E. and that is the *oneness* of all things. We can also sum up all the feelings at an event of this nature in just one word: compassion. Compassion was the central theme throughout the audience. We all felt one another's desire to be personally read, and to hear from our own deceased loved ones. We all wanted to validate that there truly is no death as James' tells us and that our life, our essence, is indeed continuous. However, our minds and our hearts *were* in that place which understood compassion. In doing so, we were able to understand that *any* readings coming through James, even for just one person, was validation for every one. Each person in attendance hoped sharing the experience with others would give us not only a greater comprehension of life after death, but also a feeling of connection to our own loved ones. It was a hope that would become a reality in the few short hours that followed his introduction.

James began his presentation to the 350 or more in attendance by telling us that he had a wonderful time meditating on Edgar Cayce's couch only moments prior. While it was his first time at A.R.E., he seemed quite comfortable on stage, perhaps from his restful meditative nap. As he thanked all those with A.R.E. for bringing him there, he mentioned that he had wanted to return to A.R.E. for many, many years. He had been a longtime member of A.R.E. and some twenty-five years prior had even belonged to an A.R.E. study group. Edgar Cayce and Ruth Montgomery were two of the people that formed the basis of his foundation for this type of work. He had remembered first hearing about Edgar Cayce when he was a child and wondered who Cayce was. At the age of nine years old, James researched Edgar Cayce in the New York City Public Library and found him quite fascinating. It seemed to him as if he knew him already. That familiar feeling came over the young James then and grew into a fascination that would eventually lead him to Edgar Cayce's couch. Coming full circle to this moment in time, James commented to the audience that he hoped to develop a film idea about the life of Edgar Cayce once he returned to Los Angeles. Perhaps by the time this book is printed, he may have started the project.

James Van Praagh said he used to be a trance medium, but that he was somewhat afraid of it. When he would go into trance, he would have various guides come through. Some of those guides were from India, as well as an African gatekeeper, and a doctor from England. However, he chose to be more of a *conscious medium* because he was, in his words, "a control freak." He did not want to be put completely under. Even though, when he gives messages, he says there is a change in his consciousness. He told the audience that at those times, he is, "a little bit out of his mind" and "a little bit out of his physical body" in order to receive messages. That was what Edgar Cayce would do whenever he would take a nap on that same couch; he would enter a slumber state of trance in order to give readings. In James' own psychic development, trance was one of the methods used to practice his intuitiveness. James stated that, "Everybody is intuitive to one extent or the other."

With James' lead, we all tested his belief with a try at psychometry later that afternoon and actually did prove it to ourselves with some form of success at it. He told us that he would also include readings in his presentation, as he does like to provide as he says, "evidence of survival of consciousness." One of the better readings was with a police officer in the audience whose past canine was apparently still with him. James kept seeing the spirit of the dog jump up and down in front of the man, and we were all emotionally moved by the special friendship that had obviously not ended with the physical death of his companion.

Like the movie, *Sixth Sense* (1999), James was a young boy when he first began seeing visions. They were always very positive ones, never negative and never violent. They were always very loving and very compassionate. He always thought everyone else could see those things, and did not know he was, in his words, "weird," until later on. He remembered that when he would say his prayers at night with his Mom, he would kneel down and ask her, "Who are those people at the end of the bed with the lights around them?" She would lovingly reply, "Oh, those are God's angels." She assured him that they would always take care of him, not to worry, and that they would always be there for him. She also told him that they were with her when she was a little girl and she would see them too. That was rather impressive for a woman of those days. Acknowledging such a phenomenon was obviously very progressive for the mother of a boy who was, as in *Sixth Sense*, seeing dead people. Had she said he was crazy, he might have ended up in a hospital for the mentally disturbed, which unfortunately happened to many psychics back then. For someone as well known and respected as Edgar Cayce was, people of his time must have thought him a little more than odd. Like Cayce, James had very positive feedback and loving family and friends to support him.

During those formative years, James could even see different colors around people. He noticed that lights would go on whenever someone smiled. He could also see very bright colors that would expand around very happy, outgoing people. However, with those that were angry or sad, the colors became dark and close to their bodies. It was an electric light show unlike any Disney parade. Of course, now we know he was seeing someone's aura, an electromagnetic field that surrounds every living thing, or as James calls it, "your own personal bubble, or your sacred space." It shows us that the consciousness of who we are is not defined by being only of the body, but rather the consciousness is within *and outside* of the body. Who we are is so much more than just flesh. Within your aura, every thought, desire, memory, feeling, and emotion can be seen and read. People who do aura readings can literally see your state of health, mentally, spiritually, as well as your emotional and physical state of being. As you are constantly thinking, experiencing, and creating, your thoughts are creating the colors of your aura. However, even if you were to have your aura photographed with the Kirlian effect, it would only be for that single moment in time. It would not be a permanent representation of you even just a few minutes after the image is taken. Remember, your aura can change with your thoughts. Thus, everything that you create within your consciousness, thoughts, and more, also affects that which is *outside* of you. Therefore, we must learn to be much more *responsible* with our thoughts. Consequently, we can actually create the world in which we live based upon our thoughts. Along with several other insightful souls, James and I discussed that very thing, how to create your own reality, and much more in my next book. My interview with James also continues in subsequent volumes on the afterlife and spirituality. However, for now, I would like to take you back to the seminar with James that afternoon by the beach at A.R.E. James began to recall some of his youth and how he eventually came to find his destiny in spirit communication.

However, at the age of twelve or thirteen, James said something happened to him. He told the audience he really was not paying too much attention to *those spirits around him*. He paused and with a straight face called it puberty. As he explained that his mind was elsewhere for a short while, we all began laughing aloud with him. The young man was growing up and all that *spirit stuff* was just not as important to him then. While he said he was not really paying spirit too much attention, he did remind us that like other children, he was naturally psychic; stating, "Every child is open to spirit." James reminds us that as youngsters it has not yet been too long since arriving from the spirit world. It is a natural way of thinking for the very young; it is their mindset.

Suddenly, a cell phone went off in the middle of his next sentence. He paused and looked around and asked if it was God paging him. Again, there was more laughter. His sense of humor would show throughout the afternoon and it made for wonderful comic relief while grappling with serious subject matters. We softly laughed with James while someone quickly shut off his cell phone. The man apologized and in his quick wit, James replied, "Don't be sorry. I am the cheapest long distance carrier." After the audience applauded, he somehow found his way back where he left off in his presentation.

James was telling us that as a young child, like so many of us, he had spirit friends or as society calls them, imaginary playmates. It is only until society starts to condition us that we cannot or should not have such friends do we experience the loss of those relationships. He believes most children begin closing off from the spirit world around the age of seven or eight because they then become conditioned by society. In his book, *Looking Beyond: A Teen's Guide to the Spiritual World*, (Fireside, 2003) James discusses how adults can embrace and empower children with this knowing. It shows us how we can teach children to remain open. Trusting our children is a big step, but I know from my own experience as a parent that it can be easier than one would think. We can teach children many things in life, but we should not disregard their intuition. After all, *intuition* means *into the soul*. It is a natural language that can be a part of early childhood if parents allow it to be. James remarked that you can choose whether to actually use it (your intuition) or not, as well as *when*. Thinking it would be better to start using it now rather than later, James suggested some fun ways in which to test it. As described even further in a later chapter on how to enhance your psychic abilities, he offered a couple of exercises such as guessing which floor an elevator might stop at, or how much a certain bill in the mail might be, and so forth. He encouraged us all to start using our psychic muscle, in the solar plexus, by simply going with our gut feeling or our intuition.

Later on, as an adult, James would find that his own intuition was becoming more evident. After trusting in his destiny, he began learning and practicing all he could to enhance his own natural psychic abilities. From reading hundreds of books on the subject and learning how out to meditate, he began seeing auras and receiving thoughts around people. He was enhancing his own natural psychic abilities.

He delighted everyone with his psychic abilities that afternoon at A.R.E. with numerous readings, and yes, we all felt as if they were for us. We all felt the connection to spirit as James reaffirmed our understanding that life is indeed continuous.

Now after more than two decades of working as a medium, James' goal is to not only assure us that there is life after death, but also that we are all from the same loving source. James avowed, "Every single person is of God." We are all aspects of that power, that energy, and that pure love which is God." To James, it is true that we *are* made in the image of God. With total confidence, he said, "It is true; we are. God is a pure loving energy. Our natural state of being is of that energy, that love. The further you get from that natural state of being, the further you get away from your true self, and the quickest way to get away from your true self is through fear." As James went on to explain how fear alone has the ability to shut things down, I reflected on the cause of most things, and people who are or appear to be negative. If you were to analyze someone's angry demeanor for example, you might find it all comes down to a fear. It might be a fear of rejection, which then fuels that negative energy. I believe that fear goes against a natural flow of being a positive, loving energy like God. Fear is definitely a blockage to personal growth.

We had talked about such fear earlier that same day in my interview with him. I had asked James how we as a people would ever be able to overcome it. "Do we just keep plugging away with positive effort, positive energy?" James acknowledged by stating, "Yes, with positive energy. I think people have to start opening up their hearts and minds to realize that God is…in everybody. God is everything…when you go 'inside'; you start to see that special part of God." The central theme in my interview with James and in his seminar is the *oneness* with God. James Van Praagh's goal as a medium is to emphasize that oneness, that connection with each other, and that we are all from the same loving source, all aspects of that power and energy and that pure love which is God. I know I felt that pure love during my visit with James and the many others I have met throughout this quest. My own personal journey has brought me closer to understanding James' message that we are *all* part of God.

Chapter 12 - The Ladies of Lily Dale

Interviews, August, 2005

Sandy had told me, "Don't just interview me; interview as many different psychics as you possibly can." Surprising to most, Lily Dale did not come to mind at first. This may come as a shock to some, but I had never heard of Lily Dale. Up until then, I had no reason to seek out such places, especially out of state. Yet, here I was, about to undertake a significant challenge, to seek out and investigate a psychic community thousands of miles away from home. Then I realized that the basis of my journey, this spiritual quest, was discovery by faith. I had to trust that spirit would lead me to the right guides at the right time, including those psychic-mediums whoever and wherever they might be.

Of course, the most famous of psychic-mediums came to mind at first. Sylvia Browne, John Edward, and James Van Praagh were at the top of the list of well-known psychic-mediums. I decided to start with them and see where it would lead me. I noticed on James' Internet website that he would soon be speaking in a town of resident mediums called Lily Dale, near another Cassadaga in upstate New York. I thought it would be a wonderful opportunity to not only interview James, but also several of the mediums in Lily Dale. Yet, even though I was beginning to get excited about visiting there, my calendar kept changing and I soon found myself scheduled with James Van Praagh in *Virginia Beach*, obviously a long way from New York.

However, the thought of visiting Lily Dale never left me. I kept planning and remained in touch with several of its resident psychic-mediums. One who I became especially acquainted with by phone and e-mail was Dr. Lauren Thibodeau. Lauren was also to join James and others to speak at A.R.E. in Virginia Beach. Her suggestion to simply visit both New York and Virginia Beach, soon lead to booking flights and packing bags.

My first trip was to A.R.E., where I met Lauren Thibodeau and interviewed both her and James Van Praagh. Stealing a few precious minutes from her patient husband and her waiting beach chair, she met me for lunch. Her generous advice and unique perspective of mediumship and psychic phenomena told me her contribution would be of great value. The following is the first of several conversations on her career as not only a much sought after spokesperson, but also as a psychic counselor and author. I am pleased to introduce you now to Dr. Lauren Thibodeau.

Lauren Thibodeau, Ph.D.
Speaker, Author, Business Intuitive,
Psychic-Medium and Intuition Development Mentor
Lily Dale, New York USA

Meet Lauren Thibodeau, Ph.D.
Interview, August 12, 2005
Leading you toward "knowing" your way in the world, "Dr. Lauren" brings compassion, integrity, insight and the inquiring, yet skeptical mind of an academic trained in the scientific method to her work. She holds a Ph.D. in Counseling, and Masters degrees in Counseling and Business. An acclaimed practitioner, she has worked with individuals, groups and organizations for more than fifteen years.

Author of *Natural-Born Intuition: How to Awaken and Develop Your Inner Wisdom*, Lauren is a member of the National Speakers Association, and the founder of the Intuitive Leadership Institute, which offers customized, on-site training in using intuition for better decision-making and visionary thinking to organizations and individuals internationally. She has taught corporate executives and law enforcement professionals to access their intuitive intelligence more effectively and systematically using her unique, grounded, pragmatic approach. The best-selling author and spiritual medium, James Van Praagh, has hailed her book, "This is one of the most informative guidebooks on intuition I have ever read. It is chock-full of natural wisdom." It has also been described by author and psychic, Stacey Wolf, as a book about intuition for logical people. Others have called it a "what about me book" since it includes many self-assessments to help readers learn about their own intuitive gifts and personal values.

A nationally certified counselor with experience in grief, bereavement, and trauma, she is a former hospice volunteer.

Dr. Lauren has been featured in hundreds of radio broadcast television programs and print stories and books. Her dissertation, "The Near-Death-Experience, Work Values, and Spiritual Wellness: A Comparative Study" won a university research award. Dr. Lauren presented the results of her research at the International Association of Near-Death Studies North American Conference (IANDS) and at the American Counseling Association national conference. She developed and continues to expand the concept she calls knowing, which is far more than intuition and much more comprehensive than traditional mediumship.

Dr. Lauren is the visionary force behind *The Seeker's Circle*, an online intuition and mediumship development community with thousands of members. A professor with Atlantic University in its fully accredited master's degree program in Transpersonal Studies since 1999, she is also a tutor with The Arthur Findlay College of Mediumship & Psychic Studies, a prestigious mediumship and psychic development training center outside London, England.

A nationally certified counselor (NCC), she holds two masters degrees (MBA and M.Ed.) and a doctorate in counseling. She is a professional member of the National Speakers Association and the International Federation of Speakers, and has been a registered medium at the renowned Lily Dale Assembly since 1996 when she passed the required tests on her first attempt, a highly unusual occurrence. Dr.

Lauren also is among the first few mediums ever to be awarded the designation of Certified Medium (Series A) of the Forever Family Foundation. This medium certification process includes independent testing and scoring, acknowledging achievement of proficiency in the ability of spirit communication through means that are neither deceptive nor fraudulent. Renowned afterlife researcher and author Gary Schwartz, Ph.D., is the President the Forever Family Foundation Board.

A graduate of the American Comedy Institute, Dr. Lauren also performs stand-up comedy about her life as a psychic medium. She has appeared at Caroline's on Broadway, Stand-Up NY, Gotham Comedy Club, the Stress Factory, and Rascal's. Why comedy? She believes that laughter is a healing force and more joy is just plain good (and it keeps her from becoming a dull, boring academic sort.), plus, as Dr. Lauren says, "The language of spirit is laughter and love."

In addition to providing private consultations, Dr. Lauren has taught many people to access their own psychic and intuitive gifts; she continues to teach in all her work and now offers coaching services for intuitive and holistic practitioners. She has presented to a wide range of groups including business executives and police detectives. Dr. Lauren firmly believes that part of being human is being intuitive and encourages people to rely on their own intuition.

Dr. Lauren believes everybody has *intuitive* talents. She said, "Personally, I don't consider psychic ability that special. I think that everybody has a good degree of it naturally. In my book called *Natural Born Intuition*, I write about that very thing and that it is a natural extension of your ability to sense. If you're a sentient being, you're psychic."

In Dr. Lauren's book, *Natural Born Intuition: How to Awaken and Develop Your Inner Wisdom*, (New Page Books, 2005) she gives you a practical, systematic guide to living through a process she refers to as *knowing* or trusting your inner wisdom. By demystifying intuition, Dr. Lauren teaches you how to bring your intuitive right brain and your analytical left brain together. I, myself, found it a powerful tool in both identifying and understanding much of what was happening in the year of my writing this book. It began as previous years, seeking and hoping, but by spring of 2005, I was experiencing the most amazing things, *psychic phenomena*, from just recognizing that *knowing*, which Dr. Lauren speaks about. I was beginning to not only recognize it, but also to some degree even develop my own *inner wisdom*. I was sensing an unseen world, even *seeing signs*, as Dr. Lauren's Mark did in her Chapter 11, *Mixed Intuition and*

Knowing, but especially acknowledging and knowing that within, which was greater than I was. This *knowing* encompasses much with only one aspect of our being, which is called psychic or sixth sense. In our conversation, I asked Dr. Lauren to help further define our sixth sense.

TRINDA: Dr. Lauren, is it true we all have a sixth sense, but some people are more in tune to it than others are?

DR. LAUREN: I don't even call it a sixth sense. To me it is *extended* sense, not extra. It is a natural extension of the senses you already possess. Most people define it in the three *clairs* called clairaudience, clairvoyance, clairsentience, but in my research over the years in teaching and so on, I have noticed there are really five different ways. Clairaudience to me is auditory intuition; clairvoyance is visual intuition, clairsentience I divide in two because I have just noticed that many people receive a more subtle form of clairsentience. Their intuition is clairsentient, they *feel* things but they do not tend to recognize them because it is so very subtle. If you have a clench in your gut, to me that is gut or visceral intuition, but that feel sensitivity, when you walk in a room and you feel that something is off. It is subtle enough that many people dismiss it. Therefore, when I work with people on using their intuition and developing their psychic abilities, I teach them first from the premise of know your own natural intuitive style. If you understand that, you are off to a good start because the way you develop it would vary depending on your strengths. Some people learn kinesthetically, other people learn by visual means, and so forth.

TRINDA: I understand my own psychic strength is clairaudience. However, I am more easily able to receive spiritual thought while *writing* rather than hearing voices. Without my logical left brain telling me that it is not of my normal five senses, I can receive spirit communication under the pretense of my own doing. So I ask you, Dr. Lauren, do you believe a good psychic has to have *all* those abilities?

DR. LAUREN: I know that once you have been working at this awhile they tend to merge. I usually call it skin-in and skin-out sentience. So that is the four types, auditory, visual, sentient (the subtle type) and sentient (the more overt type) and then mixed, which is the place you grow to.

TRINDA: How is your own psychic strength defined?

DR. LAUREN: Mine is mixed, but it depends on the client I am with and it depends on the situation I am in at that time. It depends on the people communicating, whether it is spirit guides or passed-on loved ones.

TRINDA: Is it a merge of all three?

DR. LAUREN: It is indeed. If I have a very visual client who is an artist, I tend to get much more visual data, but that makes sense because in that moment I am blending energy with them on their behalf.

TRINDA: Their spirits as well as your spirits; so, it is really a foursome?

DR. LAUREN: At least a threesome, but it varies. The situation drives it to a larger degree than people tend to acknowledge.

TRINDA: So in your thinking, it is the situation as well as the people that are there. (I was also informed that I might be recognizing one of my own guides, an angel, by seeing white wings all the time.) How much does symbolism play a part in what you do?

DR. LAUREN: If you start paying attention to how the universe speaks to you, through symbols, what pulls your awareness, why you are seeing those things?

TRINDA: Spotting a feather all the time or whatever?

DR. LAUREN: Correct.

TRINDA: As well as to look to your inner self, your own subconscious to try to figure out what that means?

DR. LAUREN: Correct.

TRINDA: So my feather could mean one thing, and your feather could mean something different?

DR. LAUREN: Precisely, and they would both be correct.

TRINDA: If you were doing a reading for someone, would you see it in *your* understanding of the feather?

DR. LAUREN: Generally, but when you learn to do this, remember mediumship and psychics are separate things, but when you're working outside the self, because psychic stuff is more from the self to the self, this (mediumship) is spirit to spirit. When you are working spirit to spirit from a mediumship level, you can direct them to show you in your own language. That is when you will hear mediums say, well sure, the person spoke French, but I hear it in English. The person may use the feather symbol that fits you. I am going to get the thing that represents the same thing as your feather to me, so it might be a silver coin, but they both represent something that is relevant. They will translate feather to coin and I will go, "Aha, this is what you mean," and present that to the client.

TRINDA: So, you really have to know your symbols and your understanding of them before you start talking with people. There is so much skepticism in this business, is it because there is so much that varies from medium to medium and sitter to sitter, including symbolism?

DR. LAUREN: You will never get away from spirit's *natural laws*. They work a certain way, but it is how you use them. If water flows downhill because of gravity, and I dam it up and water my garden with it, and you chose to let it flow freely out to the sea because you like watching the water flow. Those are two uses of the same natural law of gravity and neither one is *right* and neither one is *wrong*, but they are just different and people can chose to work their own way. I generally recommend that anybody using outside symbolism also add to that personal spiritual symbolism. You can probably talk to tarot readers and they will say, "I read the cards as they have meaning to me." They probably started using a classic interpretation and then added their own twists and interpretations later. They start with somebody else's spiritual alphabet, the classic meanings, whether its astrology, numerology, cards, you name it; some divination system is somebody else's creation. I am saying use your own power.

TRINDA: Have you ever included astrology in your readings and interpretations of messages?

DR. LAUREN: That is a symbol system and it is perfectly helpful and interesting if that is your means of understanding this universe and your connection to it, then go for it. I find it overwhelming in its minutia. Instead, I think in concepts. I am actually conversant with astrology and I have many colleagues who are astrologers who assist me with interpreting my chart and things, but I take it in and promptly let it go. It is more than my brain can hold onto. It takes up space that I would rather use for bigger ideas.

TRINDA: To whom are you speaking to in spirit, your own guides or do you not know?

DR. LAUREN: I know. I have a team of helpers who make it easier for me to receive information. They do their best in a way that an electrical line has a transducer on it to change the vibration, to reduce the current so that if you travel overseas you have to use an adaptor to get the same electrical response as you could get here by plugging directly into the wall. They help me by bringing the current to me in a way that I can best use it.

TRINDA: In addition to connecting sitters with deceased loved ones, has it ever become much more philosophical, much deeper than the acknowledgment of their mundane activities and events?

DR. LAUREN: My books are far more about that sort of thing.

TRINDA: So you answer those questions in your book, *Natural Born Intuition*.

DR. LAUREN: Yes and in other books to come. To me the philosophy is not meant to be a truth for others. It is meant to inspire people to look for their own truth. It is not meant to tell people how it is; it is *non-dogmatic*.

TRINDA: What personal revelations have you had throughout your work?

DR. LAUREN: I have never felt *disconnected* from the source, ever once in my life. I was born *knowing* I guess you could say.

TRINDA: Has it evolved since then?

DR. LAUREN: I have always communicated with them, they learn from us as much as we learn from them. What I change within me, changes the whole and it is forever transformed because I put my heart to it or my thought toward it or my intent to it. If people got hold of that idea and lived as if it were true...I have to say as if it were true, because most people have not been as fortunate as I have been to know it is true. I *know* it is true, no question.

TRINDA: In trying to communicate with spirit, deceased loved ones, ourselves, can we communicate our deepest *feelings* to them even if we lack the words?

DR. LAUREN: I cannot say how many times in my work the discussion ends up being one along the lines of, "He brings me a sense of emotional distance and talks about how he now understands how it would have been better for both parties to..." and so on.

TRINDA: The deceased ones understand us after they have crossed over and seen the bigger picture, can understand so much more, including our feelings and intentions. So we really should never think, "I wish they knew how I felt," because they do already, and just move on with your life.

DR. LAUREN: Correct, which is why, even though I do mediumship, I consider it very much a *healing service*. I think the other thing I do is teach people to do it themselves. To teach them simple, simple principles, like gravity. If you work in alignment with the natural laws, the *natural spiritual laws* that run the show. People ask, "What are they?" One *big* one is *love*. Love is all there is; it is not too tough. There is no need to create complexity around it.

According to the fundamentals of spiritualism, natural laws are the laws God has set into motion, which govern all. They are the law of attraction, the law of life, the law of love, the law of truth, the law of compensation, and the law of freedom.

TRINDA: Is that your message to everyone, to live in alignment with the natural laws in life in order to be happy and content?

DR. LAUREN: Yes, contentment comes from living in alignment with natural *spiritual* law. However, I would encourage people to first study natural law. If they cannot find a source, go within; go to *the* source.

TRINDA: What if people want to be more psychic; they want to be more clairsentient, more clairaudient, and so forth?

DR. LAUREN: That can be developed, but I think that we have to ask what it is about that experience that draws you because what you want to do with it drives the level at which it will operate. This is why people ask, "If you're so psychic how come you don't win the lotto?" It is a long story; I almost won the lotto, but I am not attached to the lotto as an outcome. I do not *value* it enough. This is all in my book. This whole idea of what we value is where the intuition thrives. If you are really *into* sports and you love baseball statistics, for example, you are going to be really good at understanding the probabilities within baseball.

TRINDA: Let you heart guide your head.

DR. LAUREN: To a point, I think you have to understand that where you put your attention becomes your intention. Whether it is intentional or not, *your attention drives your intention.*

TRINDA: Rather it is about letting your heart, mind, and focus guide you, such as in perceivable goals. Yet, concerning psychic ability…

DR. LAUREN: That *can be* developed, but also understand what your point is. To me, mediumship and psychic development always appear to be about other people, and to a large degree, they are. When you get it, that they are really a service to you as well as to other people, then you are in much better balance, and when you're in better balance, you will do better work.

In Dr. Lauren's book, *Natural-Born Intuition*, she states that, "…a wise intuitive always goes *inward* for information…" and "working from

Knowing is much more rewarding." Dr. Lauren does her rewarding work not only in Lily Dale, but also throughout the U.S. with seminars, private consultations, and live Internet chats, in addition to writing and continually working toward bringing others a better understanding of their own intuitive self and the unseen world around them. We delve into much more of the unseen world, the afterlife and her understanding of being a spiritualist, psychic-medium in further volumes to *Pieces of the Puzzle*. However, I would also encourage you to pick up a copy of Dr. Lauren's *Natural-Born Intuition: How to Awaken and Develop Your Inner Wisdom* and create your own *Knowing Journal,* as did I. Dr. Lauren writes, "Keeping a Knowing Journal moves you from a seemingly random succession of events into an observer and interpreter of the interaction between the Unseen World and the Earthly World. You begin to see the lessons in your life and put them into practice."

Dr. Lauren truly is the *thinking person's intuitive consultant.* I hope you have gained a better understanding of the work of a medium, Dr. Lauren Thibodeau, and perhaps something of yourself from my interview with her. If you would like more information on how to contact Dr. Lauren or how to purchase her book, I invite you to visit her at Lily Dale or her Internet website at www.DrLauren.com.

My next trip takes me to upstate New York where I met the lovely *ladies of Lily Dale.* Lily Dale is a spiritualist community located in Chautauqua County in the Town of Pomfret, at the north end of Cassadaga Lake, near the Village of Cassadaga. Open to the public in 1879, Lily Dale continues to welcome resident mediums and those who wish to live in this charming community. Those who want to own a home in Lily Dale must become a member of a recognized Spiritualist Church and of the Lily Dale Assembly.

Under a green canopy of tall trees, Lily Dale's quaint Victorian homes line its narrow nineteenth century brick roadways. In this tranquil environment, the community is part of a modern spiritualist movement dedicated to the religion of Spiritualism. As you now know, spiritualists believe in the continuation of life. Some spiritualists are also known as mediums and/or spiritual healers.

The spiritualist movement began in this country in the early 1800's. While there have been many *famous spiritualists* throughout our history, from mediums Lizzie Doten and Nettie Maynard to the world-famous magician, Harry Houdini, many were not mediums. Lizzie Doten was a famous spiritualist medium and a pilgrim descendant from

Plymouth, Massachusetts, believed to have channeled some of the most well known literary masters, including Shakespeare, Burns, and Edgar Allen Poe. Nettie Coburn Maynard was known as Lincoln's medium, for séances held at the White House. While it is somewhat questionable as to whether or not Lincoln was a spiritualist, he was believed to have been at the very least, extremely *intuitive* or sensitive. Weeks before his assassination, he had a clairvoyant dream of his death. In his dream, he heard a number of people sobbing and went to investigate. While he found no one searching from room to room, the sounds continued. Apparently, he then saw his funeral, complete with soldiers weeping in the East Room of the White House before waking from the dreamed vision. Supposedly, Lincoln even had a second *feeling* that seemed to indicate the same end would befall him after the war ended, and was soon after assassinated at the Ford Theater.

Yet, whether or not you too are *intuitive*, a spiritualist, or psychic-medium yourself, you might wish to visit Lily Dale, the spiritual community in which many psychic-mediums reside and work. After my conversations with those of the Lily Dale Mediums League, particularly my contact with Reverend Barbara A. Sanson, I was beginning to get the sense that there was much more to its members than simply giving psychic readings for Lily Dale visitors.

The League was founded in 1930 for promoting the religion of Spiritualism, as well as the demonstration of mediumship. It has continued to assist developing mediums while promoting Lily Dale for over 126 years. As an Auxiliary of Lily Dale Assembly, the League owns the historical building located on Library Street, built in 1890. It was in the Mediums League building that I found myself visiting with and interviewing many of the most remarkable resident mediums of Lily Dale.

I invite you now to join me in my conversations with the lovely *ladies of Lily Dale*, those exceptionally grounded women in a world of psychic phenomena.

Patty Lillis
Psychic-Medium
Lily Dale, New York USA

Meet Patty Lillis

The first of whom I would like to introduce you to is Patty Lillis. "That is Patty with a *y*," she said with a smile. As we sat together that afternoon, Patty warmly welcomed me like family. We had visited some earlier at the Forest Temple the day before and again before this interview at the Mediums building. We started talking about how she first realized she was psychic and that she believed "everyone" is psychic to some degree or another. Patty began with, "I think we all have *it*, but it depends on how it imprints on us. She said, "I always knew I was *weird*. I did not know the difference between a medium and a psychic. I had no idea until somebody told me I was a medium."

TRINDA: When was that?

PATTY: Probably in the 1970s. I used to come here (Lily Dale) off and on in the 70s, but I was not interested in being a part of this yet. You come at your own time, in your own rhythm. I just got this overwhelming desire in the 80s after doing a couple of readings that I needed to come here to expand it and to learn more about it. I came here to do development classes where they guide you. They do not tell you how to do it; they guide your own natural talent. They tell you do this, relax about that, do not worry about that, and so forth.

TRINDA: When you came here, what did you know you could already do?

PATTY: I was not sure. I knew I could do some precognition. In other words, I knew what somebody was going to say before he or she would say it. My kids would never let me play cards with them because I would just seem to know what they were doing. I think it was because I had two near-death experiences myself. I had one just before I was eight years old and again when I was twenty-four. I did not know what they were then. I thought they were cool trips.

TRINDA: What were they like?

PATTY: Well, when I was eight, I lost my appendix at school. I was very bad and there were no doctors around. They had to find a doctor. They were all at a convention. When I was twenty-four, I was on a bus and my gall bladder broke. I had some kind of tests and stuff. When my father finally talked me into going into a hospital, sometime during the night I faded. I know they did surgery and opened me from here to here. There was peritonitis (peritonitis is an inflammation of the peritoneum) and all the messy stuff. I remember floating. I remember my cousin coming to see me because he was a pre-med student and I remember thinking isn't that strange, I am floating and he's running ahead of me. He is going to get a doctor to say that I have faded. I could see him and thought it must be the drugs, yet I knew I was above.

TRINDA: Just hanging at the ceiling?

PATTY: Kind of floating and wondering where he was going. He was trying to have a conversation and I was following right behind him. That is all I remember from that part and I know that they said I was in and out for about seven days. I tell people to talk to people that are unconscious. They *do* hear you. They cannot respond sometimes, but they do hear you. You know they talk about the light. It is hard to explain it as just *the light*, and I remember seeing my grandmother with her hand like this saying, "No, you have children. No, not yet." The first one was a little bit more profound than that. I found myself turning around and when I slammed back into what they call the body, I was very mad because I had been in perfect peace, perfect love. I started coming to and the doctor was leaning over and said, "Welcome back." I said, "Where did I go?"

TRINDA: How long had that been?

PATTY: It was about the 6th or 7th day. I cannot remember exactly. My mother said she came every day and I was not really responding to everybody. I think what happened, to really make it messy, is they had pumped me full of penicillin and I reacted and everything swelled, which did not help either, but I *was* fine. Everyone was scurrying around and I was in *this space* that was so wonderful.

TRINDA: How did you *feel*?

PATTY: When you depart from your body, it is separate. When you first do it you are aware there is somebody on the bed and you have this faint attachment; if that's me, I sure am ugly. The first one was kind of sweet. I do not know if you have heard me out there (giving readings at the Forest Temple), but I have always heard music around people.

TRINDA: How old were you at that time?

PATTY: I was almost eight and I remember being in a hospital in Canada. We had a war going on. I remember that because penicillin was in very short supply. They were using sulfur drugs and my appendix had burst at school. I remember saying as a kid, that was when they had boys and girls in the same room, there was a young man across from me (he had sweet peas) and all of a sudden I remember saying, "Help," because I was feeling like I was leaving my body and I kept seeing these sweet peas. They started dropping and every time they dropped, they made this crystal note sound. It took me years to find a tape that sounded like it. It is called *Crystal Silence*. I would hear these beautiful notes and I felt myself float. There was some lady that took my hand and said, "Let's go play," and I thought "Okay, fine." I was having a good time and then she said now you have to go home. I went, "Oh." I did not know who she was and she was just a lady, but I called her the "lighted lady." She said, "Okay, that is enough time to repair you." I did not know what she meant.

TRINDA: Repair your body?

PATTY: My *ethereal* body. I floated back and came to and it was 3 o'clock in the morning. My parents were there and it is the same thing. I tried to explain to them, but you know how they said, "Sure, it is the...whatever"

TRINDA: Have you seen that spirit since?

PATTY: I saw it once; it was in a meditation. I had forgotten a lot of that; I had just filed it away. We were in a meditation called *Meeting and Greeting Your Spiritual Guides.*

TRINDA: I notice that you rub your hands when you do spiritual readings. What is that? You and John Edward have the same thing going on?

PATTY: It is like a centering. When I do readings, I ask people to place their hands just above mine so I can feel the energy in between.

TRINDA: Would you feel any energy between us for example?

PATTY: Sometimes I do, sometimes I do not. I have to be in that state. If I am not in that state, I go to sleep in a good reading. I usually tell them, this side is Dad's side; this is Mum's side. I organize them so they do not drive me crazy. The music does not mean much other than that is how I bring in the personality. It is kind of an agreement we have. Some music is the same, but then I get new ones that can even make me laugh.

TRINDA: Strong music would be a strong person. Is that what you mean?

PATTY: *Amazing Grace* to me was always a traditional hymn, so I will get a very traditional man. I will sometimes get light music like *Zippadee Do Da.* That simply means that the person was very funny, very light. I will get a motion of my feet going back and that means they were very stubborn as if you were to dig your heels in. They will give me symbols like razors if they are clean-shaven, I will feel pressure here (pointing above her nose) if they had glasses. Sometimes I will see color of hair or I will see the eyes. Mostly I bring out their personalities. If I get a hand on the hip right away, it is a very feisty woman. Usually, they tell me when I am right on.

TRINDA: When you see a hand on the hip, is it in your mind a woman with her hand on the hip, any woman, or is it just the arm and the hip?

PATTY: It is the arm and the hip and then it goes to the face and I see the height. Then I start hearing the language and say, "Don't you lie to me" and they will go, "Oh, my God." It is almost like shooting a gun. It is funny and *you can make agreements with the spirits* you work with.

TRINDA: Are they cooperative?

PATTY: Oh, yes! You are always in control. I always tell people you are never, *not* in control. Without you, they cannot channel. I always tell them that I do not want to see it past eighteen months; I do not want to influence anybody's future.

TRINDA: So you do not want to do predict the future.

PATTY: No, I do not like predictions. I have worked with parents of murdered children. I do not care for that. It is touching inward spirit too close. I can remember describing a whole murder scene, what the young man looked like and how he had his hands and it is painful.

TRINDA: For you?

PATTY: Yes. I said I am not a psychic detective. Do not come to me looking for a psychic detective. I can bring that to you only to tell you that Tim, or whoever, is here.

TRINDA: Whether he is gone or not because he is missing or dead, they want to know which it is, correct.

PATTY: Right, they knew Tim was murdered. Mostly they want to know who did it and I will get a quick flash of more than one for example.

TRINDA: In that regard, some mediums have different opinions about capital punishment; do you believe in it?

PATTY: Not really.

TRINDA: Would it be better to house them forever in prison?

PATTY: What is a worse torture? I was listening to a man who had three life sentences. He said, "You understand that I would rather be dead because for twenty-seven years I have done the same thing. I have gotten up at the same time, followed the same orders, worn the same clothes, ate the same food." He said, "That' is torture." So, to me, if they are going to make amends, rehabilitate (many prisons do not rehabilitate), but I also believe in natural progression. Whether it is right or not, when it is time, the soul will leave with any method that it can. If we choose that we are going to have a disease, unconsciously, we will have a disease. If we say that my mother is going to abort me, we will be aborted. That sounds strange, but that is what I heard.

TRINDA: Do we have "x" number of options to exiting this life?

PATTY: No, I have not. I said to myself that we make a contract. Obviously, we can renegotiate because twice I have renegotiated. Here is this contract for example, that says you will be on earth until the year whatever. Okay, and then all of a sudden for whatever reason, I am tested. You know what I mean; I am *tested*.

TRINDA: You are changing the contract.

PATTY: I am changing the contract.

TRINDA: Do you have to learn psychic *techniques* like any other skill?

PATTY: Right, there is a way of touching in where you are your own individual medium. Mediums are the same. We touch in with spirit levels, but they are as individual as their fingerprints in how they attach to those spirits. Some will write. Some will just stare at you (hopefully they blink). I have to tell you a cute story. It was my own first reading and I was about twelve. I was really excited because there was a carnival coming to town. They had gypsy tents. I thought I had to go and see the gypsy. I knew she had a message for me. I was tired of the Crystal Beach one. My mother would never allow me to do that. I told her I was going on this ride, which would make her sick. I remember running into the tent. I had the money and I am looking at her, and she is the real deal. She has the big earrings, the turban, and the crystal ball and why is she staring at me like this? I reached forward and she did not even blink. I thought I had killed her. Mum says God punishes and I have killed this woman. I was so hysterical, I threw down the money and ran out right to my mother and she said, "See I told you that ride would make you sick."

TRINDA: So you never got your reading.

PATTY: No and I never told her for years.

TRINDA: So, do you can see and hear spirit? What are your abilities?

PATTY: I sense. Clairvoyant, clairaudient, not "outside" (the physical body); I can see and hear.

TRINDA: When you hear, please help me because I have had an experience myself. Do you hear a voice or does it seem like it is coming from another room?

PATTY: If it sounds like it is coming from another room, its exenterated.

TRINDA: I thought someone from another room was calling my name.

PATTY: I had that happen to me once. It was very important that they get my attention. They said Pat instead of Patty, so I knew it was my mother's family. At that particular time, I was very cranky and very busy because I was looking for something. I went, "What?" Then I realized that there was no one attached to it. I put my hand on exactly what I was looking for, so I don't know if I was meant to find it. I was looking for family history.

TRINDA: But that is outside. What do you mean by inside?

PATTY: Internally, it is as if you are just sensing the words. Here is what happens to me. I will hear them musically, it will bring them in and I will see a blank page. On that blank page, they start to write words. I will follow the words as fast as I can because that is a fast hand that I see. Then I will get symbols and I will see partial things. I will see the glasses. I will see the razor.

TRINDA: Are your images as photographs or is it that you just *know* of an image?

PATTY: I see them. I see a blue razor or I will see a beard.

TRINDA: Is that the distinction of seeing color in our dreams?

PATTY: No, not really, some people say they dream in Technicolor, others in black and white. I just say you do a lot of work in your sleep. You can sleep eight hours and get up dead tired. I say look to your dreams because you are usually working there (on the other side). They are saying to you, "We have the answer. Just tune in." It is like a blank page and when they are finished, they are finished. I always ask for someone's hand when I have finished and I feel I am earthbound again. It is a way of stabilizing. The shake of the hand is to bring me back to this reality.

TRINDA: And everyone will do that differently?

PATTY: Yes, you will have some mediums who will swear that you are only a true medium if you can bring up a name. I will remind them, we do not have names once we go to the other side. We do not have to bring them back because we do not have emotion, therefore, we do not have an attachment. Therefore, we really would not have a name, but we can bring up the name we had here. I sometimes hear it musically. Sometimes I will hear a name and I am very grateful. I remember getting the name Ernestine one time, which was connected right to her; it was her mum. I am very appreciative of names that mean something, not names that I am throwing out saying, "Is Charlie here; is Bill here"? If people can work that way that is great, but it is not my way of working.

TRINDA: If we want to do it ourselves, do you advise meditation. If we really want to hear and see our Aunt Tillie, we want to have her sitting in the chair talking to us as if she is flesh, would we simply meditate? If we keep praying for it every day, is it ever going to come true or is it just if *they* want it to happen. How does that relationship work?

PATTY: They will come when they want to. Someone would say, why is my cousin here, where's my mum? You mum was busy; I do not know. I am just getting your cousin's vibration.

TRINDA: If we ask to see them, will they materialize for us?

PATTY: Not always, it is their will. I remember finally getting a visitation from my dad. I am a medium. I should be able to attach my family and I did not. All of a sudden, I was in a meditative state and I looked at a spirit; a visit is you are not quite sure if it is real or not. You are sort of half in a trance, floating in and out. The best time for that is when you are in that space right before you go to sleep so you can wake quickly or you can go to sleep. All of a sudden, I saw somebody walking. I saw the back of him. I saw a yellow slicker and a rain hat, and I said, "Dad"? He turned round with this big smile. He was holding a fish. He taught me fishing. He taught me how to bait a hook. That was his way of saying I love you and here I am.

TRINDA: Are they projecting an image to us. Is that how it works?

PATTY: I think so. I remember one time I was half asleep and I still don't know who the lady was and it was down in Florida. I was half asleep and half awake, it was just after 9-11, and we were all very upset. I felt a hand on my shoulder and this lady with very big earrings said, "It is going to be okay." It was as clear as that. It was external. I thought someone had come in and said something.

Patty has never sensed that woman again or gotten any more messages about the September 11, 2001 tragedy other than that one statement from a fashionable spirit telling her everything would eventually be okay. While I would imagine some of those grieving families may not ever feel completely okay, my hope is that they may become more at peace knowing and believing as Patty and all Spiritualists do in the continuity of life. Knowing that the soul survives even the worst of tragedies and that we will be with our loved ones once again is perhaps the best message that Patty and I could leave you with for now. Yet, if we "human beings" can ever get to that place which allows us to look beyond the pain of loosing loved ones to a bigger picture of the puzzle that is our existence, perhaps we will begin to understand how to more easily accept our purpose, both in living and dying. It is a challenge

tha_____nd the others in following volumes on
our_____w our spirituality and faith plays a vital
role in the comprehension of our never-ending consciousness. For now,
however, I would like you meet another lovely lady of Lily Dale, Shirley
Yusczyk.

Shirley Yusczyk
Psychic-Medium
Lily Dale, New York USA

Meet Shirley Yusczyk

A former Catholic nun, and while in a cloistered contemplative
order, Shirley had an awakening of her own personal and universal
spirituality. Since leaving religious life, she has made it her life's work to
share a greater understanding of universal truths. Shirley has studied
spirituality and healing since the early 1970s. She is a registered Medium
in Lily Dale, teacher, lecturer, and seminar leader. Shirley is no stranger to
interviews, previously featured for both television and radio within the
United States and Canada. She feels it is part of her life path to help
others to understand and incorporate spirituality and healing into their
daily lives.

TRINDA: We will start with psychic phenomena, Shirley. We call it that, but I am sure there is a great deal of misunderstanding with terminology in this field. What is your personal interpretation of it?

SHIRLEY: Psychic phenomenon is at a much lower vibration than mediumship. When we are just starting out, we learn how to be psychics, but we soon leave that behind to become mediums because mediums work at a much higher vibration. Psychics are people who get information directly from you. They look at your aura, which is the energy field that surrounds all living things, impressions they receive from you, and imperceptibly they receive body language, intuitiveness, etc. Whereas a medium raises their vibration to a much higher level and people from the spirit side of life lower theirs because they exist at a much higher vibration, a much higher frequency than we do. They lower their vibration and we meet somewhere in the middle and that is how they give us information.

TRINDA: Is your information coming from spirit in heaven or beyond that?

SHIRLEY: It depends on what your interpretation is of heaven. I do not think it as a place with white fluffy clouds and harps.

TRINDA: As far as being a practicing medium, obviously not all psychics are mediums.

SHIRLEY: Yes, all mediums are psychic, but not all psychics are mediums. You start out with psychic energy because it is a simpler, lower vibration.

TRINDA: When did you first recognize your own psychic intuition?

SHIRLEY: All my life, but I was interested in it as a teenager. I saw spirit as a child, although I was so scared of it when I saw a spirit sitting on my bed that I kicked her. I did not want to see it again, so I literally turned it off for forty years.

TRINDA: You can turn it on and off, even now.

SHIRLEY: Absolutely, you have to. You cannot possibly be walking around seeing dead people all over.

TRINDA: How do they communicate to you? Are you seeing symbols or signs? What is your expertise?

SHIRLEY: They (spirit) use all my senses. When I am making identification or when I bring someone in through during a reading, I will see or feel a presence of someone standing in a certain position that tells me the relationship to the person.

TRINDA: You ask them to do that for you.

SHIRLEY: I have it all lined up. My spirit guides line them up where they need to be as the mother, father, brother, sister, etc. My spirit guides help me; they work with me. I have like a gatekeeper who lines them all up in the right place.

TRINDA: So you say something like okay guys, we're on, let's get ready and they know their positions?

SHIRLEY: Right, when I recognize someone standing in, say, the grandmother's position on the mother's side, then I check my body, I scan my body and they will give me a twinge or a tickle or something or draw my attention to some area of the body that would distinguish how they passed.

TRINDA: Or, would you, for example, if your sitter's grandmother had beautiful hair, you would...

SHIRLEY: I would see beautiful hair.

TRINDA: The guide would be helping you to better connect.

SHIRLEY: The guide puts them in the spot where they need to be.

TRINDA: What happens after that?

SHIRLEY: Then I would see their hair color or their face, if there were a similarity to the person that I am doing the reading for. I feel it in my body. I would hear what they are saying if they give me a name or want to tell me something.

TRINDA: So, let us say they (spirit) are saying, Aunt Tillie, and you *see* someone in the aunt's position with gray hair. You would ask, "Did you have an Aunt Tillie who had gray hair? Then the sitter would say, "Yes that would be her." Is that how you do it?

SHIRLEY: Yes, basically, that is it.

TRINDA: What about the images, are they in your mind or are they projected outward?

SHIRLEY: Both, it depends on the strength of the spirit personality coming through. If they were a strong person in the living, they are going to be a strong person on the spirit side in the sense that they will butt in ahead of other people. They will be the same personality type. If they were a quiet reserved person, they will stand in the background until the end of the reading and then say, "I am here."

TRINDA: What if the person you are reading is very shy? Does that hold back anything?

SHIRLEY: No, if they were a psychic it would, but I do not tap into their psychic energy. I am way above that energy so it does not matter what they are doing.

TRINDA: So it does not matter about the sitter, interesting.

SHIRLEY: Just as long as they are open to the experience.

TRINDA: Just keeping an open mind, saying whatever happens, happens. Now their spirit, their strength, as well as your strength—would that make for a better psychic reading?

SHIRLEY: Yes.

TRINDA: Have you ever had a strange or weird experience with anyone that stands out?

SHIRLEY: I think I am always the one that is amazed at the clarity of how good spirit people come in. I will get very specific diagnoses of what they crossed from, things I would not expect or I could not make up if I tried.

TRINDA: You would not know the physical problem that happened, but also you would get those medical details? Can you give me an example of a medical reading that has surprised you?

SHIRLEY: Yesterday I was sitting doing a reading and I was bringing someone through. I was rubbing my nose right here, and I did not get a clue from it. I said, "I don't know why, but when I am tapping in with your Mum I am rubbing my nose right here." She started crying and said it was because her Mum died of sinus cancer. Therefore, it can be very unusual. It can be very specific, but I have to be aware of what they are showing me on my body. Sometimes my hand will literally scan in front of me until I feel something. Yesterday, I said cancer in the pancreas. I do not even know where the pancreas is, but it was like yes, that was it.

TRINDA: I understand that the *knowing* part of this is so hard for mediums to explain to people. If I had not had a small personal experience with it myself, I might not believe you. Can you explain the *knowing* part of being psychic?

SHIRLEY: It is almost like if I were to ask you to close your eyes and imagine your living room. You could tell me where every chair in the living room is, the colors, and of sunlight coming through the window. It is the same thing when spirit gives us an impression like that. Again, yesterday, I said, "I don't know why I am seeing racehorses with your Dad." He said, "Because we both worked at a racetrack, in the bar." They show me these things and they don't have to make sense to me, but they will make sense to the person.

TRINDA: Do you see everything, good, bad, or indifferent?

SHIRLEY: I do not get bad. I have that "rule" with my spirit guides; they do not tell me when anyone is going to die.

TRINDA: You do not want to know and you do not want to share that.

SHIRLEY: It does no good for someone to know that.

TRINDA: Would they (spirit) tell you if you asked them?

SHIRLEY: They might.

TRINDA: I have heard of a medium telling a sitter they would soon pass.

SHIRLEY: That is something an ethical medium would never do.

TRINDA: This was a long time ago and maybe there was a need to tell the sitter; I don't know.

SHIRLEY: You can always be wrong. It is not 100% because when I see things it is subject to my interpretation.

TRINDA: When you see an event occurring, a premonition, if you want to call it that…the fact that you relay that information to the sitter and the sitter hears it, it does not that change the outcome. Cannot the observer change what you are telling them?

SHIRLEY: Absolutely, quantum physics is teaching us that. I also tell people they have free will and free choice. When I look at somebody's future, the way I like to describe it is (one of the other mediums uses this example and I'll borrow it from him) if there are threads coming out of an individual and you look at the thread that has the most energy going down it. All things being equal, no one making any decisions to change it, it is the most likely course of events. Yet any way along that continuum, they can make a free choice, someone else can make a choice that alters that thread and it (destiny) hops over to another alternate reality.

A good example of how that might occur was in the 1990 film, *Mr. Destiny*, (a takeoff on *It is a Wonderful Life*) when the main character (James Belushi) chooses to hit a homerun in a pivotal baseball game verses missing it, and the rest of his life changes because of it. A fun flick if you have not yet seen it.

TRINDA: Many people are having and expressing paranormal experiences these days. They will see their grandma on the chair next to them, but they will freak out, or they will hear voices in the air and they will wonder how that is possible; they think they are going crazy or something. They may have no interest, no knowledge or desire for spirit communication, yet they have these *experiences* anyway. Some devout Christians that I know have told me personally about their own psychic experiences and worry about them. What would you tell those people?

SHIRLEY: I think in those types of situations it is generally that Grandma wants to come back and say, "I am Okay. I still exist. I am happy. I am at peace and I am still around."

TRINDA: Do you think that for some reason he or she may need to hear that from spirit?

SHIRLEY: Yes, whether it is the need of the spirit or of the individual. They love to be recognized. Spirit people love to be recognized. They are okay with it. Perhaps they had a very slight recognition of a person in the living; they were school chums. Yet, forty years later, they would come in and say, "I remember you, do you remember me?" It is like a kick for them.

TRINDA: I understand that the veil between the spirit world and our world is difficult to communicate through to us. Is it hard for them to break through that barrier?

SHIRLEY: Yes, for a spirit to materialize in solid form, that is Hollywood stuff. It is not something that happens as they show in the movies. Mediums that do physical phenomena take years of sitting in circle to try to build the ectoplasm, which is the stuff that the spirit uses to materialize. To build that enough that a spirit could actually use that; first of all they may use that to create a hand or a voice box that they could speak with, but to materialize a whole person is very, very difficult for them.

TRINDA: If they can, are they a higher spirit, a higher type of entity?

SHIRLEY: Not necessarily.

TRINDA: I *have* heard that people have actually seen that.

SHIRLEY: Sure, so have I.

TRINDA: But you have seen them almost like a see–through image?

SHIRLEY: Yes, in fact, I walked into one person one time. I was turning a corner coming downstairs, and I was coming round the corner not expecting anyone to be there and I bumped into this guy and I said, "Excuse me" and he disappeared.

TRINDA: Did he look as real as you or I?

SHIRLEY: Enough for me to say excuse me.

TRINDA: How can they sometimes materialize even partially, but not always, and why?

SHIRLEY: Sometimes it is important that they comfort a grieving loved one that is left behind.

TRINDA: How or why does a spirit move things, manipulate lights, and so forth?

SHIRLEY: It is because they exist at a higher vibration or frequency than we do. They can manipulate electronics easier because that is also a higher vibration or frequency than the earth plane that we exist in as flesh and blood. That is why they can manipulate lights flashing or radio static, things like that. There are also little spirit lights that people can take pictures of.

TRINDA: Those are the little balls or orbs that we can see on film. Is that actually the spirit entity itself, a single entity or a portion of one?

SHIRLEY: I think it is a portion.

TRINDA: They are getting us to notice them.

SHIRLEY: Right, it is just that they are around, but we cannot see.

TRINDA: You do not need a special camera or device of some type.

SHIRLEY: No, you do not need anything special. You can take it with a Polaroid, you can take it with a...

TRINDA: A digital camera?

SHIRLEY: I am sure, since I have seen pictures from a digital too. I have seen it with all kinds of cameras because the shutter speed is faster than what we see. That is why it picks it up.

TRINDA: So they are around us all the time.

SHIRLEY: Yes.

I liked the idea that spirit was with us. I felt better knowing that our loved ones and guides could always be with us. With the help of gifted mediums like Shirley, we will continue to communicate with spirit and to know that our higher self, our consciousness, or our soul lives on. If those in spirit are willing, and it seems they are, then we will most assuredly hear from them through such insightful souls as Shirley, Patty, and others like them who have this amazing ability, communicating with the dead.

The next medium that I am happy to introduce you to is Eileen McClure. Eileen is a psychic-medium, spiritual consultant, teacher and lecturer. Eileen is a graduate from the school of Spiritual Healing and Prophecy in Lily Dale, New York. Diplomas from Kent University include teaching, school counseling and school psychology. Eileen bridges traditional knowledge with her intuitive and medium work to enhance the effects of her readings. A graduate of the Institute of Light in Cleveland, Ohio, Eileen assists others in their healing process using the earth energy and grounding techniques. Her mission statement is to *empower through knowledge.*

Meet Eileen McClure

I liked Eileen the minute I saw her. Soft spoken, but upbeat, Eileen seemed happy and ready to share.

TRINDA: How did you come to notice that you had some sort of ability?

EILEEN: When I was younger, and I think you have probably heard this from many people, I used to play with spirit all the time as a child from about three to almost nine years old. At that point, I saw and interacted with spirit better than I did with a human.

TRINDA: So you had imaginary playmates.

EILEEN: Quite a lot, and I used to wake up my family in the middle of the night and say, "There's a party going on down there; let's all go on down and be part of the family." It got to the point where they would come down, look, and say, "Go on back upstairs and forget it." So then I just started to keep it to myself.

TRINDA: They did not discourage it, but they did not encourage it either?

EILEEN: That is correct. My mother was also very intuitive so she saw things periodically, but more of a premonition type of thing and not on a constant basis.

TRINDA: Did she believe you were talking to and seeing spirit?

EILEEN: She never gave a word either way. I had a unique childhood. My Dad passed almost as soon as I was born and my mother was very ill. We were passed around to many people.

TRINDA: So it was hard to get one person to understand that you had something going on there.

EILEEN: Yes, but also I saw spirit and played with spirit, the older ones and the younger ones, it did not matter. With all of us, we go through this part of our lives where I have had quite a bit of education, so I completely tuned it out while always having some good gut feelings, do not get me wrong. I laughed when I retired a few years ago as I said I have always read psychology books because I have always seen "p-s-y-c-h" and it is like I am meant to be a psychologist, but God should have given me more brains if He thought I should be a psychologist. That is my path. After I got into this again I said, "Oh, my God it should have been "i-c" at the end." Psych-ic not psych-ologist and I still laugh at that, and I still see spirit. Once I came to the fellowship school, spiritual insight training, it really did open me up again. It was in one weekend and very much instantaneous.

TRINDA: When you turned it off for your studies when you were younger, how long a time was that?

EILEEN: That was quite a bit. As you said, we have to have some hard knocks to get where we need to be. Early in life, I was studying to be a teacher. In the meantime, my husband was killed in an accident and my mother passed within the same year. As I said, I had a biological father who had passed, but I also had a spiritual father that was wonderful, and he chose to pass. Within this three-year gap, I had lost everyone significant in my life. School at that point was my saving grace. I put myself in the books. From around twenty-four to my late thirties, early forties, I spent the time in academia and that was fine. I got a degree in School Psychology.

TRINDA: You worked in the school system.

EILEEN: Yes.

TRINDA: You did that for most of your career life.

EILEEN: I taught for eighteen years and I did the rest in School Psychology. Actually, I am a retired, rehire, so I work in a rural district that needed someone, so I still do that full time.

TRINDA: So you have gone into a second career and now you are a resident in Lily Dale. How long have you been here?

EILEEN: This is my third year, so I am new, like Shirley.

TRINDA: What have you found since you have gotten here, in this *psych-ic* world?

EILEEN: My husband passed in 1978, which put me on the path. Certain things happened. We always used to argue about the Christmas tree. He liked a blinking tree and I hated it. It would be 1978 as the year I was going to put my foot down and say this tree is not going to blink. We put up the tree and he passed very close to Christmas. From that point on it blinked. This is how we communicated. I needed to feel his presence and to know he was okay because it was a car accident and I needed to know everything was okay. I went to my priest because I am a recovering Catholic; I tried to do that. Then I even tried other faiths. I said let me try Lutherans, and so on, until I ended up going to a medium, which at that point I felt so at home and so relaxed and so believing that he was okay that I started to look into this. I have been coming to Lily Dale since 1978-79.

TRINDA: So now, you have come to live here.

EILEEN: Yes, and I think all of us have this to do before we die. One of my things is to see if I could live here and see if I could be a medium.

TRINDA: You have to take a test to work here, correct.

EILEEN: Yes.

TRINDA: A special course, and what else?

EILEEN: To be a medium you would be trained outside of the Dale or a church inside the Dale and my training was inside the Dale. Another medium who works here lived in my neighborhood, which is where I went for my very first reading.

TRINDA: A neighborhood outside of here.

EILEEN: Yes, in Ohio, he was from Ohio. He had come here before me and I went to him first. I was always part of his meditation group, his development group.

TRINDA: Was he your mentor here?

EILEEN: No, but certainly in Ohio.

TRINDA: Since you have come here and experienced your own growth as a medium, which ability is your best? Would you call it clairvoyant?

EILEEN: I am more visual, so I am clairvoyant.

TRINDA: So you see spirit in your mind or projected outward?

EILEEN: I see it in my mind. Many people ask about the process. I see light shafts. Sometimes it is difficult for me to get a male or a female. I have to push myself to get that. The more I do it, the more I get the energy; it is how I am feeling with it. Last time that feeling was a male, so this must be a male.

TRINDA: So the image you see is more of a light rather than the shape of a woman or the shape of a man, and you have to feel the energy to determine whether that is a male or a female?

EILEEN: Yes, I do. It is like a cylinder. They come right down beside you and around you and that is what I see.

TRINDA: Do you have a position for them to know mother, father, grandfather, and so forth? Must they stand to your right or your left or behind you?

EILEEN: I do not. I just allow them to give me the impressions they are going to give me.

TRINDA: You are not organizing them.

EILEEN: No, probably because I am not very structured. That was how I was taught. The left means this and the right means that. I find with myself that they will give me the impressions that I need. I have spent so much time in doing testing with children as well as looking at drawings because that is the part I like best, the social and emotional aspect of the school psychology thing. I get many psychological things, so they will show me symbols.

TRINDA: They are using what you know and have learned in your life to better relate to you. What ages were you involved in the school system?

EILEEN: I retired from a pre-school position.

TRINDA: So you might have more of the pre-school graphic symbolism in your mind to give you interpretations of certain things. Are you still learning symbols even now?

EILEEN: I still am even after three years. Now that I am a retired, rehired, I go from Kindergarten to 12th grade. I am learning more projective tests and I love looking at things and picking out the symbolism in there. Every now and then, I will still get something and I will say, "Yes," I remember I was reading that manual or whatever and that was what that meant.

TRINDA: Can you give us one example?

EILEEN: Okay, let us take the house-tree-person, which is a drawing test for children. They draw a house, a tree, and a person. Your house is your family. The person is you, and the tree is your unconscious. As they draw in the tree every now and then if they put apples on, it is dependency. Spikes on a tree can mean depression. If there is a hole with an animal in it, that can just mean dependency.

TRINDA: What about a bird on a branch?

EILEEN: It would depend on what the branch looks like because the branches are very important. The clouds are important and the root systems are important. Fruit is important, but the bird is not. Every now and then, I will get a talon-shaped root, which would tell me this person is going through what I call the dark night of their soul. Where they are going through major transition at this particular time where they might need some help, or some uplifting in getting through that. The house has a number of windows, curtains; what's the roof structure like, etc.

TRINDA: What if they are just rather *artsy*, what then?

EILEEN: You can still do it because of every line and every stroke. An artist will choose their style whether it is feathered lines, or whether it is straight and consistent lines. No matter what it is, there is something there. Your personal touch came into that art to make it the way that it is.

TRINDA: You can tell the person behind the art. What a fascinating subject. So, your skill is visual, but you have the other senses as well?

EILEEN: I am getting more clairaudient (hearing) and I am really excited about it. I trust myself when I get it and I need to see if I am developing that.

TRINDA: Can you give me an example.

EILEEN: Yesterday I was doing a reading for a person, and I said, "Head trauma" and the name, John. As I was doing the reading for her in picking up different members of her family, her husband came in very much at the end and that was when he was in an accident and had significant head trauma. Those two words came through very clearly at the beginning.

TRINDA: You hear it like someone was calling out to you.

EILEEN: Yes.

TRINDA: As if from another room or right in your ear?

EILEEN: It was right next to my ear, not in my ear. John was her first husband.

TRINDA: Clear as a bell?

EILEEN: Yes, now I would like to have that for the whole reading.

TRINDA: To get the whole message that way would be so much easier, of course. Can the clairaudient person hear either with the ear or outside the ear, even far away? Can it be all those things?

EILEEN: Yes, it can be, and in the particular reading I had yesterday, it was right here outside my ear, but frequently, I would get messages or impulses that are in my head. I do not know what it means, but I will say it. This one was as if someone was talking to me.

TRINDA: Would it be difficult for them to give it to us that way?

EILEEN: I have heard that it is. They are light shafts to me and they are energy sources. So, to have this energy source really communicate in the physical vocal chord way, which we are of a low vibration, is more difficult for them.

TRINDA: Why do we not hear them in their voice, with or without an accent and so forth, but rather as *we* would sound speaking?

EILEEN: They use you.

TRINDA: It would be as if I said it. Correct?

EILEEN: Yes, that took me a while to figure out. You know how we talk to ourselves and we do all of this and I thought this is just me making it up. It took me a while to realize that, if they are going to be giving me messages and it is going to come through me, it is going to be in my voice tones, my connotations.

TRINDA: My language ability?

EILEEN: Exactly, that is why you have to be very aware of your own belief systems because many times you can imprint your belief systems on others.

TRINDA: Twist someone's truth to your slant?

EILEEN: Exactly. One of my pet peeves is infidelity, and so many times when I feel the vibration of someone being in extra-curricula activities, I have to look at the God within them.

TRINDA: You have to be non-judgmental.

EILEEN: Yes, I have to put it aside.

TRINDA: That is very hard thing to do, is not it?

EILEEN: I really did a lot of work on my values and belief systems, my own moral and ethical structure, because the messages I want to give is hope that they might internalize this in any way possible, either to do the right thing, or to be better as a person, whether they continue in the relationship or not.

TRINDA: You want your message to be helpful, non-judgmental, and truthful. That is a lot, especially since you are a human being too; you have faults. To put all that behind you, all your own luggage, and bringing a truth through you to that other person can be hard. You know the messages are being somewhat influenced by you.

EILEEN: I am sure that it is, but I hope it is just the whitewash and not the actual color. It has to because they do filter through us.

TRINDA: Perhaps the person sitting before you went to you versus someone else for a reason, maybe to get your slant on the messages.

EILEEN: That could be. I feel that anyone who comes to my door is meant to come there.

TRINDA: Should all spiritualists, mediums, psychics, intuitivist, and counselors learn to put their personal beliefs aside while doing a reading?

EILEEN: I think they need to look at what works for them. If they, as a counselor, or if they are looking for something from a religious point of view, then they need to come from their point of reference.

TRINDA: Be clear about that with the sitter, such as my faith is whatever. For example the reader might say, "I am a strong Jewish woman who is a psychic and I am going to give you the Jewish version of what I receive." That is okay, and we can have Jewish mediums, Catholic mediums, and so forth?

EILEEN: Certainly, I think you also need to tell the person who is sitting there that this is *my* point of reference. I think that spiritualists encompass, May the God in me meet the God in you, and not judge whatever behavior or whatever is going on in your life. To me, the ultimate in being in a state of grace is to realize everyone's life on this earth is hard and is a challenge. A lot of times we think you have to go through tragedy in order to be in that state, and people who can look at us having somewhat of a charmed life equally have as much hardship as anyone.

TRINDA: Different types of hardships, one example might be that their lesson in life might be to *live large,* as the saying goes these days, and another to live *somewhat smaller.*

EILEEN: We are going to get there no matter when or how.

TRINDA: I think becoming spiritual is learning not to judge people and that is really hard when society seems to encourage it.

EILEEN: Not only has the world made us judge others, but we also judge ourselves so critically. I just look at just being a woman in America. How many times do we look at ourselves and say, "Job well done. I am really proud of you for doing that." We really do not do that and yet, if you look at psychology, it takes five positives to overrule one negative. Most of the time we are critical of ourselves, let lone that of other people we deal with.

TRINDA: We even seem happier almost to hear the negative or bad news first.

EILEEN: Yes, we are trained for it, instead of saying I just accept you and I love you for the way you are.

Eileen's words rang of a truth that affects us all. Is your glass half-empty or half-full? Both our words and our thoughts are molding us into the person we will become. Are you creating the type of person you want to be? Eileen and I explore creating a reality of choice in the next volume of this series. Join me then with Eileen and the others as we continue the adventure together. For now, however, more on psychic phenomena with the next lady from Lily Dale, Jessie C. Furst.

Jessie C. Furst
Psychic-Medium and Ordained Minister
Hypnotherapist, Astrologer and NLP Practitioner
Lily Dale, New York USA

Meet Jessie C. Furst

Jessie is an ordained minister of Fellowships of the Spirit and has a BA in Human Resource Administration. She has studied mediumship and psychic and spiritual development at the Arthur Findlay College in England. Jessie has appeared on radio and television, and is a certified Professional Seminar Leader, Hypnotherapist, Astrologer, NLP Practitioner, and Registered Medium in Lily Dale. She is also a volunteer for the Domestic Violence/Rape Crisis Program, and Hospices Advocacy and Bereavement Support in Chautauqua County. A dynamic and inspiring teacher, lecturer and intuitive consultant for over twenty-two years, Jessie continues to pursue her passion in life of helping others to discover their life's purpose and to follow their own path.

Jessie and I became friends instantly. Her smile lit up the room and we chatted like old school friends meeting again after years of separation. While I realize most of the women have similar stories as to how they began to recognize their psychic abilities, each one was still unique in how they handled that awareness. When I asked Jessie that same question, she replied a little differently, stating, "I always thought that I did, but only in little ways like the phone would ring and I had already thought about that person. I would think about them and see them within a short period, but I had an interest. People always came to me, but I always thought maybe I had a little more common sense and always thought I was happier than they were. I knew that I loved helping people. When I first started opening up and wanting more of this there were no books, very few and I started out by taking a training called *Do Something Different*. I am from Michigan, and they taught an adult community program called *A Night with a Psychic*. I took that, and within a year, I was teaching it in the Detroit Metropolitan area in different schools that you would go around for Adult Community Ed. I loved it, and then I got into a hypnotherapy class and she taught a lot about awareness. Then I worked for a school system and spent twenty years as a secretary. Worked my way up the ladder and I started volunteering for a crisis center. A friend of mine was having a party for all the volunteers. She put this brochure down in front of me, *Channeling and You*, which is *Fellowships of the Spirits* now. I thought, you can *develop* this? They were coming to Michigan and to Mercy College to teach this."

TRINDA: In a college?

JESSIE: No, they rented the space and there were fifty students; that is a lot.

TRINDA: The public was coming to these classes.

JESSIE: Yes, the general public. It was advertised and that was my first training. I found it so remarkable that I could develop this more. Then they offered the next step, which was *Channeling and You, II*, I think, which is now *Fellowship of the Spirits, II, Spiritual Insights Training, II*.

TRINDA: It still goes on.

JESSIE: Yes, and it has been growing graduates for fifteen years. They have bought a restaurant and are turning it into their school. They had the second training in Brighton, Michigan, and I really loved it. I loved the mediumship more than the healing; they taught both. I went to the school and it changed my whole life. I study all the time. I take a training course every spring and every fall because spirit works through what you know or are aware of in life.

TRINDA: The more you know the more you can get from them.

JESSIE: Yes.

TRINDA: That leads me into the question of how you receive your information.

JESSIE: I see and thoughts pop in; they just show up.

TRINDA: Thoughts or words?

JESSIE: Thoughts *and* words.

TRINDA: So you can literally see lettering, as if a name or something. Is that how you would get a name?

JESSIE: Yes, or maybe it comes in so fast I just have it.

TRINDA: You have it and you are not even aware of having received it. It is just there?

JESSIE: Mediumship with me, and I am sure for others, changes all the time. If you are growing and changing, you are bringing it in differently and you are getting more receptive from spirit.

TRINDA: So even a medium who has been practicing for some time, the way they are receiving their information could change?

JESSIE: It could.

TRINDA: As they learn more techniques?

JESSIE: As they get more of anything.

TRINDA: You are the first to say that.

JESSIE: Yes, more of anything, because we're dealing with people from all walks of life and if you have a variety of things, that is a *knowing*, and when they send a symbol, you know what it means because you have the wisdom to recognize it.

TRINDA: You constantly need to be in school.

JESSIE: That is what spiritualism teaches, to always be a student and to always be learning. I am taking a correspondence course on spiritualism, phenomena, and such. That is what they encourage, and to always keep an even keel. Mediums have to take care of themselves because they are influenced by any emotional energy sitting across from us.

TRINDA: This is a good topic, as I have not discussed with anyone else yet, the protection factor. What do you do when you are receiving information and being with other individuals, so many people every day? How do you protect yourself?

JESSIE: First, I have to be emotionally stronger than they are. I work out at the gym three days a week, I take vitamins, and I try to read every day, self-help or personal growth types of books that are going to help me in my work.

TRINDA: That is wonderful, but *psychically* how do you do it?

JESSIE: You put a light around yourself. I always begin a reading with a prayer, and I try to meditate every single day for at least twenty minutes. That sets you up for the day.

TRINDA: Before your readings begin, you will do your meditation?

JESSIE: Sometimes I miss it, but that does not affect the reading.

TRINDA: If you have to protect yourself from any negative aspect of the business, how would you do that?

JESSIE: When you are coming from that intent and that light, you do not attract the negative. If there are negative people around, you are aware of them. You can put the light around yourself, but my feeling is that when you have that intent anyway you are not going to draw them to you.

TRINDA: You are drawn to the right people. When I was sensing spirit around me for the first time, I did not want any negative spirit in the house, so I asked that it be of God, from the divine light. For example, if the lights blink on and off, or this and that happens, people might fear those experiences as a negative spirit or a negative energy.

JESSIE: It is because they do not know. When you have a good healthy spiritual intent, you attract the light. Wherever the light is, there is no darkness. When you take good care of yourself and you have that strong presence about you, a spiritual presence, and intent of helping others, then you are coming from that same kind of energy.

TRINDA: The same thing would apply when we meditate and try to get closer to spirit in order to contact them directly. Is that what we are asking for?

JESSIE: I ask for the highest and best. You always ask for the highest and best, whatever that is, and for it to be heart-to-heart. When you are stronger and you have somebody of a negative energy; maybe that is like looking at the cup half-empty in a way. Yet, if your energy is strong and spiritual and you think you can work with them, then you can. If you cannot, then you let them know that.

TRINDA: Would you feel that?

JESSIE: I always had a hard time before, but I feel that spirit gives us things when we are ready and I have always struggled with that. With knowing ahead of time, because I have not always known. However, now I feel I can tell, but I will never just say, I am not going to read you because I do not think our energies would be compatible. I will take them in, I will give a couple of names, and if they do not know of the names, then I will give them something about what is going on with them. If they do not know that, then I encourage them by saying, "It does not appear that your energy and mine are working together. It is not anything wrong with you. It is nothing wrong with me, but it is the two of us *together* that is not working. If you would like to go on to someone else, you don't have to pay, but if you choose to go on with me, then you will pay." Many times it changes because they may be nervous, or may not know what to expect, and then spirit comes through and they understand and it works. You have to kind of play with it and see. I am getting better at that because I want to be in charge.

TRINDA: Even after all these years you are still learning and growing?

JESSIE: Yes, you are always growing, you never stop growing and changing and the better you get, the more you want. Is not it all about bringing in a challenge and a spark. It is wonderful and so gratifying. I have always drawn people, listened and counseled in a crisis for quite awhile. I draw many people who need counseling information.

TRINDA: That must be hard for you day after day.

JESSIE: No, I have a little black book and I have many books that I can recommend. Therefore, I can say, "Here's a counselor, here's someone who does such and such." I always have information to give them so they can help themselves, so they can be independent. We are a guide also. We are not just there. Very few people will come and just want to talk to spirit. They want a little bit of both (spirit communication and counseling.)

TRINDA: They want guidance and help. Allene Cunningham said the very same thing and that is why she offers counseling.

JESSIE: They want to know what is coming up, what they can do. Forewarned is forearmed, and they always have freewill to pick and chose as to where they are going to go with that information.

TRINDA: True, thank you, Jessie. What would you like to leave our readers with as far as an understanding of the process for those who perhaps still aren't familiar with mediumship, aren't familiar with Spiritualists or that spiritual realm for help and guidance? What message could you leave them with regard to keeping an open mind about coming to a medium?

JESSIE: I was thinking about this a week ago when I was tired. I would work all day. I did the one o'clock service and we do not have to put in our time anymore, but I want to do public demonstrations twice a day because spirit has given me information. I walk out that door and they give me three pieces of information before I get to the stump. They give me a name, an age, and a condition before I get to the stump. I give it and it is never not been taken. The minute I am done, another one pops in and it happens so fast I do not know where it comes from. I am tired, but then I am walking out with nature and releasing that energy and I feel that I have a duty because you are giving me this specific information to go out there and touch somebody's heart that has lost a loved one and prove it to him or her. How could I know the name? How could I know the background? How could I know how their mother died? That is what I want to leave. I want to demonstrate it every day, twice a day, as much as I can and give them that knowing. How can they say this is not true? Where would I have gotten it?

TRINDA: After they leave, do you feel better, emotionally or physically, once you have done this?

JESSIE: I am higher than a kite! I love it. All the way home I say, "Thank you, God, for helping me touch a heart. Let me touch a heart today."

TRINDA: All the mediums here do some daily free readings as a continuation of the tradition at Lily Dale. Do they do it also as a thank-you for their gift?

JESSIE: Yes, they do it for advertisement too, of course, but my thinking is also that the more you get out to experience the better you will get. The more they are going to give you. The more variety, the more times you demonstrate, the more you are going to get stronger at it, just like anything else. If there are any practicing mediums out there working on their stuff and they are around an area where they can demonstrate it, I would tell them to get out there and demonstrate as much as you can because that is where you are going to learn. That is where spirit is going to work through you.

TRINDA: What is next? After showing everybody that you can do it, that prove-it stage, what do you think is next?

JESSIE: We are teaching them that they can do this too. We are teaching them that this *is* possible. I tell them in their messages, "You can talk to spirit because you cannot destroy spirit."

That may be all we may need to hear for now, that you cannot destroy spirit; the soul lives on, we live on. Perhaps more will follow soon, but for now, many of us are just happy to know that we do go on, as Jessie tells us "…you cannot destroy spirit." It was the perfect ending to our conversation. Jessie and the others will join me again in an adventure of exploration into the unseen world in the next book on reality and again in other volumes with what they know of the afterlife and why spirituality is such an important piece to the puzzle. However, there are a few other wonderful ladies from Lily Dale that I would like you to meet as well.

Gretchen Clark
Medium and Clairvoyant
Lily Dale, New York USA

Meet Gretchen Clark

Gretchen Clark is N.S.A.C. certified, and registered as a medium and a 5th generation Spiritualist, and lives in Lily Dale, New York. "Offering hope and comfort to those who have sought her counsel since 1976," Gretchen is an internationally known medium, lecturer, and workshop leader. Gretchen has been heard on radio like N.P.R.'s *Savvy Traveler*, seen on television such as the Discovery Channel, and on NBC's *Strange Universe* and *Vision Channel*. She has been interviewed by many publications, including *People Magazine*, the *New York Times*, *Dallas Times* and the *Los Angeles Times*. She has lectured for the Learning Annex from Manhattan to Los Angeles and Toronto. Gretchen Clark also has several new workshops and videos available, which you can find more about on her Internet website address at http://www.GretchenClark.com.

Gretchen had an amazing presence about her. At the end of the interview, she unexpectedly demonstrated her abilities in a way I never would have expected. Join us as we talk of the paranormal and then afterward as we speak directly with *spirit*.

TRINDA: *Five* generations, Gretchen. Would tell us about your family first, please.

GRETCHEN: Five on my father's side, his great-grandmother was a medium and a worker here in Lily Dale. His great-grandparents were buried in Cassadaga, New York. They lived in a house where Pauline Kaye does now. Cassadaga, Florida, is named after Cassadaga Lakes. It was founded by people from Lily Dale; they wanted a place to go in summer.

TRINDA: I am very familiar with Cassadaga, Florida. I have had interviews with the mediums at The Cassadaga Hotel already. This is a nice tie-in to both places. I did not get that from them, the connection to New York.

GRETCHEN: They may not know that depending on who is there. The old-timers knew that Cassadaga, Florida, was owned as Lily Dale is, by an association. Years ago, the association disbanded and people bought their own property. Now anyone can live anywhere. You have to be a member of the Lily Dale Assembly to buy property in Lily Dale. You could be here in the summer, but to live here year round, you have to be a member. That is what it used to be like in Florida, which is why it is different there now, since anyone can be anywhere.

TRINDA: Thanks for the connection to Cassadaga, Florida. Now, may I ask, being psychic does not have to be generational, correct?

GRETCHEN: Correct, you are a spirit, not a body. You have all the abilities that any other spirit has. You just have to remember that. My Mum and Dad met here at Lily Dale. The cottage on Second Street where my family is meeting this weekend, there will be four generations of Mom's family tree. The Stachan family built it; my Mum was a Strachan. I think it is one of the few remaining cottages on the ground that is still owned by the original family. Both sides of the family were here, which is why it is so strong; because we were encouraged from the time we were children. It was accepted.

TRINDA: You are one of the only ones here I have interviewed so far that said their childhood was good and actually encouraged your ability.

GRETCHEN: Absolutely.

TRINDA: There were all positive experiences?

GRETCHEN: It was great. I do not remember this, but my mother said I was almost three and she put me to bed and she came in to see who I was talking to. I described the lady on the bed and it was my grandmother Clark, who died before I as born. I would tell her whom I had seen and she would say, "Who is it, what are they wearing, what do they want, and what do they look like?"

TRINDA: She was not a medium?

GRETCHEN: No, she probably could have been, but she did not have the time to pursue it. My Dad died when I was ten and she had five children. She was a schoolteacher. She was very busy and did not have time to work at it. Lily Dale is fifty plus miles from where I grew up. There were no spiritualist churches in the area then.

TRINDA: Did you see the first spiritualist church go up, formed here?

GRETCHEN: No, there were no spiritualist churches in Spartensburg, where I grew up. Lily Dale was here; it is 126 years this year. Anyway, having the background, my grandfather would let me sit in on circles with some of the old-time mediums. We were up here in Lily Dale, so it was always encouraged and talked a lot about. I had a good understanding of Lily Dale itself because I do not have just my memories of coming to visit when I was a child, but their stories as well.

TRINDA: That is awesome. You are probably one of the few mediums who had an upbringing where it was actually encouraged.

GRETCHEN: There are not too many.

TRINDA: I have not interviewed any others yet who were. They were either not encouraged or discouraged. Then they lost it for a while and picked it up again. So, if you have grown up with it, how did you deal with that throughout your education, your school life and so forth?

GRETCHEN: After school, I stopped talking about it because I realized I was different and people did not believe it. I grew up in a very fundamentalist Christian area, so, I just did not talk about it a lot, but always when the family got together, we did.

TRINDA: Did you pick it up as a career right away?

GRETCHEN: No, after college, I married and had children. We moved here in 1967. My sister Sherry was already living here. She was the postmaster. My mother had bought the house and she was going to retire here. She asked my husband and me if we would move into it and fix it up for her. We were living not too far away so that worked out well. Then Mum died and I took the house as part of my inheritance.

TRINDA: Have you practiced since then?

GRETCHEN: No, she died in 1969, and I registered in 1976. I was working as a medium. I would go to the outdoor services and the Monday circles and I worked in church and stuff, but I did not register until 1976. I worked as a healer. I did a lot of healing. Hands on healing like they do at the Healing Temple. I used to work there, but when I registered as a medium, there was not time and of course, my children were small.

TRINDA: Who of your family is here now in Lily Dale?

GRETCHEN: I do not have anyone here with me now. I am divorced. My daughter and her husband live in Springville, New York, which is not too far from Buffalo. My son and grandson live in Cassadaga, which is about a mile away.

TRINDA: What are your abilities, your skills?

GRETCHEN: Basically, I am a medium, which is what we are here in Lily Dale. Mediums in Lily Dale prove the continuity of life, which is the basis of the religion of spiritualism. I am clairvoyant and clairaudient and clairsentient, all that.

TRINDA: Do you have an understanding about where all that information is coming from, yourself personally, after all the years of doing this?

GRETCHEN: Absolutely, I always know whether it is something I am picking up through my abilities, or whether it is something that spirit is saying to me.

TRINDA: Who all is involved in a psychic reading, their spirits, yours, or both?

GRETCHEN: They bring their people with them. They pop into the room. They say a thought goes around the world three times in a second. So a spirit can be here and gone in a nanosecond.

TRINDA: So we have four or five entities present. There is your energy; your own spirit is energy, the person, their spirit and so on. How do you perceive all of that? Is it coming through as whatever strength that person has, as far as visual or audio?

GRETCHEN: What I receive has not anything to do with the person I am reading. They attract their people with them. I am not a mind reader, I am not a telepath and I am not a psychic.

TRINDA: It does not depend on their energy or abilities.

GRETCHEN: No, not at all.

TRINDA: Some mediums have told me that if the person they are reading is more visual, for example, then the medium might also be *more visual*.

GRETCHEN: That is interesting. I did not know that. It does not work that way for me. Everyone sees these things differently. Every medium receives things in a different manner. Sometimes I see spirit as clearly as I am seeing you. Sometimes they are a little more ethereal. Sometimes they are just *kind of misty* there. Sometimes I see a very bright spirit light or a tiny little light.

TRINDA: So you have *clear seeing*.

GRETCHEN: Right, but I also hear spirit. I am clairaudient, so I can hear them talking to me. Sometimes, and its funny, it is as if one channel is busy so they come in on another line. If I am talking to your great-aunt Claire here and your Uncle Mike wants to say hello, he will say, "Mike".

TRINDA: They are cross talking.

GRETCHEN: Yes, they come in on a different line, on a different frequency.

TRINDA: So you could be hearing on the left side and on the right side from someone else.

GRETCHEN: If I am seeing someone, I may hear someone else. I do not see two people unless they are interrupting each other, which can happen as well. Sometimes, I sense them so strongly that I can identify them. I can describe exactly whom I am seeing, but I am not visually seeing them.

TRINDA: When you have that image where you can see and hear them almost as clearly as you see and hear me, is that ability yours, theirs, or a combination?

GRETCHEN: Theirs, but it has a little bit to do with me of course. A lot of times when a medium cannot get names, maybe the people coming through to her don't know how to say it. It is not necessarily the lack of ability of the medium, but the lack of ability of the being coming through. Generally, the longer someone has been in spirit, the stronger they become and the better able to communicate.

TRINDA: I thought it might be the other way around.

GRETCHEN: No, when somebody first dies, you may hear from him or her the first week or week and a half and then maybe nothing for a couple of years. They have to learn to accept the fact that they do not have a physical body. They go somewhere and dissimulate for a while. They make atonements they feel they need to make and they learn to communicate all over again because they are used to talking with a physical body and mouth, and they are not doing it that way anymore.

TRINDA: That is interesting because some people think that the longer they have been gone, the harder it is for them to communicate with us.

GRETCHEN: That has not been my experience at all. Sometimes when somebody has been gone a while you do not hear from him or her. I have never heard from my great-grandmother, but my great-grandfather said that she had reincarnated. Basically, he said that she had picked up another body, so I guess she got bored or something.

TRINDA: So, do not think they do not love you or want to speak with you as they might have reincarnated or are off on a journey or something?

GRETCHEN: Exactly, there could be many reasons. I did a reading for a woman and asked if she had any questions. She said, "Where's my mother?" I sent out a thought for her mother and said, "I am sorry, I cannot find her," and she said, "I am not surprised; we did not speak for twenty years".

TRINDA: Yet, that would not be the reason because they love us no matter what happens here.

GRETCHEN: Right, or since her daughter did not really want to communicate with her, she just did not bother. You are the same person you are when you die; you have just taken off a suit of clothes and walked out the door. You are still the same. However, the longer you have been gone the more chance you have adapted, you have progressed, you have lost some of your picky little problems.

TRINDA: What about psychics who predict a hundred years in the future, can they know that this or that is going to happen?

GRETCHEN: If nothing changes, you can see things that are going to be the outcome, but it is not as if this must occur on this day at this time, no!

TRINDA: So when it does not happen, people say she must be a phony.

GRETCHEN: She saw what she saw.

TRINDA: It changed because of freewill.

GRETCHEN: Exactly, I saw a woman getting married one time and I told her I see a third wedding ring on your hand. She said who would want an old, one-eyed Jew. I laughed. She was blind in one eye and was eighty-three. I said he is a rich Texan. She laughed. This woman never left Manhattan. At Christmas time I got a little package from Texas and inside was a note, which said, "Just wanted you to know, Dearie, I said, no, but I did get a proposal last night and he is rich." I clearly saw that third wedding band on her finger. She chose not to put it there, but she could have. Therefore, I saw a probability or a possibility, but *you* have to make it a reality.

TRINDA: Just the fact that you are receiving the message could change the outcome of those things predicted.

GRETCHEN: I make sure that I always tell people, "This is what I am seeing at this moment. If you don't change anything, chances are this is the logical outcome." Like anybody else, when people in spirit come through and give you advice, they give you advice when you are living and they give you advice in spirit. Whether or not you listen to it and take that advice is up to you.

TRINDA: They are there to help us, to tell us what things we can correct. If you said something negative to them, it would be as a warning, correct?

GRETCHEN: If I see a negative occurrence in the future it is almost always there as a warning, sure. Spirit does not usually tell you about things if you cannot change them, if they are negative, things like, your Mum is going to die in two years or something. They do not tell you that unless you are not supposed to be at that spot.

TRINDA: So they might warn you of something that they would like to see prevented. If you knew about it, you would act accordingly.

GRETCHEN: Exactly, this chain of events is set in motion. If you do not want this occurrence to happen, this is going to, unless you do something. The cake is going to burn if you do not take it out of the oven in time.

TRINDA: How wonderful that they give us that much. We are always thinking that we are not supposed to know the future. Some say I should not know the future and that is not for me to change.

GRETCHEN: It is your life. You are in charge, you, and spirit. It is not a definite future; it is a possibility.

Ah, the possibilities, I thought. If that were true and we *are* in control of our destiny, what are the endless possibilities before us? There are those who have taken control over their lives and actually changed the course of their future. Lives are being altered by the power of prayer, thought, and faith everyday. I have met a number of individuals who have done just that, taken control over their reality and changed it to their expectations. The ladies of Lily Dale and other unique individuals share how they have actually created their reality of choice in my next book as they describe their own personal journeys toward enlightenment.

After my conversation with Gretchen ended, I thought my visit with her was over until she paused to recognize that spirit was with us. It seems that we had an unexpected guest with us. Gretchen turned her head ever so slightly to her right and said, "We've had company." I wondered who it might be. Normally, when I get word of my mother's presence, she is usually on my left, but this spirit was to Gretchen's right. As she tried to interpret the female energy's name by sounding it out, only the first part of the name was immediately clear to her. Gretchen told me that her name began with a *haaa* sound. She tried listening to spirit's communication for the rest of it, but before she could finish sounding out the name, I blurted out, "Hazel"? I know, I know, I am not supposed to give it up that quickly, and I don't even know how *I* knew it was Hazel, but it escaped uncontrollably from my mouth as I thought of her. I asked Gretchen if it really was Hazel, the first psychic-medium I had ever met. She said that yes, Hazel was indeed with us the whole time and she simply found our conversation *interesting*. I was surprised and curious as to Hazel's presence, so I asked Hazel myself why she came to visit. Gretchen replied with subtle Hazel gestures and spoke for her saying, "Why, where else would I be?" Gretchen remarked that after all, we were in the Medium's League building and Hazel had been a medium, so it made perfect sense. Happy to have had such a surprise visit from both a special soul and fellow spirit medium, Gretchen and I smiled and hugged good-bye. I only hoped Gretchen knew how truly thankful I was with her for bringing Hazel's comments to me. I was, to say the least, *inspired* by the moment.

That last unexpected confirmation of spirit's presence led me to realize the scope of my work. The interviews were not only of importance to those of us here, but apparently were of interest to those in the spirit world. I was extremely pleased to have had met with such lovely women in both body and spirit while in Lily Dale. Hazel had been a blessing over twenty years ago and as she was during my interview with Gretchen. My sincerest thanks go out to Gretchen for reuniting me with a long ago, but not forgotten and fondly remembered medium called Hazel. Remember, those you know and love who have *gone home* have not left us forever; they simply may wait patiently for the opportunity and appropriate time to meet once again.

However, I had not heard the last of Hazel. A little over two months later I would think of her again. I was returning home one evening after a long drive when a thought came to me to make an unexpected stop at a library to research Hazel's obit. I was near the only county library that housed obituaries for our local newspaper. Once in the library, I asked for assistance and the information receptionist directed me to their reference section. As I approached a few women at the reference desk, I addressed them all while asking for help with newspaper obits. One of the women offered to help and we proceeded to the card catalog. The librarian asked for her name, smiled, and then began fingering through the cards. She turned to me and asked if I knew the year of her passing. I did not. A daunting task lay before me; I had to find an unrecorded woman's obit without a date of death. I believed from Hazel's age when last I saw her that she might have passed away in the 1980s. In addition, some time ago I had read in the newspaper that there was no record of her in their digital format after 1988. That meant she must have died in 1988 or before. I had seen her last in 1983. Her death would have been sometime between 1983 and 1988. Nevertheless, five years of weekly obits adds up to a large number of newspapers to search through. I would have been overwhelmed with the task, had the year 1984 not popped into my mind. That was it, the year of Hazel's death. I just *knew* it. After I suggested the date to the librarian, she began to search the microfiche records again. She placed the slide in the machine and within only a few seconds found Hazel's information and her date of death, which was indeed in 1984. Amazing, we now had a date and were able to search for the newspaper. As the librarian reached for a box of film around the week of her death, she looked at me and said, "Let's try the following week first." Excellent *intuition* on her part as it was there; she found it! It was such an easy hunt for having so little information. After she handed me my copy of the paper, I said, "I am sorry, I want to thank you Miss, and your name is?" She flipped her badge around. Her name was Hazel. She had been waiting for me to ask. We just smiled and I thanked her again. When I think of the odds of her name being Hazel, an old name at that, I have to think spirit had something to do with our encounter and in leading me to find Hazel once again.

Before I introduce you to the remaining ladies of Lily Dale, I would like to include one more *psychic* event. I had called my niece on the ride home from the library. After I told her that Hazel had guided me to yet another Hazel, she was happy to hear of another validation of spirit.

However, to my surprise, she had a story of her own, which I would like to share with you now before concluding my interviews with the ladies of Lily Dale, especially the next meeting, which held a surprise occurrence for both of us.

Recently, my niece and her husband were at their daughter's Air Force graduation ceremony. As proud parents, they watched from stadium seats knowing their daughter was among the many graduates on the field. It was a special moment for them, but someone very dear was missing that morning. His mother, whom I shall call Mrs. B had passed away sometime ago, but was sorely missed for this special occasion. When Mrs. B passed away, her granddaughter had gotten a tattoo of a butterfly in her memory. Butterflies were their association with Mrs. B due to her love of gardening and the frequency of butterflies in her flower garden. As my niece and her husband sat watching the graduates, she clung to a pin she wore of Mrs. B's and silently prayed for a sign from her mother-in-law. At that moment, three butterflies circled them both, lingering in the moment. Shortly afterward, my niece noticed a section of the stadium's field covered with hundreds of butterflies. She knew spirit was with them, but kept praying for something much more specific to ensure that Mrs. B was truly there. After the ceremony, parents and guests gathered onto the field to meet with the graduates. As they approached their daughter to give her a hug, they were delighted to find a large Monarch butterfly clinging to their daughter's blue uniform.

My niece paused, *knowing* it was a sign from her mother-in-law. They just smiled in the belief that their mother must surely be with them. Knowing that there were hundreds of butterflies at the other end of the field, the odds were likely to have a butterfly, two, or even three appear that morning, but what I have yet to tell you is she was the *only* graduate with a butterfly on her *throughout the entire service*. It is at the very least cause for wonder.

As you may know, butterflies have long inspired the spirituality of humankind with their symbolic metamorphosis of change similar to spiritual growth and rebirth, as well as freedom and inner beauty. I was truly happy to hear of their special reunion that morning, but happier yet to share it with their daughter's great-grandmother, who seemed to find quiet comfort in the possibility of *spiritual signs*. Throughout my journey, family and friends have blessed me by sharing their own stories of hope, love, and mystery. It was a touching moment for them all and I thank my niece for sharing this true and uplifting story of everlasting love.

Please join me now as I meet with yet another of the ladies of Lily Dale as we speak of such mysteries as the divine, mediumship, psychic phenomena, and much, much more.

Reverend Donna S. Riegel
Psychic-Medium
Lily Dale, New York USA

Meet Donna S. Riegel

As an ordained minister, Donna has committed herself to the path of a mystic. She hopes to serve us all, myself included, while recognizing that we are divine, unique beings, all on our own spiritual path. In this life of service to others, she has devoted years to developing the gifts of communication with spirit. Specifically, she has chosen to serve God and humankind with the gifts of intuitive mediumship and healing.

Donna tells us that, "Each of us is a divine, unique being on a path in life that is solely ours. Many times, we have questions and doubts. 'Why me, what next?'" Our inner self knows the answers; what we must do is search within to discover the nature of existence. Sometimes we are best served by seeking assistance in our search. While exploring the possibilities of the knowledge within and the love expressed by spirit, I pledge to work with sincerity to unfold the mystery and bring through the joy of enlightenment."

Please join me as I speak with the Reverend Donna S. Riegel, a registered medium and intuitive healer at Lily Dale.

TRINDA: Let us talk briefly about auras, Donna. I have seen many, but the first aura I ever observed was around my husband one afternoon by our pool.

DONNA: It is like going down the road on a hot summer day in Florida and you can see that heat wave. Everything in life is a vibration; everything in existence is a vibration. The word universe means one world, and when God created the world and spoke, "Let there be light," it was created by vibration. Everything that we know as our real world is vibration. Atoms make cells, cells make tissues and tissues make organs. It does not matter if it was a tree, a plant, or a person. We are all combinations of atoms, cells, and so on. Even plastic and crude oil comes from fossil fuel, which is that physical remainder of what was once living organisms. What probably happened when you were sitting by the pool and saw your husband's aura is that you reached a point of relaxation. You were out in the sun, focused, and your mind saw a spirit connection to that vibration. It is what we perceive, it is how we feel; it is our emotions and what we are connected to. The brain is the computer of all past experiences. It is the physical part of our body, which allows us to express our mind. Therefore, when we get inspired, as you are, meaning in spirit, everything that ever was, is, always will be, and always has been, everything is *out there* for us.

TRINDA: Everything is known to us?

DONNA: It is *already* known to us. When Edison created the electric light, he was inspired. He imaged that there was a way to contain this energy so that it would be a safe way of illuminating without having to burn or create flame to do it. It took him half his life, but he had an image in his mind and he kept working at it until he created it. If you hold it in your head, you can hold it in your hand. When we focus on the mind, which is what happened that day when you were relaxed, you were away from your brain and you gave up calculating. You enjoyed for that moment the pleasure of mother earth, the warm sun, and the warm energy. Your husband's movement created the ability for you, through your mind's eye to immediately envision that energy or spiritual essence or aura of your husband. It is psychologically and physiologically understandable.

TRINDA: Even though I was seeing it with my physical eyes?

DONNA: Yes, because your physical eye and your third eye, for that brief moment, became one. That is also how we have true clairaudience, like when you hear someone call your name.

TRINDA: I have had that happen, too. It woke me up. I thought that my husband had called to me from another room.

DONNA: I call those wake-up calls. Every single human is a spiritual being. We choose to come into this lifetime. We choose our parents. We are spiritual beings incarnate. When we leave, we leave the physical part of our body behind and we are inter-carnate or in spirit whenever we go. What we were before we came here, we are when we leave. Communication with spirit is the proof that it is so. It is irrefutably so that we are contacting people when we get wake-up calls that touch our physical senses. Most mediums work clairvoyantly. Think about it. If we were to have that much physical noise around us for great hours, it would be too much for the central nervous system. It would become too hard to differentiate between that which is occurring psychically or physically, but some mediums do work as clairaudients, some of the mediums here.

TRINDA: We would start thinking of it as this reality and we would get the two mixed up. All I heard was a name, but I wanted a whole sentence or a whole thought.

DONNA: Sometimes you get it all, but it can be very disturbing and you can become crazy from it. I was back from Florida staying with my Mum, lying on her bed, and I heard a woman, just as plain as we are talking now, but speaking to me in Italian. I do not speak Italian, but I understood what she said and I cannot explain it.

TRINDA: Was that because the spirit was Italian and you understood it telepathically?

DONNA: It had to be. In other words, somewhere in my vast super consciousness, I have experienced Italian, became aware of it, or heard enough of it.

TRINDA: I have not talked to anyone about languages yet. How do you think we all communicate with one another in spirit? Telepathically with thoughts and images?

DONNA: It is the clairvoyant; it is the seeing and the knowing whenever mediums say, "They are telling me or they are showing us." A picture is worth a thousand words. People have long since known and understood this. As I am working with a person and all of a sudden, for example, I will see a bridge with a rainbow over it, it is giving me something to say to this person. When we dream, there actually is no language in dreams. We dream in these "picture" clips.

Donna went on to explain that every medium has his or her own perception of how we communicate with one another in the spirit world, be it telepathically or otherwise, as well as how we visually exist, with and without form.

DONNA: It is rather like the concept of God. If you believe in a personal God entity, then you will have one picture, for example, seeing a very old man with a long white beard down to his feet sitting on cloud nine and so on. However, if you truly address, accept, and embrace an idea of an infinite intelligence, of a non-entity, have an understanding of a greater source that goes beyond our understanding, then you realize that God, and the spiritual part that connects each of us, are all of a greater energy, which is the piece we cannot explain. So, if your concept of God is one of infinite intelligence, I do not believe that spirit has to maintain a form. I do believe that they can relate and they can take on form so that they can better communicate with us, but I do not believe that they need it or have to have it, in my opinion. You will get as many different opinions as mediums with whom you will speak.

Donna's opinions mirrored many of the other mediums at Lily Dale in a few fundamental ways, belief in an infinite intelligence and in spirit communication with and without form through a variety of clairvoyant methods such as seeing, hearing, and simply knowing. However, it is their belief in everlasting life, an everlasting survival of the consciousness, which we will explore in later volumes that may challenge the way you look at life.

After my interview with Donna, I retired that evening to my room and began packing for the trip home. Even though I was somewhat saddened to leave Lily Dale and bothered with not having yet spoken to Barbara, it was an unbelievable and truly *spiritual* weekend. I would speak to Barbara, that I knew, and I would be leaving *knowing* so much more than when I arrived. I had found out so much about not only the mediums that work and reside in this mystic town, but also about myself. Meeting such insightful souls as the ladies of Lily Dale, seeing spirit, and now finally *knowing* that there is much more to our existence that meets the eyes had left even *me* speechless. I was not only recognizing an unseen world, but now acknowledging it from knowing.

The next morning, I tossed my bags in the maroon mustang, checked my maps, and slowly drove out of the Lily Dale community. The tree-lined road led me back around the lake and eventually out of the town of Cassadaga. Driving a little slower than the posted speed, I tried to take in as much of the countryside as possible. I was comforted to see the lush greenery and cleanliness of the roadways. Even though I felt the visit went better than I could have ever expected, I began to tear-up the farther I got from Lily Dale. My visit had been all that I had hoped for and so much more. It had been a fantastic adventure and I did not want it to end. Everyone had been so gracious and kind. They opened their doors and their hearts, all in the hopes of helping others. Their stories were shared not for fortune or fame; they could do that on their own if they wished to. The mediums and residents of Lily Dale gave their heart and soul not just for my spiritual benefit, but for yours as well. They live and work in Lily Dale for the betterment of others. They love what they do and they love the place in which they do it. They share it with others for the love of all.

That love, which penetrated my very soul, was what I would miss most. Being in an environment that emanates so much love makes one feel whole. Leaving Lily Dale at that moment felt like I was missing some part of me. I wiped the tears and turned on the radio. The music playing was an old Beatles song that I had never heard before. *Coincidently*, it sang of the love of God and oneself and it was then I reminded myself that I could take that feeling of love with me. I could share it others and get it back again ten-fold. I could feel it at any moment by simply remembering how wonderful everyone had been, and all of my experiences. It also gives you the knowledge that *you* matter to others, that *you* have value and a purpose in this life.

When you share an *unconditional love* with others, they in turn can share it with others and so on and so on. Love is a powerful energy in itself that keeps growing and evolving. My visit had been an amazing affirmation of both love and everlasting life. It was deeply appreciated. Please appreciate the unconditional love that you receive from others and remember then to pass it on.

I finally let out a deep breath and felt much better. In fact, I was beginning to get excited about sharing my paranormal, now spiritually, normal experiences with others, especially through my writing. I had not only come away from Lily Dale feeling loved and valued, but with a confirmation that there is indeed more to us than the physical bodies we possess.

Through my own profound experiences, I came away with knowing what is within, out of, and around the body. I was able to acknowledge an unseen world and some of what it entails. For most, it is not every day that one senses, sees, or speaks with spirit. However, after actually having experienced all those things, I can honestly say that I will forever believe in life after physical death. I was anxious about the trip when I planned it and had simply hoped for a good weekend of interviews. Little did I know how truly enlightening it would be or how spiritually motivated I would become by my visit to Lily Dale. It was a surprisingly miraculous time, and I am truly humbled by my contact with spirit and those that I came to meet along the way. I would only hope that both the mediums and especially those of the spirit world know how much they have filled me with an everlasting gratitude and purpose, but most of all, with such an abundance of love.

Once home, that love lingered with me as I reflected on all the wonderful souls I had met. Yet, there was one remaining lady to speak with, my hostess while visiting Lily Dale, the Reverend Barbara Sanson.

Reverend Barbara Sanson
Psychic-Medium
Lily Dale, New York USA

Meet Barbara Sanson

Barbara Sanson enjoys working within the realm of spiritual healing and has been the Chairperson of the Healing Temple for over a decade now. Working in the field of healing since 1970s, Barbara has also worked with hospice, Therapeutic Touch, Reiki, Touch for Health, and NLP. As an ordained minister and graduate of the School of Healing and Prophecy, she is a founding member of Keepers of the Heart Project. She enjoys traveling, lecturing, and working with youth on various aspects of healing. Barbara is frequently sought after for interviews and featured on the television show *Medium*, which aired a few weeks after our conversation.

I first met Barbara through e-mail and phone calls. Every call and every message was warm and inviting. She responded to my questions with an open heart and welcomed me to Lily Dale like an old and dear friend. I knew our meeting would be a special one.

In my first meeting with Barbara, we instantly hit it off. I was no longer a stranger at the doorway, but a friend within her home. The afternoon I arrived in Lily Dale, she personally guided me to the Temple where my first experiences with the mediums of Lily Dale occurred. She had introduced me to the ladies of Lily Dale, reserved use of the Mediums League Building, and arranged all of the interviews for me. I had found yet another earthly guide among strangers. Yet, in all our meetings and conversations together, we never had time for her interview until after I left Lily Dale. A few weeks later, we finally found valuable minutes for that long and heartfelt talk by phone. Our conversation covered a great deal, from her understanding of this reality that we call life, our existence after death, and what *true* faith is, as well as her life's work, mediumship, and spiritual healing.

TRINDA: Please tell us, Barbara, how you came to be a medium and in Lily Dale.

BARBARA: In 1971, I was diagnosed with cancer and had surgery. A friend, who I knew was into spiritual healing, came into my room and prayed with me. She gave me a gift of a Bible. We prayed together and she did a spiritual healing for me. I really believe that it had a lot to do with the positive outcome of my surgery. It really changed my life because after that occurrence, I realized deeply and profoundly in my heart and soul that my life was not just for myself, but it was to serve the spirit of life, God, or the creator in some way.

I went home from that surgery with internal stitches. A few days later, I had profound hemorrhaging. The hospital was sixty miles away. My mother had called the doctor who was ready to send an ambulance if things did not improve. I looked up at the corner of the room and saw my grandfather's face. I saw an ectoplasm energy swirling and swirling in a golden light and thought, "Oh, Jesus, I am going die!" I thought, well, if that is really what is going to happen, God, I guess I am ready to meet my maker. I was very calm and saw what I thought looked like the outline of my grandfather's face in that vision. He said to me, "Don't worry, you're not going anyplace. You have got more to do on this earth. Just relax, healing is going to come to you and you're going to be all right."

Barbara told me that within five minutes the bleeding had completely stopped.

TRINDA: How did you hear your grandfather speak?

BARBARA: It was like *an inner knowing*, but the image of his face was so real, as if I could reach up and touch it.

TRINDA: Amazing. Many people have had similar experiences, but do not speak of such things because either it seems so unbelievable or goes against their religious upbringing. A woman I know, by the name of Iris, has had similar visions of her deceased grandfather and relatives, and the experiences frightened her. During the middle of the night, they would suddenly appear at the foot of her bed. When people have these experiences, people of various backgrounds with similar stories, what recommendation would you have for them? They are so afraid that it is not of God, that it might be another type of entity or influence or thinking. How can they be sure it is of God?

BARBARA: By saying, "If you come in the name of the Christ light then I embrace you in love, and you embrace me in love and if not, be gone." It is as simple as that. The white light of the Christ mind or the white light of creation is about a higher good and about a higher collective consciousness. If it is negative and you are thinking higher thoughts, it is not going to stay attracted to your thought form. It is going to leave.

TRINDA: Aren't people seeing visions and speaking of them more than ever before?

BARBARA: Absolutely. Life is an evolution, a spiritual progression on this planet and in other realms of existence, it is happening. You know, we are manifesting those things; we are calling them to us. It *is* happening.

TRINDA: You know while I was in Lily Dale, *I saw spirit.* Surprisingly, I was not nervous, shocked, or excited, but rather quite calm about it. Then I tried to interpret what it was that I was seeing. When I leaned over to the medium next to me, all I said was *cool*, and kept watching spirit. I saw not one, but *three* spirits and never became excited, which was so surprising considering the experience. I was wondering if you can explain *why* I reacted the way I did, and why the only place I have seen spirit is in Lily Dale.

BARBARA: You know there are high-energy places on the earth plane. People go to Niagara Falls and people feel the power of the falls, all that energy and they say, "Wow the energy in Niagara Falls is really powerful and great." It is really magnanimous.

Other places such as the Grand Canyon and Yellowstone Park are vortexes of powerful places. Many places in this country and on our earth have evolved over time like Lily Dale in spiritual intention or prayer or spiritual consciousness. The native people that were indigenous to this part of the world traveled through here and made settlements and encampments. There are sacred mounds here that are thousands of years old. The intention of spiritual energy in this part of the country, or this part of the county, is very high. There are sacred places all over the U.S. I think there is a vortex of powerful energy in Lily Dale with the water and all the elements earth, wind, fire, air, wood; they are all very powerful. People come with prayer intentions, love intentions, creation intentions, and there is energy that is not always necessarily seen, but it is emitted from spirit above and around us. The thought forms of people's minds have produced a very powerful place.

TRINDA: A very calming place.

BARBARA: It is very powerful in the sense of healing. Not everybody feels *calm* here. You were looking for that and I feel that was part of how you were feeling in your journey. If people come here and say, "Oh, my God, I cannot sleep, I have been up and I am awake. I am so energized and invigorated. I am so alive that I have trouble going to sleep." There is a duality to life, so you are calm and someone else may be wound-up. Both can be right. I think it is what you are seeking in your spirit. That is a mirror of who you are, either being or choosing what you want to become is what you get. So you got calm.

TRINDA: Yet, how was I actually able to see spirit? Was it just because of the environment or something more?

BARBARA: If you want a right-brain answer, I would say that in your wish, in your heart, you wanted to see something. Remember, in everybody's chemistry, it is as you believe. If you *believe* spirit is there and it is possible to see it, then in some way a shape or a form is going to identify with you. Just like the heat wave on the asphalt on a hot day, that is energy too. You wanted to see the outline of a definition of spirit, not only in your heart, but also in your spirit and mind. There is also a collective consciousness here with the same intention. I think the energy was beautifully set up for that to happen.

TRINDA: So, even though I was not *consciously* looking for spirit, my subconscious desire was being supported by a collective consciousness, all in an ideal environment.

BARBARA: I believe so, absolutely.

TRINDA: I feel blessed to have seen spirit.

BARBARA: Not everybody sees it though. Some people feel it and some people who are clairaudient hear the messages of spirit, or do automatic writing. There are many variables to the expression of spirit.

TRINDA: As a practicing medium, how do *you* sense spirit, clairaudient, clairvoyant, or is it a combination all?

BARBARA: In my prayers, I'll say, "May I be guided to be your instrument of healing and inspiration to those who come seeking in any way and that it is healing and beneficial to them, as well as healthy for me."

TRINDA: How do you experience that?

BARBARA: I am very *clairaudient*.

TRINDA: Tell me about the process.

BARBARA: It all works together. I will see a picture, a spirit level will identify with a picture and they may give me one or two words. If I am not filling in the blanks with the message they want to convey, then they might stop it and show me another picture. It works in a combination of all methods, clairsentient, clairaudient and clairvoyant. They all work together and I think ultimately that as mediums, we should strive to develop them all.

TRINDA: Yes, many have said the same thing, and to better connect with whomever you may be reading.

BARBARA: So we can be the best example of a message bearer, to be the best in mediumship, and to advance and accelerate mediumship. To be able to demonstrate that loved ones are not only all right, but that their love and their healing will continue on in another plane. They wish our spiritual progress here to be as easy and without strife as much as possible. However, not everybody in spirit is in a happy place, but I do not ask to talk to those people.

TRINDA: Are there things that you do not want to do, such as see predictions or see someone's death or something very negative? Do you have any *limitations* of your own for spirit?

BARBARA: No, I do not ask necessarily to be told if somebody is going to die, but occasionally, they will show me a picture, and remember, I am the message bearer and so it is up to me to find the most harmonious and loving way to present information. If you have experience in that type of communication, you will know how to do so from your heart, to do it with respect for the person who is receiving the message. There are ways to say things that are loving and kind while still being truthful.

TRINDA: There is a skill to that though.

BARBARA: There is a skill and that is why I believe in the evolution and standard of excellence for mediums. It is not just about giving a message from somebody who has passed on from this life.

TRINDA: There is training before becoming a medium and coming into a community such as Lily Dale, correct?

BARBARA: Yes, there is all kinds of training.

TRINDA: How can individuals, laypeople, contact their loved ones directly, without going through a medium? How might you suggest the best way to do that, if we all have some intuitiveness already?

BARBARA: I think it is possible because we are evolving on this planet and the time and space of other places are evolving. Just like twenty years ago, they would not have had cell phones and now they have discovered how to make that happen. People are constantly discovering what is already there. The links between this world and the spirit world is simple. It is about the vibration of love. It is very simple, but people like to complicate it by making it a complex situation when it is not at all.

TRINDA: Would you recommend meditation for communicating to deceased loved ones?

BARBARA: Meditation is a very good way to open yourself, clear yourself, to let things bubble up to the surface that need to be cleared from your energy field with intention, focus, and love. In mediumship, it does not mean that people cannot get their own messages from their loved ones. I encourage many of my clients to talk to their loved ones who have left this life, but where a medium may be necessary is in the outside validation that your loved one exists. In other words, getting a message from a medium that validates what you already know about your father, your grandfather, is a validation that a person would totally understand in their heart and soul. That is why I tell people that, one good message is all you need.

TRINDA: It can be about anything.

BARBARA: Exactly.

TRINDA: The message itself is the actual validation, not the content of the message.

BARBARA: Yes, if done truthfully. I may not make sense of somebody else's message necessarily, but if given with honesty, intention, love, and not with ego, but with heart, you can make life-changing things happen for people, absolutely.

TRINDA: Many mediums describe their communication with spirit as *raising their vibration*. Can you explain what they mean by raising their vibration, perhaps scientifically if that is possible?

BARBARA: No, honey, I got low marks in physics. I spent my time in the art room. I wanted to be an artist. However, there are known frequencies and vibrations and everything has a scientific measurement of some kind. What we have not deemed viable in the past has become more and more witnessed, like white noise, which I knew about twenty years ago. One of my teachers taught me about that and was very involved in communications and the enfoldment of white noise, evidence of people's faces on television screens. It is becoming more and more evident with people recording and making such phenomena public. So why not, they laughed at Marconi. They said that he would never be able to transmit a message in a wireless situation, and of course he did. They laughed at Edison and Alexander Graham Bell. Bell was going to have people speak into an instrument and transmit it for miles. Everything is being discovered, as it is already out there to discover. Who would have ever believed in cell phones? *Now* you can talk to anybody all over the world.

Barbara's words mirrored much of what Sandy Anastasi had previously told me in the belief that much of our existence is already *out there* and we are just now discovering those things. Barbara was forthright about her understanding of *how* she was able to communicate with spirit. Yet, another medium explained the use of the words *raising their vibration* or energy to simply mean that mentally, they are praying to and striving to reach the highest and best of spirit, which is also known as the Christ consciousness. I explore our understanding of the process of spirit communication further, in my next book on *our reality*.

I reflected on how much humankind has already learned in the last few decades and wondered what might be next. What old and new mysteries await our exploration? What missing pieces of the puzzle to our existence are yet to be revealed? I am anxious to see what the future holds for humankind. I hope the answers to some of life's mysteries will manifest into more than just material marvels, a deeper sense of purpose perhaps, a greater knowing, or most of all, love. Perhaps we will become even more intuitive, more easily able to recognize that which we could not begin to comprehend yesterday, including spirit communication, and some of what the unseen world entails.

Psychic-mediums today are those who are just naturally more *sensitive* to those things beyond our current, normal range of perception. After experiencing a few of those things myself once thought of as psychic or supernatural, I realized how close we *all* are to that enhanced awareness. As the paranormal becomes more normal, more *real* in our thinking and knowing, we will be able to experience much more of what is unknown today. We are all uniquely *intuitive* and possess the real ability to not only sense, but to *know* of those things not so long ago unimaginable. Without a doubt, we are finally becoming more *conscious* of an unseen world around us, including spirit and of a continuous life.

I hope by somehow demystifying that which psychics can do—communicate with the dead and a great deal more—we will see the person behind the psychic-medium as simply a sensitive soul blessed with just a little more natural, intuitiveness. No one psychic will have all the answers we seek, but some, from their enhanced, natural abilities, may hold valuable pieces of the puzzle which will lead us all to a better understanding of our existence and our purpose in living and in *living on.*

These gifted souls are trying to comprehend the bits and pieces that they do get from their ability, including hints to our mortality and the connection with not only one another, but also with the divine. The enhanced abilities of psychic-mediums, like those that I have introduced you to, show us that in finally *knowing* that life is continuous, we can become one again. We can grow to be more loving and caring and less fearful of those things that hinder us from becoming all that we already are, a truly unique and wonderful spark of a divine oneness that is here to simply learn how to love unconditionally through living.

How we live our life is a direct result as to how we use not only our freewill, but also our natural *intuitive* abilities. Will we learn to recognize and use our intuitiveness in life or blindly charge ahead without direction or intention?

It is up to us to stop and listen to that divine intuitiveness which speaks to us. The art of listening has been achieved intuitively every day and by millions. From the neighbor down the road who intuitively knew to bring me flowers for my birthday, to the many mediums that psychically reveal the smallest details of your life and loved ones. Messages were there for them to recognize. If only more of us knew to look for them. Yet, how do we do that? Actually, there are a number of ways, but you must first start by acknowledging that each of us is unique and you too have this *ability* to some extent or another.

Then you must be *still* and attune yourself to hear that within which whispers of messages and truths. Through desire, patience and practice, you will begin to recognize the divine and that of an unseen world around you, including spirit's communication. To help you in your own quest for enlightenment, however, I have asked those mediums introduced to you how to enhance your own psychic abilities. What steps can you take to seeking your own messages or purposes in life? From my own beginner attempts to the meditation suggestions of the renowned psychic-medium, James Van Praagh, you may recognize even more that is within and around you. Their suggestions follow, after one of the most amazing demonstrations of mediumship I have ever witnessed. It is an example of spirit communication, a true marvel for the minds of non-believers and believers alike. Please join us next in church, as we welcome spirit in lively patriotic song.

Chapter 13 – Blindfolded Billet Reading

Meet the Reverend Phyllis Dee Harrison, Psychic-Medium
February 26, 2006

> *Glory! Glory! Hallelujah! Glory! Glory! Hallelujah!*
> *Glory! Glory! Hallelujah! His truth is marching on.*

The voices of dozens upon dozens grew louder with each verse of the *Battle Hymn of the Republic*. As a sweet, little lady played the piano, the Reverend Phyllis Dee Harrison stood at the center of the altar of this quaint spiritualist church downtown. She was preparing herself for messages from the spirit world. First, she placed a strip of first-aid tape horizontally over each closed eye, then another piece of tape vertically over each eye. Lastly, she placed a red velvet mask over her face and cinched its back tie. We were all standing now, clapping and singing, *Glory, Glory, Hallelujah*. Focused intensely on the Reverend's every move, I had not realized I was singing so enthusiastically. I am usually the one who mumbles the words to even the most well known hymns and sits quietly during services. I have been a bit *reserved* when it comes to church singing, at least in years past, but not today. Caught up in the moment, I joined wholeheartedly in vibrant song, singing the *Battle Hymn of the Republic*. It gives me *chills* every time I hear, *Glory, Glory, Hallelujah!*

This was the first time I had ever witnessed such a phenomenon as a blindfolded billet reading. While I knew that a billet was a question for spirit through a psychic-medium, I had never seen a medium blindfolded to do so. Why would she do that? How would she be able to read the billets, and was it all just a show for those in attendance. Confidence from Reverend Harrison spread to the other Reverends and among the pew-filled believers. We practically held our breath waiting for her to begin.

Chester appeared from the pews to help hold the basket of billets for the Reverend, each one folded neatly in half. On them, you would address a single question to someone in spirit and sign it with usually only your first name. Each of us wanted to hear from our loved ones and guides, and this uniquely talented medium would help us receive spirit's messages. Her spirit teacher had taught her years ago to trust more in both herself and in the divine by learning to communicate with spirit using a blindfold. This was not a theatrical flair, but the disciplined training of a faithful student.

As the Reverend Phyllis Dee Harrison fully developed her natural clairvoyant abilities, she continued to give spirit messages in this way. It allows her to focus more thoroughly on spirit's communication and more precisely relay their messages, thoughts, and names with unfailing accuracy. I have not yet met any other medium, famous or not, that can relay names as well as Reverend Harrison. While I realize that receiving names are not to be the judge of a skilled medium, nonetheless, it is an ideal way to validate that certain loved ones are still with us.

As the Reverend reached into the basket, she would select a private billet and hold it to her forehead. You could hear a pin drop. We strained to hear her softly ask of spirit, "What's your name? What's your name, please?" There was a pause and then ever so assuredly she projected out loud, "Is there a Frank in spirit?"

"Yes, that is my father," echoed a voice from the back of the church.

"Okay, are you Joyce?"

"Yes!"

"Okay, your father says that you will be going back to school soon. Do you understand?"

"Yes."

"He also says that you are thinking about taking a vacation next month to Maine."

"Yes."

"Good, that is a nice time to go; go and enjoy yourself. Okay, dear?"

"Yes."

"Thank you, next please," as she hands the still unfolded, slip of paper back to Chester who walks it back to Joyce. She has heard from her deceased father and smiles widely in this validation of continuous life as she takes back her billet.

Next, Chester holds up the basket to Phyllis' outstretched hand. Another slip of paper and her quiet question once again to whom in spirit is with us. Silence fell as she questioned the audience. "Is there a "Frieda?"

No, it is Trinda, thinking I have to work on my handwriting. Somehow, I just *knew* it was for me.

"Did you write to a Gloria?"

"Yes!"

"She says 6 to 8 days. Do you understand?"

"Yes, I do, thank you."

I had asked my mother, Gloria, how long I would be at Camp Chesterfield in the spring. I was hopeful of going to Camp's Spring Seminar, but unsure as to how long I should stay. The Reverend had moved on to the next person while I was still reflecting on my mother's answer. I could no longer hear her words, my mind was swirling. My mother, who had passed over twenty-four years ago, once again came through to speak with me. I knew she could. These past years of similar experiences had repeatedly proved what a normal occurrence it was. Yet, it still surprises and delights me each time I hear from her. It is an amazing experience to say the least. Now that I truly know such things are possible, and yes, real, I believe that life is indeed continuous and our loved ones watch over us. Yet, I still yearn to affirm her presence and of others in spirit, and this one blindfold billet reading had given yet another validation. For me, one question had told me our loved ones are still with us and know what is happening in our lives. It gives great comfort and a renewed belief in an unseen world. It strengthened my faith in the afterlife, in spirit, and in God. It was a church service like no other, and I went back the next Sunday and the Sundays that followed.

If you would like to know more about the blindfolded, psychic-medium, Reverend Phyllis Dee Harrison, her services, the spiritualist churches in which she gives messages, or Camp Chesterfield, please join us for my personal interview with the Reverend in following books on reality, the afterlife and spirituality. We discuss her clairvoyant abilities, beliefs and understanding of spirit and the unseen world after a lifetime of unique, psychic experiences. I will introduce you to Camp Chesterfield, its history, activities and services, as well as several of the psychic-mediums that both reside and work there. Home to spiritualists, mediums, channels, and like-minded folks, it is a picturesque historical spot for spiritual learning, healing, spirit messages, and much, much more.

Founded in 1886 as a Spiritualist Church, Camp Chesterfield is home to the Indiana Association of Spiritualists. Spiritualism is the science, philosophy, and religion of continuous life based upon the demonstrated fact of communication by means of mediumship with those who live in the spirit world. For more details, you may visit the website on the spiritualist center of Camp Chesterfield at http://www.campchesterfield.net. It lists their activities and classes, as well as an opportunity to request prayers of healing. In addition, the site lists several of the mediums that reside at Camp. However, I hope you will join me in my next book where I will personally introduce to you to them as we talk of their abilities and their understanding both of this reality and an unseen world in which there are those who can and do help guide and watch over us each and every day.

In the meantime, let those we have met thus far show you how you too can develop your own psychic abilities. Learn how to speak directly with your deceased loved ones, spirit, and those of the divine. Their easy suggestions and practices will introduce you to new and wondrous souls and places. The ability is within you; you need but only look within to find it.

Chapter 14 - Psychics Tell How to Enhance Your Own Psychic Abilities

While I am not a psychic-medium, I feel compelled after my own successes and failures to include a little of my attempts at enhancing my own natural psychic abilities. I offer my humble layperson's perspective, as well as the advice of spirit and psychic-mediums throughout the country. I hope all of it will help you in your own attempts at becoming more intuitive or sensitive to the unseen world.

From all the conversations and interviews with psychic-mediums, you now know that many believe we all have a natural psychic ability within us. Yet, how can we develop it? Can a "How to" class bring out the abilities of a psychic-medium, or must someone simply be born with the gift? I believe the answer depends on a number of factors, including the freewill of both you and spirit to work together. It would also have to be possible within your life's plan and physical capability. While you may have the heart and desire, and an accommodating life plan, your body's chemistry, for example, may not be ideally suited for the work of a psychic-medium.

However, I believe as many psychic-mediums do that we are all born with a natural ability to directly communicate with our deceased loved ones, spirit, divine entities, and with God, or the divine intelligence. Through our thoughts alone, we are heard. Of course, there are many practices or rituals that someone can perform, but know that your *thoughts alone* will reach them. I have proven it to myself thousands of times. I would also like to suggest that if you wish your thoughts addressed to a particular spirit, be it a loved one, a guide, even Jesus, you might find it much more *real* to you if you simply request that before just sending your thoughts *out there*. If you have a prayer or message for Jesus alone, you could first direct your message or prayers to Him before beginning. I think the *formality* of addressing someone and the organization of your thoughts will help your purpose, as well as your ability to understand the experience.

The question that troubles us most is how *spirit* communicates with us. How can we know *their* thoughts? How can we hear, see, and sense spirit, including our deceased loved ones? Psychic practices may lead us to discover that communication can occur in a number of ways. If spirit comes to you without formal attempts on your part then, by all means, please acknowledge and appreciate it. However, if you have prayed, meditated, or even performed various religious rituals and believe that you are *not* receiving communication, please think again. Perhaps you have, but just not yet learned how to *recognize* those results. Remember, Sandy Anastasi told us in her interview that, "The difference between a psychic and a layperson is not in getting the information to begin with; it is the fact that they recognize it." Throughout my life, I have been receiving messages from spirit, but it has only been recently that I have learned to recognize those messages.

James Van Praagh has written and spoken of how he used to test his newfound psychic abilities in the simplest ways. From riding on an elevator and *guessing* what floor people would get off at, to ultimately *knowing* how many people would be in a meeting. Such tests are your simplest attempts at *recognizing* your intuitive or natural psychic abilities at sensing the unseen world around you and in spirit communication. More times than not, I have surprised myself with accurate *guessing*. Even after all that has happened, I am still trying to recognize spirit's attempts at communication. There are many examples that I could give you of this, but one that comes to mind is when an intuitive feeling comes over me that something is about to occur. Some call it women's intuition.

One morning while driving to my office, the thought of a visitor or visitors came to mind. Someone new to me was going to visit at my office. I did not know who or why, I only *knew* that there would be a visitor or visitors there that day, which is not the norm for that office location. I *recognized* the thought and wondered if it were true. Validation came the minute I walked in the door when the receptionist announced that her father from out-of-town would be visiting that afternoon. She was excited about his visit and wanted him to meet all of us in the office, her new family of co-workers. Not only would her father and her family visit us, but two other co-worker's families unexpectedly stopped by on the same day. We had a full office of family and friends all day long, truly a most unusual occurrence. Women's intuition, coincidence, or sixth sense—you decide. Either way, the thought or *communication* just simply popped into my head on my drive to the office that morning. I had nothing to lead me to think that, except it being my *recognition* of either spirit's communication or in simply knowing what was yet to be.

Perhaps we somehow already know what is *out there* or is yet to be. Are the events in our life previously planned, or simultaneously occurring? Is all that we are contained within an infinite existence, an infinite oneness? Most assuredly, we all connect with one another. Our lives are intertwined with one another and affect who and what we are; that much we know. What we think, say, and do connects us all within an existence of a divine oneness. Can we then learn to recognize that which is already a part of us? Perhaps we are just now learning how to recognize such possibilities as we walk through this mysterious matrix of life. If we were to try to become more intuitive or more *sensitive* to all that is around us, we might easily recognize the oneness, including the past, present, and future. We need only be alert to it and learn how to develop it.

However, I believe, the secret with all of this is subtlety. More times than not, I have had the quickest and most subtle messages come to me while I have dismissed them in their entirety. They are those quick and quiet thoughts that come and go that may lead you to a thought or decision. They are creative ideas and unexpected thoughts of loved ones than come to mind. It has been my experience that most of the time spirit communication is extremely quick and subtle. While they could even be yelling at their end, we are hearing it *psychically* at this end. Occasionally, the layperson may hear, see, or sense spirit, physically or psychically. However, more times than not, spirit will speak to our mind with thoughts of them and we will just *know* they are with us, and at times, when we learn to recognize them, we will recognize their messages.

How can a psychic sense spirit so easily when the average person cannot? Many psychic-mediums have told me that they were just born with the ability, but learned to recognize it more and more and began developing this God-given gift. When I asked Shirley Yusczyk, one of the mediums of Lily Dale, if she thought anyone could learn to be more psychic, she said, "Yes, everyone can be trained in this."

"Like a beginner pianist?"

Shirley replied, "Right, but not everyone is meant to be Mozart, but you *can* get better."

Does our own life's path and natural abilities determine how good we will get at it, how skilled we can become? I asked.

Shirley replied, "I believe that if you are a spiritually based person that you are going to do better at this, but it is not necessary. People who are not really spiritually based can still tune into spirit."

However, in my interview with Allene Cunningham, she believed, "They pick us. We don't pick them."

Of course, she was referring to being a psychic-medium. As far as the layperson is concerned, however, I believe everyone has been *picked* to receive God's messages of love and peace. Some people just may choose not to listen. Yet, if we are trying to develop our psychic skills, experts tell us that we can.

Dr. Lauren Thibodeau reminds us that while you can develop it, she would advise us to examine what is it about doing so that draws you to enhancing your own psychic abilities. She asks us to understand why and, "What drives the level at which it will operate." Is it that you want to connect with your loved ones directly, eventually become a medium yourself, or something else? *Why* do you want to become more psychic? To me, wanting to become more psychic should not be about fortunetelling or winning the lotto, but simply about *finding God*, finding the God within you that connects us all.

What we do with our natural psychic ability would be the next concern, but to recognize it you must first know that you already have this divine ability within you. Some, like Allene Cunningham, even believe that the older the soul, the stronger their intuitive abilities.

Nevertheless, most agree that practice is vital to enhancing psychic abilities. It is not a *"use it or lose it"* process either, as you can regain your psychic senses at any time. However, if you do not seek to develop your abilities, you may not *recognize* spirit communication as easily or as often. In order to be more psychically connected, you must practice tuning into spirit. As stated early, mediums understand that spirit communication occurs at a higher vibration than human communication. We must *both* work at matching our frequencies or energies in order to communicate better. It sounds logical enough, but in my household, the dogs are the only ones able to hear the frequent calls from spirit. Yet, there are courses with professionals who can teach us how to become more receptive to spirit.

I asked Donna Riegel of Lily Dale how she thought the average person might become more in touch with spirit, more psychic.

"You can't become more or less than what you are. Every one of us is a divine spiritual being. *Desire is the key that opens the door.* If they choose to become knowledgeable about the nature of themselves, their body, their mind, and their spirit, they will begin to open that door to be more sensitive to the world around them."

Most psychic-mediums recommend meditation as the best way to communicate with spirit. Here are a few other responses from mediums of Lily Dale.

Gretchen Clark: I think everyone has the ability. Some people, no, no, no. Everybody can sing, yet some can barely carry a tune. However, there are the Pavarottis, the Streisands and Beverley Sills, all with different abilities of the same talent. Practice it. Remember the first time you ever drove a car and what it feels like today, same thing – practice. Get into development circles and meditate. If you are in a building with elevators, guess which one is going to be there first. Save a parking spot for yourself. Little things like that. Practice and use it. The ability is there for you; why not utilize it to make your life easier and better.

Patty Lillis: When I first heard from spirits, other than the near-deaths, I was meditating, I just opened myself and asked if anyone was around who can give me any kind of proof you are around. I actually felt a physical touch, came right out of the meditation, and was as white as a sheet. I said, "Don't do that. I'm not ready for that." I went back into the sleep.
There are many ways of doing it. I always did it with music; it took me right there. I just visualized and said to myself, "I'm sitting on a beautiful beach, protected by the sun; it's like a beautiful archway." I did what they call creative meditation. I said I am ready for anybody to join me. All of a sudden, my grandmother came in. She was on this bench in a beautiful quiet place and I felt her very strongly. Interestingly a few days later, my mother handed me some jewelry that was my grandmother's and she said, "I think my mother wanted you to have this." You can get it in several different ways. I like other people to give me messages, because it is like a doctor has to go to another doctor, a medium has to go to another medium, because you are more comfortable. I do a lot of prep before I do readings. I do a lot of *long meditation*, and I do have my own way of touching in with my relatives and asking for their guidance. I pray for people that need healing. I have a healing list that is a mile long, but I shorten it if I need to. I try to touch in with those who have gone before me and visualize them in families.

Shirley Yusczyk: I think meditation has scared a lot of people. They try too hard. I think people get stuck, "I have to sit and meditate and I can't think of anything." You can meditate anywhere. You know where I tell people to meditate, standing in line at the grocery store. Close your eyes for a second, take a deep breath in and another out, feel peace, and feel love surrounding you. It is as easy as that. If it lasts only a moment, that is good. If you can maintain this peace and feeling of love, even better. We can hear that still small voice within, an imperceptible inspiration. If we spend a half hour, we are trying to meditate, we count backwards from one hundred, we do the deep breathing or whatever we do and nothing happens, we think, "I'm a failure, I'm not good. I can't meditate," but what will happen is later on, when you are doing the dishes or whatever, all of a sudden that inspiration hits. That is because we have opened that connection to the beyond or to the divine. We have made an attempt and they know that. Every action has a reaction, so when we open up, something comes. Nature abhors a vacuum, so when we put negative energy out of us, positive energy will fill us if that is our intent.

Dr. Lauren Thibodeau: Understand what your point is. To me, mediumship and psychic development always appear to be about other people, and to a large degree, they are. When you get it that they're really a service to you as well as the other people, you're in much better balance, and when you're in better balance, you'll do better work.

Not surprisingly, meditation and prayer are believed to be the best methods to commune with spirit. Simple thought alone will do, but meditation is the best and foremost-recommended method at reaching those in spirit.

Why is meditation the path to successfully communicating with spirit? I never really understood until recently, when my *attention became my intention* to learn of such things. As you may know, when we enter a state of meditation, our brainwaves change from a beta to alpha state. Our understanding is that when you function from the beta level, you are using only part of your immense mental potential. However, when you regularly go into an alpha state of consciousness, you learn to use more of the mind. In alpha, you are more relaxed, calm and *ready to open your self up to much more*, simply becoming open to spirit communication.

Therefore, one of the most recommended practices by psychic-mediums for receiving spirit messages is through a relaxed state of meditation.

James Van Praagh and other notable mediums have repeatedly said the best way to communicate with spirit is to "meditate, meditate, and meditate." I know some of you might think ugh, m-e-d-i-t-a-t-i-o-n. In my interview with James, he explained *why* he believes meditation is the best way to communicate with spirit.

> That is the first thing that I do, meditation, meditation, meditation. Because what happens is, you begin to close off the rational mindset and open up your heart and you can only hear from your heart. That is the way to get to that space or receptivity. Then you are open to those other realms. You really are. It is really developing it and doing it over and over again. It is discipline, discipline, discipline. You can also set up signals with your loved ones. Every night before I go to sleep, I will say something like, please come to me in my dream state. I have a journal next to my bed and that works really well. Set up things with them like with signs also. Okay, when I see a blue jay, I know it is my father. I don't know how the animal kingdom works with them, but I know they do work with them. - - James Van Praagh

Yes, meditation is indeed one of the best ways in which to communicate with spirit. For most, it is not difficult and you would be surprised how successful at it you can become. Although the first dozen or more times that I tried, I kept falling asleep, skipping alpha and going straight to delta in only a few brief minutes. Of course, then someone told me not to do meditation in bed or at bedtime. I changed lying down to sitting up in bed. No, that did not work. Then I tried sitting up in a chair in the bedroom. No, that did not work either. The dogs would come over and lay their paws on me as if to say, come on, you do not really want to meditate; you would rather play with us instead.

I thought it was hopeless, until my meeting with Dr. Walker. Dr. Walker is a guide in the spirit world for Mike Mellott, a psychic-channel I will introduce you to in my next book on *our reality*. Our meeting was one I will never forget. Dr. Walker's response to my failed attempts at meditation is as follows:

DR. WALKER: For those like yourself who may have difficulty removing the thoughts, perceptions, and frustrations of the day's situations, they may wish to consider Tai Chi, possibly Yoga, or perhaps even Pilates. Those things in which the body must be doing one thing while the mind is doing another will make it much easier to enter into the realm that is your desire. There are times when an individual is doing the dishes and staring intently out the window when for some period of time he or she recognizes I have lost track—yet, the dishes have been done—so where was I? This indeed, my child, is the *true* meditation. It is the leaving, if even momentarily of the body from the mental realms. This is what you must strive for, my child. For an instrument (body) such as yours, you may find yourself needing some form of physical activity, which will lead you to that place you wish to be.

It was an excellent suggestion to the say the least. In addition, please do not think you do not have a place or time to do a much more structured meditation. You would be surprised at where and how I have found time to meditate, if just for ten or fifteen minutes each day. Can you meditate in any room in your house? Yes. Can you meditate outside of your home? Yes. You can mediate anywhere you want to, but feel safe, comfortable, and still, without interruption. It is that simple. Find a place you can call your own and begin there.

However, one suggestion from several psychic-mediums is that you make it your *sacred* place. Perhaps the décor or ambiance of the space can be modified to create the mood or state of mind that helps put you in a more peaceful place. Sit rather than lay down, unless you do so without falling asleep. Relax and then just be *still*. That alone is challenging enough for most of us. We are always running both with the body and with the mind. Instead of television one or two nights a week, find your fifteen minutes or half hour that you can just sit and be still with yourself. Does is sound too boring? I promise you it will not be. Probably, for the first few minutes you may just think of all the chores you still have to do, or of the day at work. You should conclude any thoughts of the day before you begin.

Remember to turn down the phone and pagers. Then, once your mind is quiet, you can begin anyway that you wish to, but starting with a prayer would be best. Asking for God, the divine light, or all that is good and loving to surround and protect you is an excellent way to deter any unwelcome or negative energy. Several psychic-mediums have stated that you can enclose yourself and your environment in a bubble of white light or use mental mirrors to reflect any distractions. The premise is to surround yourself with goodness and not allow any negative thoughts while asking for those of the highest and best level of the divine to approach. Once you feel you have *secured your transmission*, you may begin to address those in spirit or simply calm the mind to receive whatever it is you need to know.

Once in a positive meditative mental state, many methods can lead you to spirit communication. Even though I know in times of grief or great sadness, being positive can be challenging, but meditating will actually calm you. One common practice is to envision being somewhere peaceful, perhaps sitting on the beach watching a sunset, or walking through a magnificent forest at daybreak, or sitting in gazebo surrounded by green grass, flowers, and trees.

Wherever you wish to go, it should be a safe and peaceful place. Once you are there, you can begin a number of thought processes that may introduce you to spirit. You may wish to envision your loved ones joining you, or wait until other divine spirits or guides comes to you; any method of thinking is acceptable. As you practice the fine art of meditation, your mind may wander at times, but if you refocus and keep meditating, spirit will notice that you are inviting them to join you.

Create a place with your thoughts that you can envision yourself and your loved ones in and allow it to happen. Yes, you are creating a *real* place that your *etheric* body, your spirit, can travel to and meet others. I periodically go to a healing room that I have created and invite spirit doctors and healers in for various issues. Of course, we should also look to those doctors and healers in this life that help with the health needs of the physical body. I think a combination of the two is necessary to overcome whatever may ail you. In meditation, however, many psychics suggest that you should create as much detail in that environment as you wish in order to make it real.

I envision my doctor's office with soothing colors, comfortable chairs, and soft candlelight—a very warm and relaxing room rather than the stark white walls of most of today's clinics. If only medical facilities would implement such comforting décor aspects as color, scent, and sounds. If only they addressed the mind and spirit as well as the body in order to create a total healing environment. I understand some have, especially for birthing rooms and children's hospital wings. I hope others will also address this issue. I will continue to envision future institutions with beautiful and restful colors, soft and soothing music, and pleasing scents throughout their hallways, and hope you will too. Perhaps then, such positive changes will actually occur.

Nevertheless, as far as your success with meditation goes, I really believe, as most mediums do, that from practice, patience, and dedication, you will eventually be successful. Trying to meditate a couple of times now and again may not always bring you the success you wish. It may take weeks, months or even longer, but please do not give up. I also do not believe time is of relevance either. You may spend only a few minutes or perhaps longer at meditation. Time is not the same for those in spirit. It is more the effort and *thoughts that matter most*. Of course, spirit may also come to you without formal meditation practices or rituals, but if *you* want to make the effort, you must continue to regularly practice. Remember *dedication* is the key to being successful at meditation. My hope is that you will eventually come to know spirit in that perfect place you create in meditation.

Meditation Practices

A common meditation position that many mediums offer asks that you begin by sitting and putting your hands on your lap, palms up, with feet uncrossed, flat on the floor. Meditative practice will usually begin by simply taking a few moments to just be still and quiet. Allow yourself a moment or two to clear your mind.

James Van Praagh asks, "Why cannot we just learn to be in the moment"?

Being mindful of the moment is the secret; living in the *now* is being open to that which is already around you. If you are worried about whom you might contact before you even begin your meditation for spirit communication, you might miss those who are already here to meet you.

Before you begin to meditate, try to be more aware of the energy that is already within and around you. For example, try closing your eyes and hold your hands, palm sides toward each other a little less than arm's length apart. Put your mind, you sense of awareness, in the space that is between the palms of your hands. Just become aware of what that space feels like. Does that space have weight or volume? Mentally take note of how it *feels* to you. Now, slowly, move your hands closer together. Subtly, you will be able to notice how that space changes the closer you bring your hands together. Notice the change and the difference in how it feels to you. As you bring your hands closer together, you may even begin to feel a certain polarity or charge from your palms. You can feel that energy and even play with it like an accordion, changing with the varying distance from hand to hand.

With your eyes still closed, place your hands over your heart just a few inches away. You may actually feel the energy that surrounds and comes from your heart. Once you have relaxed, let your hands drift away from your heart as far as out they might go with the push of that energy. See how far that energy will go out from your body. Characteristically, the heart is the center of unconditional love and can expand out as far as you allow it. Keeping your eyes closed, and your awareness of that energy that comes from your heart, place your hands down on your lap again.

James suggests you imagine a beautiful, green crystal ball in front of you. The color green is associated with the heart chakra, which deals with the higher consciousness of love and healing. In that green crystal ball or beautiful green light, place the image of a person or those with whom you wish love and healing. You may also focus on the color green whenever there is desire for change, growth, and freedom to pursue new ideas, finding a new state of balance for protection from others.

Everything is made up of electromagnetic energy, vibrating at different frequencies, which corresponds to sound, and light. Frequency is the number of waves or wavelengths passing a given point, and the wavelength is the physical property of waves that allows us to see different colors. Those colors represent different wavelengths of light. The color frequencies of green and blue are associated with healing of various forms. Green may bring about a greater balance of emotions. It is also an energy that aids with broken bones, the growth of tissue, and areas needing stimulation. Therefore, you would not want to work with green, but rather another color for cancer patients, perhaps blue, which is good for cooling, calming, and reconstructing or white for general healing. It is also advisable to ask the person if he or she wishes help with any healing. Working together would be more helpful. It encourages their participation, an active role in aiding the healing of him or her self. However, when you are not together, you may still include your loved ones or others in your meditation and prayers, and surround them in a healing light of love.

James reminds us that, "Love brings us together and fear separates." Bring that love to those you may wish to help. You may even wish to bring into that light a situation, whether at work, at home, or perhaps elsewhere that needs forgiveness and illuminate it with a light of unconditional love. Heal the situation with understanding and forgiveness. Lastly, put yourself—your own image—in that beautiful green light of unconditional love for the forgiveness of self. Forgive and heal your own heart center. As a spark of the divine, you too are worthy of healing. For some, this may be the biggest challenge yet.

If you wish communication with spirit or deceased loved ones, you may take the next step toward meeting them in the spirit world. First, allow your conscious doubts and fears to fade away to your subconscious *knowing* that it is possible to meet. In your mind's eye, see before you a place, which brings you comfort, peace, or contentment, whether it is a pristine beach or a green spirit garden with all the flowers and trees in bloom, colors more vivid than you have ever before seen. Feel the love that comes from the nature that surrounds you. Take it all in and become aware of the life within that beach or spirit garden. It is in every speck of sand or in every flower within the garden, every petal, every leaf on the tree and blade of grass beneath your feet. It is all a part of oneness. You are a part of that oneness and it is a part of you.

As you become aware of the life force of all, standing in front of you is a wonderful being of light that becomes clearer and clearer until you see one of your spirit guides. You recognize them, as there is something familiar to you. They have been with you for some time and love you for just being you. With their help and through the divine, ask for heavenly blessings through them. Ask for the guidance and answers to any questions you hold. Thank those spirit guides for joining you and ask for their help and assistance as you come together in the spiritual realm. As you open your heart and mind, you may see others with your spirit guide of healing (doctor or chemist), other guides and teachers, as well as your family and friends. They are all there, looking much more youthful and alive than ever before. They love you and want you to know that you are never alone. They see and know you, and want you to be as happy and healthy as possible in this life. They want you to know their love is with you always.

As you see your family and friends, you may ask them questions, if only a single one at first. When you are ready to hear them with the answers to your questions, see a letter, a single folded piece of paper, which they hold in their hands. As they give it you, take it, and when you are ready, unfold it for your answers.

Thank spirit and your loved ones for being there with you and bless them. Know they can always be with you. You can revisit with them at any time and ask any question you wish. They will meet with you again as they are always there for you, emotionally and spiritually.

As you end your visit, take a deep breath, exhale and then become aware again. Become aware of your physical body and your heart center filled with unconditional love from the highest and purest light of love and energy. Slowly open your eyes and come all the way about to full consciousness.

As you practice and become more experienced in meditation, less preparation or meditative exercises may be required. However, repetition and practice are keys to successfully reaching a relaxed state of mind for meditation. Even repetitive almost hypnotic motions such as focusing on breathing, brushing your hair, stroking your pet, or rocking in a chair can induce meditation.

Finally, once you have mastered the fine art of meditation, all that may be necessary is to simply, sit in silence with rhythmic breathing to tune into your own higher awareness or higher consciousness. Remember, it might take practice and dedication to reach this level, but it is within your reach, that I promise you.

Prayer

A family member of mine has a portion of her living room set up for her own meditation, prayer and religious practices of Nichiren Buddhism. She routinely prays and chants each day focusing on a Gohonzon (the object of devotion in Nichiren Buddhism) to bring out her innate Buddha nature and to build a solid state of happiness. Remember, there is always time for a few moments with the Buddha, Jesus, the Divine Source, or whomever in spirit you wish to address. Thinking about how you want your day to be and what good you may be able to do for others, is another wonderful way to begin each day. You can do that from the foot of your bed. I make a regular practice of praying each morning before my feet even touch the floor. My simply prayer is, "May Christ guide my way as I live this new day." It only takes seconds, but the results have been life altering. I no longer rise to the moans and groans of back pain and dreading the chores of my workday. My outlook on my both my health and my daily activities have improved enormously. Not only am I feeling better, but I also feel more connected to God, spirit, and loved ones than ever before. It is a refreshing and positive approach to each new day. Remember, positive thoughts and actions can only yield positive results, including spirit communication and the recognition of a divine oneness. It is then that you will lose any negativity that dwells within you and welcome the happier, wiser soul within. To help you shed the dullness from your soul, I offer you a prayer, which can be said during your daily bathing.

Refresh Me Lord

Bless this water, I ask of the divine,
to cleanse my body, soul, and mind.
Wash away my doubts, tears, and fears,
and guide me, please, to happier years.
Let me go forth to be a soul that shines,
someone who is truly loving and kind.
Refresh me, Lord, please, I ask of thee,
that I might clearly see, the divine light in me.
Amen.

Prayer has been with man since the beginning of time for a reason. It is our inner most desires, hopes, and dreams that we wish to share with our creator. We are like children seeking understanding, approval, love and support from the divine, our loved ones, and each other. Through prayer, we can express our truest feelings and emotions. It is in prayer that we see not only our true selves, but others as well. Please continue to pray, as God and all those in spirit who love you, do hear you. To help you in your practice of prayer, I would suggest you pray to the highest and best in spirit, especially when asking for blessings—for yourself or others. Yet, when your day is done and you are ready to give thanks for all that has been bestowed upon you, I offer you this evening prayer of thanks.

Evening Prayer of Thanks

As I end my day, I give thanks to the divine,
and to all those who have enriched my spiritual mind.
As I learn to see which was once unseen,
I hope to find a renewed heart sublime.
I thank thee now for all that has come,
but especially those blessings this day of kindness and love.
Amen.

Remember, prayer is speaking to spirit while meditation is listening to spirit. I hope you explore those practices through both meditation and prayer that can introduce you to the highest and best in spirit, to God, and particularly, to your own higher self. May these prayers and meditation suggestions not only enhance your own psychic abilities, but also enlighten you in your own spiritual journey. I would like to leave you with one last prayer, which comes directly from the spirit world.

May the power, the glory, and the love of
the ones who have passed into the afterlife
be with you here and now.
May you carry with them blessings, which
are laid upon your head and your heart,
now and forever more.
That you may be in the loving arms of
their holy protection, always and forever.
Amen.

Conclusion – Learning How to Recognize the Unseen World around Us

In reflection of my journey thus far, in particular, the exploration of psychic phenomena and spirit communication, my experiences and lessons still overwhelm and humble me. From all of the years of *unusual* experiences, including sensing and *seeing spirit*, I am a changed soul. There is no going back now. It has been a thrilling adventure so far, and I thank God, and all of the divine, especially our guides and teachers in both spirit and flesh, who want all of us to know that we are indeed more than we appear to be, and that there is more *out there* still to discover.

We pass so fast through life that we may miss much that is around and within us. Yet, as we learn how to recognize some of the unseen world, we may come to recognize the limitless possibilities for a better tomorrow. It is a tomorrow filled with answers, amazing answers to some of life's greatest mysteries, including our purpose in living, and yes, in living on.

As all those introduced to you have led us to *know* life does continue. We continue with our loved ones in a world only partially seen. Those in spirit have given us a sense of our greater self and an awareness of a continued consciousness, but more importantly, great comfort in knowing that our loved ones are still with us. For every person who has lost a loved one, know that he or she lives on. For every person who thought he or she were only of the body, know that you are *much*, more. For every soul that desires purpose in life, know that you have value in just being you. For every soul that cries out, know that those in spirit hear you. These things did not happen for the few alone, they happened for everyone. Spiritualist's, Christians, Buddhists, Jews, anyone who truly believes in an unseen world, knows we never walk alone. It is a knowing that comes from within and around us. However, you must come to that realization on your own. I can write, speak, and jump up and down proclaiming this and proclaiming that, but until you have come to that place of *knowing* for yourself, you may never believe it. Whether you see spirit or not matters little in coming to know the truth that lies within you.

All I can do is tell you I found answers, as well as my spirituality, through not only personal tragedy and faith, but from finally recognizing, that which has been present all along. From all the tragedies came triumph. The paranormal became normal and the supernatural, *spiritual.* Ultimately, from that knowing, came an all-encompassing inner peace. I wish you that same inner peace, not only through hope and faith, but also from truly knowing. *Know* then that there is more, that *you* are more, that life continues and that you are not alone in this world. Know that you are a valuable piece of the puzzle that is our existence. It is as simple as that.

In speaking the truth and putting pen to paper, I risk much in the process. I have spent a great deal of time contemplating my purpose in writing this book and the volumes that follow it because this project of love has literally consumed my life. While I desire a great deal from the work, the underlying reasons have remained the same. Staying faithful to cause, the purpose is to not only search for the answers to some of life's greatest mysteries, but also to acknowledge those answers that ring of truth. From all that I have experienced thus far, I have come to a place in my journey where my heart and my head now know that we are more than just the body and that life is continuous. With the knowledge that we are part of bigger picture, which is a divine oneness, I have found my spirituality and faith in God, as well as in each other, renewed.

If you found this book helpful in your own journey, then I have been successful. If you found it mystifying, I hope you at least found cause to seek out your own answers. If you found the experiences similar to your own, I join you in truly *knowing* there is more *out there* for us still to discover. Together we can learn much from each other. Together we can explore the many wonders of this life and our purpose in being here. Together we can form a positive force toward a more spiritual, peaceful, and loving existence. Living and progressing on life's journey is difficult, never mind doing it alone, yet can be so joyful at times, that it must be shared. I hope you will continue to join me in exploring and sharing some of life's greatest mysteries, including our purpose in living, and in *living on.*

In the following volumes, new and familiar psychic-mediums, authors, scientists, religious leaders, filmmakers, philosophers, and others in both body and spirit join us as we continue to search for answers to some of life's greatest mysteries, especially of this reality, the afterlife, spirituality, and faith, which play a critical role in our future together.

Lastly, as a spiritual phenomenon ourselves, I hope you feel blessed as I do, to be an amazing *piece of the puzzle*. Thanks for joining us and let the journey of a lifetime continue.

Work Cited

Anastasi, Sandy. Personal Reading. 5 March 2005.

Anastasi, Sandy. Personal Interview. 28 May 2005.

Barnes, Peggy. The Fundamentals of Spiritualism. New York: National Spiritualist Association of Churches, 2002.

Brief History of Cassadaga Florida - Microsoft Internet Explorer
        http://www.cassadaga.com/history/
        October 23, 2005

Camp Chesterfield – Microsoft Internet Explorer
        http://www.campchesterfield.net/index.htm
        March 19, 2006

Camp Chesterfield. Chesterfield Lives. Indiana: Camp Chesterfield, 1986.

Clairvoyance – Encyclopaedia Britannica – Microsoft Internet Explorer
        http://www.britannica.com/eb/article-9024160
        April 17, 2006

Clark, Gretchen. Personal Interview. 20 August 2005.

Cunningham, Allene. Personal Reading. 26 June 2004.

Cunningham, Allene. Telephone Interview. 15 July 2005.

Definition of clairvoyant – Merriam – Webster Online Dictionary – Microsoft Internet Explore
        http://www.m-w.com/cgi-bin/dictionary?clairvoyant
        March 5, 2006

Dictionary definition: medium – Yahoo! Education – Microsoft Internet Explorer
        http://education.yahoo.com/reference/dictionary/entry?id=M0
        195100
        August 15, 2005

Definition of phenomenon – Microsoft Internet Explorer
> http://www.brainydictionary.com/words/ph/phenomenon2020
> 99.html
> August 15, 2005

Dr. Lauren – Microsoft Internet Explorer
> http://www.drlauren.com/
> November 12, 2005

Edward, John. *After Life: Answers from the Other Side*. New York: Princess Books, 2003

Fodor, Nandor. *Between Two Worlds*. New York: Parker Publishing Company, Inc., 1964.

Furst, Jessie. Personal Interview. 20 August 2005.

Gretchen Clark Medium Home Page – Microsoft Internet Explorer
> http://www.gretchenclark.com/
> October 30, 2005

Hazards/Climate Extremes – Microsoft Internet Explorer
> http://www.ncdc.noaa.gov/oa/climate/research/2006/mar/haz
> ards.html#Focus
> April 22, 2006

http://www.colorado.edu/philosophy/vstenger/Quantum/qmeta.html - Microsoft Internet Explorer
> http://www.colorado.edu/philosophy/vstenger/Quantum/qmet
> a.html
> February 11, 2006

Janet M. Reynolds, Intuitive Counselor – Microsoft Internet Explorer
> http://www.bluefeather.net/
> January 11, 2006

Kirlian effect – technology, tricks and the truth – Microsoft Internet Explorer
> http://www.thiaoouba.com/kiref.htm
> September 17, 2005

Larry King and Guest, Jane Seymour. Interview. Cable News Network (CNN) LP, LLLP, a Time Warner Company. Near-Death Experiences. Aired May 23, 2005 - 21:00 ET

Lillis, Patty. Personal Interview. 20 August 2005.

Lily Dale Assembly – Lily Dale, NY - Microsoft Internet Explorer
        http://www.lilydaleassembly.com/
        October 23, 2005

Lily Dale Home Ownership - Microsoft Internet Explorer
        http://www.lilydaleassembly.com/homeowner.php
        October 23, 2005

McClure, Eileen. Personal Interview. 20 August 2005.

NIV Bible: Passage Search Ecclesiastes 12:6 – Microsoft Internet Explorer
        http://www.ibs.org/niv/passagesearch.php
        May 27, 2005

Official site of Edgar Cayce's A.R.E. - Association for Research and Enlightenment - Microsoft Internet Explorer
        http://www.are-cayce.com/
        August 16, 2005

Orellana, Iris N. Personal Interview. 11 May 2006

Philomena. Personal Reading. 10 January 2004.

Philomena. Personal Interview. 15 May 2005.

Physical phenomenon – Wikipedia, the free encyclopedia – Microsoft Internet Explorer
        http://en.wikipedia.org/wiki/Physical_phenomenon
        August 15, 2005

Psychic Allene Cunningham – America's Top Radio Psychic – Microsoft Internet Explorer

http://www.esphelp.com
September 4, 2005

Riegel, Donna, Reverend. Personal Interview. 20 August 2005

Remote Viewing Training and products from David Morehouse
Productions and Remote Viewing Techno – Microsoft Internet Explorer
http://www.davidmorehouse.com/
August 12, 2006

Reynolds, Janet, Reverend. Séance Attendance. 14 May 2005.

Reynolds, Janet, Reverend. Personal Interview. 9 January 2006.

Sanson, Barbara. Telephone Interview. 29 September 2005.

Search Results for spiritualism – Encyclopedia Britannica - Microsoft
Internet Explorer
http://www.britannica.com/search?query=spiritualism&ct=
April 5, 2006

She saw dead people – Microsoft Internet Explorer
http://oldcolony.southofboston.com/articles/2005/10/29/news
/news02.txt
April 5, 2006

Spiritualism – Wikipedia, the free encyclopedia – Microsoft Internet
Explorer
http://en.wikipedia.org/wiki/Modern_Spiritualist_movement
April 5, 2006

Taylor, Carol Ann, Reverend. Personal Interview. 15 May 2005.

Thibodeau, Lauren, Ph.D. Personal Interview. 12 August 2005.

Thibodeau, Lauren B., Ph.D. *Natural Born Intuition: How to Awaken and
Develop Your Inner Wisdom.* New Jersey: New Page Books, 2005.

Van Praagh, James. Telephone Interview. 13 August 2005.

Yusczyk, Shirley. Personal Interview. 20 August 2005.